AF248808

Staying Up Much Too Late

Gordon Theisen

Staying Up Much Too Late

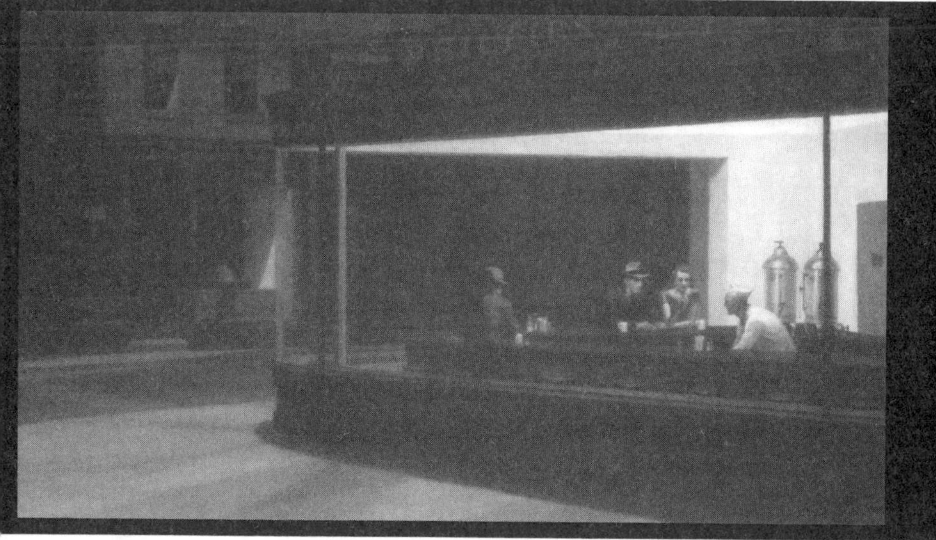

Edward Hopper's **Nighthawks**

and the Dark Side of the American Psyche

THOMAS DUNNE BOOKS

St. Martin's Press   New York

THOMAS DUNNE BOOKS.
An imprint of St. Martin's Press.

STAYING UP MUCH TOO LATE. Copyright © 2006 by Gordon Theisen. All rights reserved. Printed in the United States of America. No part of this book may be used or reproduced in any manner whatsoever without written permission except in the case of brief quotations embodied in critical articles or reviews. For information, address St. Martin's Press, 175 Fifth Avenue, New York, N.Y. 10010.

www.stmartins.com

Designed by Kathryn Parise

Edward Hopper, American, 1882–1967, *Nighthawks,* 1942, oil on canvas, 84.1 × 152.4 cm. Friends of American Art Collection, 1942.51, The Art Institute of Chicago. Photography © The Art Institute of Chicago.

Edward Hopper (1882–1967). *House by the Railroad,* 1925. Oil on canvas. 24 × 29". Given anonymously. (3.1930). The Museum of Modern Art, New York, N.Y., U.S.A. Digital Image © The Museum of Modern Art/Licensed by SCALA/Art Resource, N.Y.

Edward Hopper. *Automat,* 1927, oil on canvas, 71.4 × 91.4 cm. Des Moines Art Center Permanent Collections; Purchased with funds from the Edmundson Art Foundation, Inc., 1958.2.

Edward Hopper. *Approaching a City,* 1946. Oil on canvas. 27⅛ × 36". Acquired 1947. The Phillips Collection, Washington, D.C.

Weegee (Arthur Fellig). *On the Spot,* photograph, 1940. Hulton Archives/Getty Images.

Edward Hopper (1882–1967). *Night Shadows,* 1921. Etching. 17.6 × 20.8 cm. Location not indicated. Collection of Whitney Museum of American Art, Josephine Hopper Bequest. Photo Credit: Art Resource, N.Y.

(Copyright permissions continue on page 234.)

LIBRARY OF CONGRESS CATALOGING-IN-PUBLICATION DATA

Theisen, Gordon.
    Staying up much too late : Edward Hopper's *Nighthawks* and the dark side of the American psyche / Gordon Theisen.—1st ed.
        p. cm.
    Includes bibliographical references and index.
    ISBN 0-312-33342-0
    EAN 978-0-312-33342-3
    1. Hopper, Edward, 1882–1967. Nighthawks. 2. United States—Civilization—20th century. 3. Alienation (Social psychology)—United States. I. Hopper, Edward, 1882–1967. II. Title.

ND237.H75A74 2006
759.13—dc22
                                                                2006040393

First Edition: June 2006

10   9   8   7   6   5   4   3   2   1

For Sue and Keith

Contents

Staying Up Much Too Late

Introduction

Optimism in America, more than a widespread character trait, is a core tenet of the national faith: what we know to be true, how we experience the world. If stocks go up, they will continue to go up, and if stocks go down, it is only a matter of time before they will "regain their footing" and go up once again, as is only right, what stocks must and should do. What merely appears bad will soon be revealed as good, as with the lengthy spate of increasing postwar violence in Iraq (at least as far as right-leaning pundits are concerned). So Franklin Delano Roosevelt seemed inclined to defeat the Great Depression with an ever-present grin as his sword and with the very idea that he and we together could and would climb back out of that unaccountable valley and resume our ascent to the very summit of human possibility. And Ronald Reagan arguably led us to victory in the Cold War by declaring and making us believe, with the unshakable confidence the former movie star easily achieved, that it was, once again—following the twilight of recession and lukewarm liberalism under former peanut farmer Jimmy Carter—"morning in America."

Not that optimism is enough: There are always practical measures to be taken as well, business to drum up, products to be designed and refined and sold, programs to be funded, missiles to be built, enemies to be defeated. We are excruciatingly productive, all in the name of progress accomplished and yet to come, buttressing our belief in the immense capacity of human beings for improvement and our special status as the avatars of such improvement, both as individuals and as a nation united. This same belief influenced the most romantic of the country's founders, Thomas Jefferson, in writing the Declaration of Independence. The sentiments contained in that document—and the implication that "moral sense" and "justice" are not imposed by society or learned but "innate" in each of us (as Jefferson once maintained in a letter to John Adams)—were commonplace among preachers of the day. They had inherited the spiritual fires lit during the Great Awakening, an orgiastic religious revival in the early eighteenth century that theologian Jonathan Edwards thought resulted from a spreading awareness of heavenly glory, a sign of cosmic good fortune.

The Great Awakening, incidentally, helped spread the rigorous Baptist tradition in which the primary subject of this book, Edward Hopper, was raised. Hopper could, however, trace his family's heritage further back, to Dutch traders who arrived in what was to them a New World in the mid-seventeenth century, a period we now identify almost exclusively with the Puritans, and for good reason. We might trace America's extraordinary vision of itself to those stern forefathers and their surprisingly resilient belief that this virgin territory gave them the unprecedented opportunity to found an exemplary "city upon a hill," a New Jerusalem cleansed of the catastrophic history they had left behind and peopled by a divinely chosen elect.

If this fantastic metropolis never quite materialized, it nonetheless became our supreme goal, a beacon blazing throughout the development of a uniquely American culture defined by more than hope. It was the promise of something greater, something transcendent—not in some ghostly afterlife, but here, in fact, upon this solid Earth. We can hop, skip, and jump along. During the Second Great Awakening, in the early part of the nineteenth century, evangelist Charles Grandison Finney exhorted tens of thousands of listeners at open camp meetings that they should and could become "as perfect as God." Around the same time, one Joseph Smith of Palmyra, New York, founded the Mormon Church, now America's fastest-growing religion. Revelations entrusted to Smith from on high located the Garden of Eden in Jackson County, Missouri; directed the construction of a New Jerusalem on the Western frontier; and (in an elegantly aphoristic restatement by the church's fifth president, Leonard Snow) proclaimed, "As man now is, God once was; as God once was, man may be." Less ambitious than Smith, but still remarkably exuberant, the mid-nineteenth-century philosopher Henry David Thoreau advised his readers to build their "castles in the air" first and then "lay foundations under them." Poet Walt Whitman witnessed the nation's "turbulent, quick, and audacious" drive away from rusticity and toward urbanization and industrial prowess following the Civil War, and he predicted a "new race dominating previous ones and grander far."

We can note Manifest Destiny—the belief that this vast continent was granted to us to overspread and cultivate—and the pioneer spirit that continued to push us onward following the settling of the West in the 1890s, to invent, to build roads, highways, and ever-taller skyscrapers. We can note the forward-looking, epoch-making names given to political agendas throughout the twentieth century: Woodrow Wilson's New Freedom, John F. Kennedy's New Frontier, Lyndon Johnson's Great

Society, and Newt Gingrich's Contract with America (among the latter's provisions: an Act for the Restoration of the American Dream). We can go from the left to the far left and swing back to the hard right, politically speaking, and still find variants of the "city upon a hill." There was the "beautiful symphony of brotherhood" prophesied by Baptist preacher and civil rights leader Martin Luther King, Jr., and there were the half-million hippies who gathered at a farm outside Woodstock, New York, in the summer of 1969 for "3 Days of Peace & Music." More than a festival, Woodstock was a "demonstration," as participants would later term it, that nonviolent togetherness was feasible and might be emulated throughout the country—or better yet, throughout the world. Then there were the free-market fundamentalists and corporate cheerleaders who saw no reason the boom-boom nineties, fueled by increasingly cheap, increasingly fast information technology, should ever end. Rather, they expected final and irrefutable verification of the classical economic theories of Scotsman Adam Smith, who published his *Wealth of Nations* the same year as the signing of the Declaration of Independence. Smith argued that the "progress of opulence" depends on "natural liberty," i.e., the unfettered pursuit of self-interest, the resulting competition forcing manufacturers to fit their products to customers' evolving desires, to the ever-increasing satisfaction of . . . everyone!

Maybe so, but the Dow did not rise to 36,000 (as the title of a 1999 bestseller, now evidence of mass delusion, declared it would). Instead, the much vaunted "invisible hand" guiding stocks upward wavered or was never there or revealed a twisted sense of humor, and trillions of dollars disappeared. But the optimism endured and continues to shape every aspect of our lives, giving happy endings to the enormously expensive movies we watch, a triumphant sensibility to our careers (Millions laid off?

A highly adaptable workforce!), sports, news, and bouts of intercourse (note the preternatural erections provided by tantric methods for the organic crowd and Viagra for the rest of us). This optimism inspires us to stop smoking and start jogging, return to college, recapture our youth, try yoga or plastic surgery or both, buy an HDTV (progress: If the shows aren't any better, the picture sure is).

We create our own Web sites despite the Internet's apparent failure to found a communal-cum-commercial utopia. We actually think that the most recent war could and should be the last. We take out loans for new houses we can't quite afford with large garages for the new SUVs we can't quite afford because the payments won't seem so bad after the promotion we presume is coming our way very soon. And even if no one visits our Web site and a new war starts and the promotion does not come tomorrow or six months or six years from now, still our optimism shall be our guide.

What we need is to get back in touch with nature for a weekend, go on a better diet, find a better job. We need to think of growing older not as a heading toward death but as an opportunity to continue pushing further ahead, improving. We need to take up mountain climbing, to feel better than we've ever felt before.

> The Planet drifts to random insect doom.
> —WILLIAM S. BURROUGHS

A preordained belief rather than a lesson learned, American-style optimism hovers above setbacks. But any faith breeds doubt, and in the case of such high-flown expectations, even a minor distress or just the apprehension of potential distress may cause full-fledged skepticism. Like the husband in a Nathaniel Hawthorne story, driven to despair by a birthmark on his otherwise beautiful wife, we then take on a vision as dark as our faltering optimism was bright. We might have discovered an underground carnival run by Satan directly beneath Disney World, its Mickey Mouse–like mascot a monstrous undead rat, its Snow White a sneering Martha Stewart doppelgänger decked out in S-M fetish gear and wielding a bullwhip.

The whole program may come into question: Not only is my own life nothing like a sitcom, with its harmless pranks, warm, fuzzy feelings, and tidy morals, no one's is. The so-called city upon a hill is built at the bottom of a strip mine, the American dream a nightmare in disguise, our castles in the air collapsing all around, history a revolving tragedy from which there is no escape. Stocks will not recover; we are headed into a second Great Depression. Postwar Iraq is a Vietnam-like quagmire. Our country shines no beacon of moral purity but is irrevocably blighted by racism, poverty, slavery, and genocide. Or perhaps it's not the whole program. The program is intact; it's just that some will not make it to the city upon a hill. There's only so much room. Real estate prices are somewhere above the ozone and only going up. The Puritans who conceived of this earthly paradise were Calvinists after all: They were not really interested in everyone's salvation, only of those whom God happens to favor with His grace. The rest, termed reprobate (condemned) or preterit (literally bygone, i.e., left behind), are the damned, the unchosen. Why? Our sad lot is not to know why, only to suffer accordingly, though we can see clues, evidence of how the preknown and predetermined outcome (God being omniscient and omnipotent) has come out. Who can afford the mansion by the sea, and who seeks cover beneath wet cardboard in the alcove of a vacant storefront? Who drives a shiny Mercedes, and who a beat-up Chevy compact? Who dines on sirloin and single-malt scotch at the Four Seasons, and who slurps mush in prison?

Success and failure are their own sufficient proofs of grace or lack thereof, and we may begin to suspect we are on the wrong side of the line, that we won't keep up with the bills, get the job we wanted, find true love, catch the dream. It's enough to make us a little anxious, or very anxious indeed, to interfere with our sleep, to keep us up late at night; our once comfortable bed comfortable no longer—it might as well be someone else's. So with a sigh we may rise, dress, and head out onto the darkened streets, to wander, "get some air," think things over, to wonder if we went wrong, where we went wrong. Instead, we notice only how decidedly imperfect the city in which we live out our decidedly imperfect life is, with its cracked sidewalks and refuse-strewn gutters, chipped brick, cold granite facades, and padlocked metal gratings, none of which have anything to say about one solitary person's newfound fears. How very different from the little hometown of many a legend and mass-media myth, with the white picket fences and trenchant but necessary values based in family and church and nutritious dinners with our loved ones every evening. How did we get from there to here? And where to turn now for the warmth we lack?

A glow from a corner: an all-night diner. There we will find temporary succor, sit on a padded stool at the counter, and, not hungry, order a hot cup of coffee that's poured from a large silver urn by a handsome blond young server in a white uniform and hat who does not smile. The coffee, however, will only keep us up still later, make us even more anxious, when we really should stop this foolish thinking about things so much, get our head straight, get back to bed, and get some rest so we can be effective come morning. "Tomorrow is another day!" But as the night reluctantly slouches onward, as if the dawn were a dreaded intruder, our coffee intake increases and we become curious about the other customers. There are a few: a woman with rich red lips who seems vaguely repulsed by the thin remnant of a sandwich she holds in her hand, one man with a hawkish face and lit cigarette, another bulky, hunched over. Who are they? What's their story? A rare bout of insomnia? Unemployed? Addicts? Thieves? Nothing better to do? Might one of them suddenly decide to rob the place? They are utter strangers, their past as opaque as their present, as our own must be to them.

One thing: They don't look especially friendly, and they don't look as if they are enjoying themselves. More: They don't look as if they are headed anywhere in particular, that their lives are on an upward trajectory, that they harbor expectations. Rather, a sense of disaster pervades everything: the diner, the customers, the server, the empty street outside, the buildings across the way. They inhabit a different America, a flip side of the one we are used to, a cooler, jazzier, deeply shadowed America hidden behind the giant billboards and manicured lawns and wide toothy smiles and Norman Rockwell townscapes. Freedom is a form of rootlessness there, while experience teaches futility rather than hope, and people fail to make more than fleeting contact with one another or find a place in a society that guarantees every wish and whim is within easy reach but remains utterly unconcerned with their actual fate.

Defined by a pessimism that simply would not fly in a TV commercial ("Life's a bust! Drink Coke!"), this other America is everywhere suppressed and everywhere denied ("Pay no attention to those naysayers!"), but nonetheless appears everywhere. Or peeks out from under. Consider the film noir of the late 1940s and 1950s, with its morally compromised men and unscrupulous women attempting to escape decaying and corrupt cities but always coming to a bad end. Note how this plays off the form the American dream took at the time: detached dwellings with a car in every garage and gleaming appliances allegedly available to whoever works hard, the city upon a hill reimagined as newly minted, crime-free suburbs. Or consider the junky antiheroes of novelist William S. Burroughs, wending their ways from urban mazes to rural enclaves marked by bigotry and hate, using heroin because they have no "strong motivations in any other direction." Consider the stark imagery of hard-boiled 1940s photojournalist Weegee: individual lives made suddenly meaningless by tenement fires, murders, and car crashes on the streets beneath New York's glittering office towers. The irascible genius Miles Davis, playing love ballads in a detached, muted tone, as if giving in to their sentiments (and how we want to!), would merely be setting himself (and us) up for loss and pain. There's the mélange of poverty, drug abuse, promiscuity, and random murder on the seedy margins of righteous, clean-living Mormon Utah in Norman Mailer's *The Executioner's Song*. There's the "crumbling beauty" of a cocktail waitress from a Tom Waits song, who has "that razor sadness that only gets worse with the clang and the thunder of the Southern Pacific going by." There's the small town of Jim Thompson's 1952 pulp novel, *The Killer Inside Me,* where deputy sheriff Lou Ford spouts a string of clichéd platitudes—"if we didn't have rain we wouldn't have rainbows"—but gets his kicks from torture and killing, by, say, extinguishing a cigar in a beggar's palm.

This America holds no glorious future, no New Jerusalem, just alienation, an endless supply of gadgets to buy, and the pretense of success in the face of increasing despair. It could bear the name that Andy Warhol gave to his multimedia road show from 1966, "The Plastic Exploding Inevitable." It does offer a kind of hero, but rather than a has-been with one last chance, he's a never-was with no chance at all, like the alcoholic, down-and-out boxer Billy Tully in John Huston's movie *Fat City*, the overall look of which was directly inspired by Edward Hopper's desolate 1942 masterpiece, *Nighthawks*. Haunting but immensely popular (in a country where high art is not highly regarded, useless as it is), this painting of lonely figures in an urban diner late at night might be a window onto an America that never became what America once might have been.

Me, Hopper's Nighthawks, *This Book*

Only vaguely aware of *Nighthawks* as a unique painting someone actually sat down, planned out, and committed to canvas, I first saw it a few years ago at the Art Institute of Chicago while there for an exhibit of the somber work of German artist Gerhard Richter. (Now there is someone, as the descendant of men and women who abetted the Holocaust and lost two world wars, for whom pessimism is an obvious refuge.) Richter made for satisfying, museum-style viewing, but when I came across *Nighthawks,* I paused and thought, simply, There it is, that painting. I had seen it countless times before, reproduced in however many books and magazines, on posters and postcards, in many an homage and pastiche. An episode of *The Simpsons* alludes to *Nighthawks.* Austrian artist Gottfried Helnwein's *Boulevard of Broken Dreams* (1981), kitschy staple of dormrooms, pizza parlors, and neighborhood bars throughout the land, reproduces the painting while replacing the people in the diner with Humphrey Bogart, James Dean, Elvis Presley, and Marilyn Monroe. A similarly conceived French version replaces the people in the diner with characters from the comic strip "Tin-Tin." Accurately detailed, three-dimensional versions of *Nighthawks* served as sets in Wim Wenders's *The End of Vio-*

lence (1997) and the lip-synch musical *Pennies from Heaven* (1981). Reflecting the feel of Hopper's painting, the latter movie's downbeat narrative plays off the optimism of Depression-era songs: Steve Martin plays a lying, selfish, and destitute but always optimistic (he *believes* in those songs) traveling sheet-music salesman, who is executed for a murder he did not commit.

I was, in sum, prior to seeing *Nighthawks,* already familiar with the painting's determinedly dejected sensibility, which is, it turns out, common to Hopper's work, and a common topic of Hopper criticism, along with his distinctly American outlook. It is a sensibility he has to a large degree bequeathed to us, for Hopper's influence has been broad and significant. Artist Eric Fischl uses a Hopper-like aesthetic to plant loneliness and angst in the postwar middle-class suburbs of his youth. Sculptor George Segal did his own dreary diner using his signature white plaster figures (*Diner* [1964–66]). The great abstractionist Mark Rothko based some of his early works directly on Hopper paintings. Red Grooms's *Nighthawks Revisited* (1980) shows the diner during the day, with piles of plates and cups, a calendar, flypaper, and newspaper, and on the street outside a jumbly profusion of litter, trash cans, scrawny cats, pedestrians, and a car with 1950s-style tail fins. For the man facing us from across the counter, Grooms inserted Edward Hopper himself, with cigarette, coffee, and disapproving frown. Hopper also inspired and influenced the painters David Hockney and Willem de Kooning; photographers Robert Frank and Gregory Crewdson; poets Lawrence Ferlinghetti and Mark Strand; fiction writers Paul Auster and Walter Mosley; and moviemakers Paul Schrader, Terrence Malick, Todd Haynes, and George Stevens, who directed James Dean in *Giant* (1956). Hopper influenced the look of Charles Addams's wonderfully macabre cartoons detailing the antics of the Addams Family, which initially appeared in *The*

New Yorker in 1938 and later became the basis for a television show and two feature films. Singer Tom Waits put out a live album called *Nighthawks at the Diner* in 1974. The opening track, "Eggs and Sausage (in a Cadillac with Susan Michelson)," begins with the lines: "Nighthawks at the diner / of Emma's '49er, there's a rendezvous / of strangers around a coffee urn tonight."

Hopper was also a favorite reference for directors and designers of film noir, and through that bleak genre influenced such noirish (or "neo-noir") movies as *Chinatown* (1974), *Blue Velvet* (1986), *Basic Instinct* (1992), *Pulp Fiction* (1994), and *The Matrix* (1999). *Basic Instinct* happens to include, I noticed recently, a late-night diner scene. Underrated by critics, *Basic Instinct* achieved easy notoriety for combining torrid sex with horrid violence, but is truly unnerving for its desolate, amoral view of late-twentieth-century America. The movie's rogue cop protagonist lacks a single sympathetic trait: He's shot a couple of tourists by mistake, has but one friend, gets kicked off the force, and does not hesitate to "fuck," as the dialogue insistently puts it, a sleazy serial murderess he plans to arrest. Sometime between the sex and the arrest, he and his loud, crude cop partner meet for no particular reason in a neon-lit diner and do little besides offend the other patrons. In the next scene, a car chase, he runs a vicious leather-clad lesbian off the road, killing her.

After that day in the Art Institute of Chicago, and before I got to know Hopper and his place in art history better, I started to think of such moments in our movies, TV shows, and books—maybe influenced by Hopper and maybe not—as evincing that same, peculiar, America-gone-all-wrong feel to them. The opening sequence for HBO's *The Sopranos,* which depicts northern New Jersey as an overdeveloped industrial wasteland, would be one example. Others include the almost apocalyptic urban back-drop of many a 1970s police drama on both small and big screen (I grew up with these), as well as the awful resignation that im-bues Ernest Hemingway's spare prose in *The Sun Also Rises* (1926), and the opening of Herman Melville's dire epic, *Moby-Dick* (1851), in which his suicidal protagonist, Ishmael, wanders the empty, unwelcoming streets of a whaling village at night, humbly seeking rest and food. Miles Davis's melancholy *Kind of Blue* (1959), one of the greatest and most popular jazz albums, nicely complements *Nighthawks* as a sort of soundtrack.

All of which suggested to me that what keeps *Nighthawks* fresh and striking despite its familiarity is that it evokes a gener-ally unacknowledged side of a nation that touts its optimism, and offers up hope and progress as its very reason for being. This, however, only begs the question of why *Nighthawks* in particular, with its dejected sensibility and desolation, can seem so uncannily representative.

The painting is undoubtedly a great work of art, likely the great-est realistic painting this country has produced. Moreover, as I shall argue in the pages that follow, *Nighthawks* is deeply relevant to essential aspects of American—especially twentieth-century American—culture. In a single, cogent, concentrated image, *Nighthawks* manages to reflect our attitudes toward individuality, cities, technology, nature, freedom, sexuality, women, money, ex-perience, success, and religion. But it does so darkly, through its de-jected sensibility, its desolation.

To try to understand what this means is to undertake a negative case study, to analyze a trend by focusing on where it collapses. We might, for example, see a cheerful, chatty, sunny-voiced, bright-eyed car dealer—"Have I got the *perfect* deal for *you,* my friend, and *I mean* PERFECT!"—after a long day, near the Dumpster off in the lot behind his gaudily decked-out showroom. He is silent, standing there, pensive, puffing on a cheap cigar, his eyes lowered and his cocky grin so utterly gone it's hard to remember what it looked like. He is surprisingly, shockingly sad, rather, and lonesome. We are forced to wonder: What is the relationship between how we knew him when we bought the used Plymouth Reliant with the like-new shine that needed the radiator replaced a day later (he seemed so frankly well intended yet must have been aware of this) and what he is revealing now?

This book is just such a negative case study. It attempts to understand America by deliberating on a painting that depicts us precisely as we insist we are not but that, nevertheless, as an icon—our icon—reveals what, at least on some level, we are: *Nighthawks* is us.

Chapter One

The Making of the Painting,
or How to Be a Stranger in
Your Own Land

> Nothing is at last sacred but the integrity of your own mind.
> —RALPH WALDO EMERSON

1. The Artist

Edward Hopper began *Nighthawks* in December 1941, shortly after Japan attacked Pearl Harbor. How difficult to imagine: like photographing a flower garden on the afternoon of September 11, 2001, not because a flower garden expressed certain feelings about the cataclysmic events of that morning, but because photographing flower gardens is your thing, is what you would have done anyway. While the country as a whole, pretty much overnight, committed itself to total war, "Ed," as his wife, Josephine "Jo" Hopper, recorded in her journal, "refused to take any interest in our very likely prospect of being bombed. . . . He's doing a new canvas and simply can't be interrupted."

Come what may, devotion to a self-imposed task evokes the archetypal American hero: Think of John Wayne in John Ford's 1956 classic western, *The Searchers,* striding across an arid Texas landscape for seven long years in quest of Scar, the Comanche who kidnapped and ravished his niece. He has put all else aside, cares only about doing what he knows is one absolutely right thing to do. Or think of Raymond Chandler's obstinately moral private detective, Philip Marlowe, who takes on cases with little chance of payment—he may even refuse payment because he cannot be bought, committed as he is to the interests of his client (even when that so-called client hasn't actually hired him or attempts to halt his investigation). He gets a job done and done well because it is his duty, however ridiculous he seems when everyone else is for sale because that's the best way to get by. So the fifty-nine-year-old Hopper, world war or no world war, meticulously developed a scene based on a Greenwich Avenue restaurant that he spotted during one of his meandering strolls through lower Manhattan.

He had labored in obscurity for some two decades following his graduation from the New York School of Art in 1906, supporting himself by illustrating advertisements, magazine articles, and movie posters. He despised this work and refused to do it more than three days per week to save time for his more personal artistic endeavors, but received scant attention for the few group shows he participated in. He was invited to contribute to the "Exhibition of Paintings and Drawings by Contemporary American Artists" in 1908, along with such up-and-comers as George Bellows and Rockwell Kent. But while the other artists displayed American views, Hopper—somewhat perversely, given the exhibition's stated theme—chose to display paintings inspired by a recent sojourn in Europe (mainly Paris), where he had traveled to visit museums and round out his education. He was duly ignored by the press. Not quite unjustly: The work was too derivative of French impressionism, which he greatly admired. Perhaps he needed the failure, the ensuing isolation, to keep to his own course, mature his style, and find his artistic identity.

He made some notable breakthroughs. The massive (36" × 72") near-masterpiece *Soir Bleu* (1914) portrays a voluptuous, heavily made-up prostitute surveying the customers in a Parisian café through narrowed eyes. She might be a demon searching for a soul worth stealing, and presages Hopper's career-long fascination with the enticements of very shapely women. *New York Corner* (1913) shows a group of faceless men in black hats and overcoats milling in front of a corner saloon on a gray, wintry day, the ice blue silhouette of a factory in the distance. At once ordinary and desolate, the painting won him some early praise when exhibited in 1915.

Wider recognition did not come until 1923, when he exhibited a series of brilliant watercolors at the Brooklyn Museum, done in and around the picturesque town of Gloucester, Massachusetts. These paintings dovetailed nicely with critics' increasing interest in often idealized American settings done in a plainly realistic (i.e., not avant-garde, not European, and hold the flourishes) style. Now in his forties, Hopper suddenly achieved renown as a portrayer of the "American scene." In 1930, the Whitney Museum of American Art paid the then-impressive sum of $3,000 for *Early Sunday Morning* (1930). This aggressively mundane, if sunny, depiction of a block-long redbrick row building with a barber pole, fire hydrant, and a strip of pale blue sky above but no people in sight, makes for a vision so silent and still it suggests some mysterious vitality, the existence of which we are but latently aware and cannot name.

Hopper's reputation grew. In 1933, the Museum of Modern Art hosted his first retrospective. But recognition, even on this scale, did not compromise what critic Lloyd Goodrich called Hopper's "unwavering integrity" and "consistency," his almost defiant sense of himself as cleaving to a singular vocation, however propitious (or not) the trends might be. He would not give in to the art market any more than he gave in to the market for commercial illustration, which he would never again resort to. He continued to work slowly, completing only a few oils per year, always waiting until he was certain he had a fresh idea and would not be repeating himself. And he continued to spend a long time on each canvas, thinking a project through thoroughly before stubbornly painting and repainting, until he got precisely the intended effect (he liked working in oil, he said, because it facilitated "corrections and changes"). As the Great Depression continued, sales dropped off, and he faced financial strain, Hopper seemed to become even more selective, more afraid of simply coasting, of having nothing left to say.

When Hopper did get going again, it was 1940, and the war in Europe took up much of the public's attention (Germany conquered France in June of that year), but he was entering arguably the most powerful phase of his career. Six weeks after Pearl Harbor, he completed what critics often point to as his most accomplished painting, one the artist himself counted as a favorite. *Nighthawks,* unlike many twentieth-century masterpieces, has won admiration from those who champion the often inaccessible experiments that make up much of modern art, as well as those that do not. This is in many respects a deeply cold and alien work, despite its immediately recognizable subject matter: a nameless, nondescript diner late at night.

The diner is brightly lit from within, lending a whitish glow to the yellow walls and a shine to two large silver coffee urns on the far ledge of a mahogany counter. Three stray customers—a man and woman together and another man sitting across from them with his back to us—are being served by a younger blond man in a white uniform and hat. This scene is at a moderate distance, as if glimpsed while passing by, on the sidewalk perhaps, through the diner's plate-glass window. Above the window is an advertisement for Phillies: ONLY 5¢. AMERICA'S NO. 1 CIGAR. To the left is a section of the sidewalk and street outside the diner, empty of people and cars, of anything but shadows cast from inside the diner and by unseen streetlamps. On the other side of the street, across from the diner, is a two-story redbrick row building, with some windows on the top floor, their blinds partly drawn and impenetrable darkness beyond. On the bottom floor are a couple of storefronts, utterly vacant, as far as we can tell, except for a single ghostly cash register.

The casual if not quite relaxed image of a big-city diner in *Nighthawks* certainly exemplifies what someone might mean by the term "American scene," as much as would, say, a small-town soda fountain or sandlot baseball game. The painting has a definite sense of place to it, one that depends upon, and even helps to define, an American way of living. But Hopper came to reject the term: "I don't think I ever tried to paint the American scene." This was partly a matter of professional pride. He did not want to be regarded as a distinctly American painter comparable only to other American painters. He wanted to be on level with world art, to be compared with Claude Monet as well as Winslow Homer. But Hopper's feelings also had to do with how he thought about art, his own and in general. As he succinctly put it,

"The man is the work." Schools, movements, and groups, like regional identity, were anathema to Hopper, or at least irrelevant. Great art, he felt, was about the individual artist behind the work trying to give his unique, innermost being an objective, communicable form on canvas: "I am trying to paint myself." Thomas Eakins was, Hopper said, "our greatest American painter" not because he provided a facsimile of his surroundings but because he was "a profound personality" who "speaks to us through his art."

This notion might be applied to any artist from any nation or period. But it is characteristically American in the sense that Walt Whitman is characteristically American: not because he gave one of his poems the title "Song of Myself" but because all of Whitman's poetry could be gathered under that title. One value American culture continually and predictably holds up—we might even say rigidly conforms to—is the value of nonconformity, of the individual following his or her own heart. The individual is paramount over teachers, over friends, over family, over circumstance: Today we have made popular literary genres out of confessional verse, the memoir, the personal essay, and first-person journalism, in which events being reported occasionally recede in importance before descriptions of the reporter's efforts to report them.

"Whoso would be a man would be a nonconformist," wrote Emerson back in 1841. This was in "Self-Reliance," one of a series of philosophical essays in which the first-person singular makes a repeated and more than incidental appearance: We cannot even speak of truth as existing apart from the individual who is perceiving that truth. And Emerson's dictate could serve as a motto for "maverick" CEOs who "think outside the box" (and have themselves been publishing a lot of memoirs of late) and trendy pop stars, as well as the willful radicals who jump-started the revolution and the Puritans who left everything they knew behind in order to practice their own brand of worship without harassment.

This is not to say that Hopper's notion that art expresses the artist's innermost self was facile, only to suggest—his own denials aside—that such an American notion should hardly have kept him from portraying the "American scene." For Hopper, who was too diffident for merely confessional self-exposure, it was quite the opposite; "painting myself" meant painting the external world in accordance with his "personal vision" of it. He felt that abstract painting fatally lacked the artist forging connection between himself and the facts of his environment.

To mean something, anything, art must provide a specific sense of where you are and where you have been, of your particular take on the larger history of which you, willingly or not, form a part. Hopper's first title for *Skyline Near Washington Square* (1925), an unpeopled watercolor of a multistoried building seen from a lower rooftop, was *Self-Portrait*. Immediately after he complained to an interviewer about having "the American scene pinned on me," he detailed his ancestry: "Like most Americans, I'm an amalgam of many races," but mainly Dutch, specifically "Hudson River Dutch—not Amsterdam Dutch."

The artist who painted *Nighthawks* knew well his pedigree and heritage. And if he was capable of pursuing an emphatically personal vision even at the onset of war, *Nighthawks* gives ample evidence of the importance he granted to being in a specific place at a specific time. For unlike an image of a sandlot baseball game or small-town soda fountain, which might easily assume an aura of being outside both space and time, of being mythic rather than historical, the urban diner Hopper portrayed is securely rooted in the early 1940s. Diners, for example, were a twentieth-century phenomenon, increasing in numbers through the 1920s and 1930s and reaching their heyday in the 1940s and 1950s. The whitish glow within the diner, meanwhile, has the unvarying flatness of fluorescent lights, which had only a year or so previously attained widespread use in stores and restaurants. Advertisements like the advertisement for Phillies cigars, which tops the diner, became ubiquitous in the early decades of the twentieth century. Phillies themselves could be sold for "Only 5 cents" because they were rolled by machine rather than by hand, an innovation that came about in the 1930s, when cigar interests were trying to regain market share from cigarettes, which had been rolled by machine since the mid-1880s.

The soft, brimmed, dark-banded hats worn by the diner's male customers—fedoras—were, along with their suits and ties, practically mandated wear for men in midcentury (they were originally worn by women, back in the late nineteenth century). The way that the female customer's tight burgundy shirt exposes the lengths of her arms and her neck down to beneath her collarbone, and how her hair spreads out to her shoulders, reflects the way women were supposed to look in an era that gave rise to such pinup queens as leggy Betty Grable and Rita Hayworth.

All of which, while typical, may well have lent itself to a personal vision for an artist for whom such details were remarkable because of who he was and where he had been.

2. The Man

Hopper lived in Manhattan for sixty-odd years—his entire adulthood—in a fourth-story walk-up apartment off Washington Square Park, and *Nighthawks* is one of many paintings of his that directly reflects life in a big American city in the twentieth century. But he was born on July 22, 1882, in Nyack, New

York, a small town on the west shore of the Hudson River, twenty-five miles north of Manhattan.

He was raised there in a handsome, if relatively plain, two-story clapboard house with a large front porch. Built by his mother's grandfather, the Reverend Joseph W. Griffiths, in 1858, the house was sited on a rise near the river, and from his bedroom window Hopper could watch the ships sail past. In 1856, this same Rev. Griffiths had founded Nyack's Baptist congregation, which the Hoppers attended. Hopper's father, Garret Henry Hopper, a friend of the minister, served as trustee, and Hopper himself attended Sunday school there. Garret Hopper was, for his part, the descendant of Dutch traders who had arrived in America in the mid-seventeenth century; his mother was a zealous Methodist.

Hopper's experience of Nyack was as the eldest son in a family that had roots in the town for three generations and in the nation for more than two centuries, lending him a sense of tradition, of being where he belonged, with a deep, rigid faith as central to his identity. Critics would later note an austerity in his painting they would term "Puritan," and there is evidence of sexual and emotional repression in the Hopper household. Hopper's younger sister and only sibling, Marion, would die in 1965, having never married or moved from their house in Nyack. Hopper was self-conscious and reserved (even late in life, renowned and respected, he could sit through entire dinner parties hardly uttering a word) and did not sustain a serious relationship until his early forties. But repression was hardly unusual or frowned upon in their era, and the Hoppers were prominent members of the local middle class, while the town itself was, initially at least, busy and bustling enough.

Nyack was incorporated in 1872. Two years earlier, tracks

were laid, connecting Nyack to New York City. In addition to being a busy port for steamers and for a ferry that crossed the Hudson, the town served as a rail hub, with some thirty passenger trains a day passing through during Hopper's childhood. (The trains impressed Hopper and would become a recurring motif in his painting.) Nyack also boasted six shoe factories, three cigar factories, a carriage manufacturer, a piano factory, a church organ factory, as well as three shipyards, which captured the young Hopper's imagination. Showing an early talent as a draftsman, he thought of becoming a marine architect. At fifteen he designed and built a sailboat; soon after, he made his own canoe.

The financial panic of 1893 gutted local industry, however, and Nyack never recovered. It became something of a touristy stop for those wishing to escape to a relatively placid and pristine example of Victorian America. But the Hoppers did not depend upon local industry or on Garret's dry-goods store, where the town's housewives purchased fabrics to sew clothing for themselves and their families. Hopper's father had no head for business, and his store never made much money. But Hopper's mother, Elizabeth Griffiths Hopper, had inherited enough to keep them comfortably ensconced in the God-fearing and well-mannered (to us, restrictive) lifestyle of their standing and their time. Meanwhile, however, the country as a whole surged ahead, full-bore.

Change occurred so fast and along so many different lines in the last decades of the nineteenth and beginning of the twentieth century as to make any attempt at summary seem insufficient for omitting significant examples, yet overblown for ignoring both long-term antecedents and striking continuities. Even today, the nation is dotted with small towns where families like the Hoppers, with set beliefs and socially conservative predilections, exist in great numbers, albeit with such arguably superficial differences as cars and microwave ovens. But still: If the ubiquity of rail service had been a seventy-year project that had finally come to fruition by 1900, when some 190,000 miles of track worth $10 billion threaded the country, peak use would not arrive until the 1920s. This was the era that saw such dramatic, world- and worldview-altering innovations as electricity, telephones, cameras, movies, phonographs, and lightbulbs. The internal combustion engine was put to use in cars, airplanes, and tanks, while the ancient dream of traveling underwater, embodied by the submarine, finally became reality. Indeed, an entire panoply of technology and machinery that both defined what we call progress and allowed us to fight a pair of wars that involved most of the globe and left millions dead came into being.

This was also when the Wild West was parceled out and closed off while immigration soared: 788,992 arrived in 1882, the year of Hopper's birth. Rapidly growing cities crammed with factories and tenements absorbed the excess workforce and much of the rural population as well, replacing farming communities as the nation's cultural centers. Which is why, in part, there appears to have been a decline in religious belief. The immigrants, many of them non-Protestants—whether Asian or, more often, Jewish or Catholic—tended to dilute the American-style Christianity in which boys like Hopper were raised. The applications of scientific methods to human beings, both hard (Darwinism) and soft (psychology, sociology), provided alternatives that drew academic resources away from theology. What was really happening was not a drop-off in church attendance— America continued to have, as it has now, a higher church attendance rate than Europe—so much as a decline in the attention paid to religion by educated elites. If they did not consider religion a pernicious hodgepodge of superstition bypassed by new ideas (à la Marxists and Freudians), they deferred in a modernist-relativist manner to a stew pot of various creeds, none of which could be said to be more valid than any other.

Secularism, popular among those whose ideas and activities had a certain preeminence, did coincide with a breakdown of social mores. Women left the home and joined the workforce, smoked in public, and agitated for the right to vote.

They also wore less clothing, moving, for example, bit by bit from the full-body bathing suits of Hopper's youth to the bikini in some fifty years. Divorce rates went up, marriage became for many not a sacred union but a "companionate" civil contract to be ended as soon as either partner became dissatisfied. The country was already headed in the direction of sexual tolerance that would explode in the 1960s and give us pornography as mainstream entertainment by the 1970s.

Increased mobility reduced the importance of towns such as Nyack and local ties to neighbors and to relatives. Technology-driven business activity was remaking a renegade democracy into a capitalist-industrial powerhouse overseen by such multi-millionaires as Andrew Carnegie and John D. Rockefeller, generating a host of new opportunities for success and wealth. But these opportunities were mainly in cities, where vice and crime were also concentrated, and where a young man from a small town would confront the modern world on his own.

In the summer of 1899, Hopper, now a lanky (six feet, five inches) high school graduate of seventeen with blue eyes, brown hair that he parted down the middle, and surprisingly full, sensual lips, decided to take advantage of his talent for drawing. He did not and could not simply declare himself an artist in the higher sense. His parents' values were too staid, and although comfortable, they were not rich. His immediate goal was to support himself. This meant skipping college and trying his hand at the then burgeoning field of commercial art. It meant commuting from Nyack to the New York School of Illustration on West Thirty-fourth Street in the biggest, busiest city of all.

It didn't last: The lessons on offer there were far too limited for his talent and need to express himself. With his parents' approval, Hopper spent the next six years studying at the New York School of Art, much of this time under the tutelage of one of the best-known and most inspiring teachers in the country, Robert Henri. Henri advocated originality in painting and celebrated the messy energy of contemporary life, encouraging his students to go out and find fresh subjects that would free them from the past and from the academy and give them greater scope to put their own unique imprint on their work. These were lessons that Hopper would ultimately follow. Many of his paintings represent extensive wanderings through the crowded and quickly evolving streets of Manhattan, vacations along the shores of the Northeast, and long drives across the country. He was always looking out for something that he could put on canvas and make thoroughly his own, while displaying an attentive eye for detail—his having been there at that specific place right then.

But Hopper's paintings would not of themselves pay the rent—not yet. He took up commercial illustration after all, joining C. C. Phillips and Company, a recently established firm on East Twenty-second Street. Later, after three trips to Europe to polish off his education, he became a freelancer, which gave him more control over his schedule but also involved scrapping about for short-term jobs with magazines and other clients. This gave him firsthand experience with what might be somewhat righteously termed the "hard reality" of America: making and buying and selling—the subordination of self to meet the demands of commerce.

Meanwhile, his ambitions for serious art and the connections he made among his classmates kept him in touch with the more bohemian element. He counted as a lifelong friend fellow alumnus Guy Pène du Bois, himself a talented painter and also an insightful critic who would be one of Hopper's early champions. Hopper was also friends with the novelist and sometime socialist John Dos Passos, author of the trilogy *U.S.A.* (1930, 1932, 1936). He spent summer vacations at Ogunquit and Monhegan Island, Maine, and (later) Cape Cod, where New York's artists and writers gathered away from the heat. He continued to read widely, as he always had, in classic American and English literature. He was dedicated to Emerson in particular, but he also kept up with recent works, and was especially fond of E. B. White and the poet Robert Frost, whose often dark, unadorned aesthetic resembles his own. He knew French well enough to enjoy poets like Rimbaud and Paul Verlaine in their native language, and was a fan of Thomas Mann, Goethe, and Proust. He accepted Freud. He did not attend church. He became an avid moviegoer, as if to unify his intellectual and artistic interests with his professionally acquired knowledge of popular tastes.

The cultural and commercial ferment of New York could be said to have suited Hopper, and given his drive and capacity, it was perhaps a necessary relief from the provincialism of Nyack, which he once described as "intolerably stupid." But he hated the restrictions of commercial illustration, and hated as well the consuming efforts at self-promotion required of a freelancer, often needing a job "for money and at the same time hoping to hell [that he] wouldn't get the lousy thing." And he never gave up his ties to Nyack, retaining until his death the house his great-grandfather had built. Among his fellow artists, Hopper was known as excessively quiet, as if he was holding something back or keeping his surroundings at bay: Lloyd Goodrich noted his "monumental silences," du Bois his "refusal to compromise," i.e., make small talk, "for social reasons." He remained regular and relatively sober in his habits, smoking some but spending no time in bars or drinking to excess. He was frugal, staying in the same small Washington Square apartment for decades, eating out—but cheaply, and buying secondhand cars. He did have a summer house with a studio constructed on the still-undeveloped coast of Maine in 1934: His single luxury was a space far from even casual contact with other people. Hopper was also that relative rarity among artists, a staunch Republican. And while he was an artist during a period when promiscuity among artists provoked no great scandal, he did not have much, if any, kind of sex life—not until forming a romantic liaison with one Josephine Nivison.

Nivison, who went by Jo, was an artist herself, who had studied under Henri at the New York School of Art in 1905 and 1906, the last two years of Hopper's attendance there (she remembered Hopper, she later said, but did not know him at the time). A "passionate prefeminist" with "quicksilver intelligence," according to art critic Brian O'Doherty, she was in many ways Hopper's opposite: a city girl and a joiner, who taught public school and acted onstage, as peppy as she was short (she reached to just over five feet), and almost excessively chatty. She did not hang out in bohemian circles reluctantly (as Hopper seems to have done) but enthusiastically, including among her acquaintances photographer Alfred Stieglitz and painter Marsden Hartley. However, she was still a virgin at forty when she struck up a friendship with Hopper while on vacation in Gloucester in July 1923. Yet nude sketches Hopper made of his wife over the years testify to a sustained erotic charge between the two of them, and to her willingness to let Hopper explore his sexuality.

She helped him in more practical ways, as well. It was Jo who got him his first big break by convincing him to submit some of his new watercolors to the Brooklyn Museum exhibit. They married soon after, without ceremony, on July 9, 1924, and she was his constant companion from then on, reading the same books he read, traveling with him, and more. She would encourage him during his often frustrating dry periods, suggesting subjects and even starting a painting to get him to paint. She was the model for all the women in his work, while he used himself as model for the men. As his fame grew, she became something of a personal assistant, handling his mail and requests for interviews, during which she often added her own comments to make up for her husband's reticence.

Jo became, in brief, exactly what Hopper required, a mediator between himself and society-at-large. With her there, he was able to overcome his dalliance with French impressionism and replace it with a more clear-eyed style that directly confronted his surroundings. This enabled him to produce a remarkably wide-ranging record of the country, from the Northeast to the deep South and on into Mexico, from the eastern seaboard out into the West. He painted small offices and row houses, train stations, gas stations, movie theaters, the rooms and lobbies of hotels and motels in cities and along highways. He painted hulking tenements near a drab but eerily lit factory along the East River. He painted an Automat, a barber shop, and a corner drugstore. He painted banks and cafeterias, mountains, coasts, and forests, waitresses, and sunbathers. He painted a bright red neon sign burning behind a pair of flappers eating in a Chinese restaurant, a man sitting on a stoop smoking a cigar before a darkened storefront, and even a stripper prancing across a stage in a G-string and high heels. He captured farms and suburbs, along with the streets and byways of small towns and rural enclaves. He painted cramped inner-city apartments and two-story clapboard houses like the house he grew up in (he revealingly titled one such painting, of a pair of plain white houses with white picket fences, *Two Puritans* [1945]).

But if Jo helped make his career, their marriage, however close, was not happy. According to Goodrich, who knew the Hoppers, they could "be appalling frank with one another" and "to hear them sometimes one was convinced they were at the breaking point." From critic Robert Hobbs we hear of Jo's "imperiousness" and of "the constantly bickering, jealous female" whose "failings" Hopper did his best to "understand." But however much the harpy Jo was, she seems to have had reason to complain. Hopper was, it turns out, too old-fashioned to take to the idea of a woman artist, much less compete with his own wife for attention. Her career, which had been going well, took a backseat to his. Worse, he often denigrated her talent, and despite his increasing clout, did not put forth any effort to get her noticed by dealers or gallery owners.

The bedroom was also a problem for Jo, as we learn in Gail Levin's *Hopper: An Intimate Biography*. If she was willing to indulge his sexual interest, he seems to have had little or no interest in her sexual desires. In her journal, Jo recorded an ongoing bitterness at what she felt she had given him being met with so little in return. The conflict between the couple was not only vicious, painful, and persistent, but also physically abusive. They had violent, knockdown fights, with him slapping her and throwing her around, and once dragging her forcibly from their car onto the ground after she had gotten into a minor accident. She, for her part, made up for her deficit in strength by scratching and biting, even drawing blood.

Yet, as Goodrich puts it, "there was no mistaking their deep mutual attachment and dependency." Hopper did love his wife, in his way, writing her notes of endearment in French after fights, doing her portrait, being her constant companion as she was his, and at least helping her out in small ways: She would ultimately testify that "he has had a lifetime stretching canvases for me." But perhaps for the very reason that he depended so heavily on Jo, he resented her. Even in marriage, and in such intimate, daily contact with another human being, Hopper needed to maintain a certain distance. He could not entirely relinquish his independence for his wife any more than he could ever quite fully acquiesce to New York City, to commerce, to the lefty artistic milieu in which he found himself, to the modern world. "One was aware," according to Brian O'Doherty, "in his presence, of a slight displacement in his experience of his own person." A part of him arguably remained alien to what he had become, i.e., something other than a boy from a religious family in a small, decorous, Victorian-era town.

But what kept Hopper apart also made him acutely aware of contemporary life and caused him to portray life as he saw it, without resorting to what he considered faddish strategies, such as cubism and surrealism, employed by so many of his fellow painters. Hopper's distance also explains why, rather than moving forward, he retreated from impressionism to a version of his other great influence, nineteenth-century American-style realism (especially Eakins and Homer). It also explains how he could bring drama to ordinary subjects, such as a diner, making extraordinary images of them: It gave him a skeptical perspective on the new liberties and multifarious changes he saw around him. If Hopper's genius lies not in this skepticism as such, it lies in both the subtle and the blunt ways in which he expressed his skepticism, like a lone guerrilla warrior using whatever lies at hand to discomfit an infinitely more potent enemy.

If he painted the very movie theaters he often attended, he portrayed them as garish, too large, overly ornate. If he painted a row of picturesque houses on a rise along a suburban street, he included a small, forlorn "for sale" sign and a bunch of unsightly telephone poles. He might slice through a group of buildings by placing an iron bar in the foreground, or cut off the view entirely halfway down with a concrete wall, making certain to place fire escapes along their sunlit facades, perhaps a billboard off to the side. The cafeterias he painted were clean (too clean) and impersonal—places people ate without talking or enjoying their food. If he painted a train station he included no train, no sense of the muscular force and excitement of technology, but portrayed it at night, darkened, vacant, a place that no one would go if they could avoid it, except perhaps to hide. His women are often busty, made-up, with their cleavage and sexy shapely legs on display, but they are not flirty, not inviting. Like his men, they are often dejected, looking downward, alone and lonely, or simply blank, as if their surroundings have robbed them of their very being, or pushed it so deep inside there was nothing of it left on the surface for anyone else to see.

So it is with *Nighthawks*. We are clearly being shown an image of a diner in a big city. But the people in the diner do not seem particularly pleased to be there, and what gives the diner such presence is not details like the matching fedoras on the male customers or the billboard, though they do ground the image. It is, rather, the same thing that makes the expressions on the faces of the people (surly for the man facing us, angry for the server, detached for the woman) seem appropriate: the dark, empty backdrop. This backdrop undercuts the glow within the diner: What is electric lighting but a poor modern contrivance?

Ironically, however, the diner stands out like a beacon against the weirdly desolate backdrop because of the lighting. The modern, after all, gave Hopper his subject and made his austere, old-fashioned realism significant.

3. Both Old and New

"I am trying to paint myself," Hopper said, and he was aware that a kind of cultural collision between old and new was inextricably tied to who he was. He explicitly engaged this collision in paintings such as *House by the Railroad* (1925), which rather brutally juxtaposes an antiquated mansion with train track.

The mansion is sober yet luxurious. Three large stories with a turret that once, no doubt, provided a panoramic view of the surrounding scenery, a sloping mansard roof with three bright red chimneys, and a colonnaded veranda rise up against a bland sky of light blue and white. But we see the mansion from the front, shadowed as if in consternation, its base abruptly cut off from view by a rust red rail atop brown dirt. And that's it: no birds, no people, no clouds. The painting could be pure allegory, or (as critics have argued) nostalgia for a nobler past all too conveniently disavowed in favor of what has been passed off as a great leap forward.

This interpretation is fine as far as it goes, except the mansion is a bit too much, too sober, too luxurious—an example of what Raymond Chandler once referred to as "jigsaw gothic." Hopper's background was middle class, not aristocratic, and his mansion does not embody some hypothetical Victorian owner's upstanding character and impeccable moral hygiene. Rather, it seems designed to contain secrets, immoral in kind, which may one day burst forth as if from a decaying estate in a horror story by Edgar Allan Poe. It is more appealing than the train track, but as *Nighthawks* and the careful attention Hopper gave to painting the track suggest, he had no problem portraying the conventionally ugly. *House by the Railroad* does present a collision between old and new, but without sentiment, without judgment, and without resolution. The mansion rears up as if affronted by the unmitigated audacity of the track in presuming to exist within its purview—those red chimneys are like spots of rage—while the track, sure of purpose, blithely ignores the mansion's dated claims.

The painting is itself contemporary. However skeptical of the modern he may have been, Hopper was not especially nostalgic and never tried to re-create some fantasy idyll of small-town life à la Norman Rockwell. He avoided historical topics. Mansions like the mansion in *House by the Railroad* still stood in 1925, though as in other Hopper paintings, they might be reduced to taking boarders or serving as redoubts for rumrunners. But still: That mansion looks pretty commodious, not just functional like an apartment in the city to come home from work to and sleep and eat breakfast in before going off to work again. It is where we might feel deeply and think freely, where we might live life as an end in itself, something to wallow in rather than use up. The track, meanwhile, provides an awkward path for strolling. Trains are about getting as much material and as many people as possible from A to B with all due haste because we have things to get done, business to take care of, or, if lucky, vacation with family and friends to maximize before getting back to business again. The train sets the pace, and we accommodate ourselves to it as best we can, with its schedules, seating, and compartments.

The modern takes us over and redefines us: The diner in *Nighthawks* is no more accommodating of the customers' particular needs and desires than Henry Ford's assembly lines were of the long-term development of individual skills and knowledge of his employees. Biographies, blood ties, and social status would have been important to the original owners of the mansion in *House by the Railroad,* as they were to Hopper's sense of himself. But trains don't ask about the pasts of their passengers, and diners do not care where you came from or where you are going, do not care whether you are married or not, do not wonder about your values or your religion. The only thing any diner needs to know is what you want to order and whether you have the money to pay for what you order. We are at liberty but disconnected, isolated, and transformed from particular people into generic units.

Modern art movements were attempts to come to terms with this or to rediscover something enduringly human. Dadaists in Zurich during World War I were intentionally offensive, obscene, and irrational: Painter Marcel Duchamp purchased a ceramic urinal from a factory outlet, turned it upside down, signed it R. Mutt, and submitted it as sculpture to the Independents exhibition in New York City in 1917 (the urinal, called *Fountain,* was rejected). Cubists such as Picasso and Braque tried to beat change at its own game, showing an impossible multiplicity of perspectives in a single painting. Italian futurists used a similar method to celebrate the modern as an exhilarating confluence of speed, energy, and violence. Surrealists looked inside to the presumably premodern phenomena of dreams and the libidinous unconscious. Abstract artists reduced painting to its formal elements: shape, line, and color. In New York after World War II, abstract expressionists such as Jackson Pollock reintroduced content, of a sort: They painted emotion itself, passion itself—the primal something-or-other in all of us.

Hopper would have none of it, up to and including the brilliant innovations of Picasso, whom he regarded as "capricious," a chic trickster: If you follow your heart, you will get where you want to go, we tell ourselves. To "be a man," as Emerson declared, means not conforming; means photographing flower gardens on the afternoon of September 11, 2001, because that's what you were going to do in any case; means come-what-may devotion to a self-imposed task. It is easy to imagine that an enormous amount of frustration must attend such an ethic, most of it hidden by failure and death: Bucking trends can be a form of self-destruction. But in insisting on making accessible pictorial paintings long after it made any sense to do so, Hopper evolved a vision at once archaic and distinctly modern by portraying the lost place of the individual—of his own stubborn, willful self—in the twentieth century.

The people we see in the diner may be overwhelmed by their surroundings, may feel dejected, sullen, angry. But they are not part of their surroundings the way the Hoppers were part of Nyack in the late nineteenth century. They only happen to be there. Any one or all of them could just as well be in another diner in another city, on the subway, entering a movie theater, or in a bar in, say, Kalamazoo or San Francisco. This accidental quality is all the more powerful because Hopper gave them such a solid, three-dimensional presence. Those customers and that young server in his white uniform are what keep *Nighthawks* from being only an exercise in atmospherics. We want to know more about them. How much does the server hate his job? What is the man with his back to us thinking about? They allow us to enter into the painting, to wonder something similar about ourselves: What do we think and feel when we pass through such establishments or wander down such empty streets, and, also, does it matter?

That what we think and feel may not matter—while it would have been pretty much all that matters to those living in a mansion like the one in *House by the Railroad*—lends *Nighthawks* a subliminal jolt and suggests one way Hopper might be said to prefer the past.

4. The American Scene

Whether Hopper actually did prefer the past, a perception of him as something of a throwback to a purer version of America had much to do with his increasing fame and respect in the years following World War II. His paintings sold well: *Nighthawks* itself was purchased shortly after completion by the Art Institute of Chicago, where it remains on prominent display. He was elected to membership in the National Institute for Arts and Letters in 1945. Hopper retrospectives were featured at the Whitney in 1950, the Philadelphia Museum of Art in 1962, in Arizona in 1963, and in Detroit and St. Louis in 1964. New work was exhibited in Detroit and Boston in 1950, and Hopper represented the United States at the Vienna Biennale in 1952. He received top prizes and honorable mentions in a variety of shows and was granted three honorary doctorates: from the Art Institute of Chicago in 1950, Rutgers University in 1953, and the Philadelphia College of Art in 1965.

But perhaps his most significant recognition came when his picture adorned the cover of *Time* magazine on December 24, 1956, because it underlined his popularity outside of artistic circles and the attraction his work held for people who rarely set foot in a museum. A section of the adoring article within, entitled "The Champion," venerates Hopper as the latest chapter of what the writer implies is the sole authentic American style of art, here termed "searching realism." Hopper proves that "for the past two centuries" domestic painting "has stood on its own two feet, comparing favorably with the art of every nation except France." This, of course, flatters the attitudes of the magazine's readers. They would also presumably appreciate that Hopper "denies none of the Anglo-Saxon attributes which are so strongly built into his character" or that while painting has become the plaything of "clattering egos" (the arrogantly recondite avant-garde), he remains as steadfast and straightforward as "a tree growing on Main Street."

Predictably, Hopper thought little of *Time*'s efforts to immortalize him—would he ever escape that "American scene" stuff? One can sympathize with the touchiness, the wish to be taken on his own terms, period. But it was as a portrayer of the American scene, and because of how far Hopper took traditional American realism, that he had an enduring effect on other artists and on writers and movies. And if the "tree growing on Main Street" metaphor is a bit too homey, his accomplishments did require a rooted resistance to shifting winds of taste.

Hopper further demonstrated this resistance by not being affected much, if at all, by fame and fortune. He, for one, did not move to a large house on Long Island, eat in the finest restaurants, buy the best of everything, or dally with younger women. He stuck to his routines, his parsimony, and the wife with whom he continued to fight. His art had made him more than an artist; he became a public figure of some stature. He was invited to the inaugurations of John F. Kennedy and Lyndon Johnson (he refused both). But his interest never ceased to center on art, and he did not coast but remained as meticulous, and as displeased, as ever. "There is a loneliness about him," wrote artist Raphael Soyer, who met Hopper in 1963, "an habitual moroseness, a sadness to the point of anger." His last works included *A Woman in the Sun* (1961), in which a woman stands naked, lit by sunlight in a sparsely furnished bedroom, smoking a cigarette, and looking sad and distracted, as if being naked in the sun meant no liberation, gave no pleasure. In *Sun in an Empty Room* (1963), sunlight is the only sign of life, but it is pale, not warming, and not for anyone. The painting might be a dryly ironic anticipation of Hopper's own death, which occurred on

May 15, 1967, in the studio of his Washington Square apartment—where else? He was buried back in Nyack in a family plot on a rise with a view of the Hudson River.

What we are left with is what he left us—his paintings, and mostly *Nighthawks*. More than any other Hopper, and arguably more than any other American painting, *Nighthawks* has moved beyond art and made an indelible impression on the national imagination. If you mention Hopper's name to Americans, *Nighthawks* is the painting they will recall, the one they have not so much consciously considered as much as simply accepted as part of their cultural heritage. It did matter, despite his own skepticism, what Hopper felt and thought: This is a work in which he managed both to sum up and to give a unique and powerful take on who we are.

Chapter Two

One Man,
One Big Damned City

We may admit to the merits of *Time* magazine's attempt to claim Hopper for the middle class as the latest paragon of American realism—as *their* artist—and that we can easily see *Nighthawks* as a credible view of America at midcentury. Yet the painting is startlingly original, so stripped down and idiosyncratic it could almost be a version of the early 1940s fantasized by an artist born in the 1960s or later. We might then suggest that *Nighthawks* captures the timeless essence of New York, and we do recognize the feel and the atmosphere of it even today. But we still have to wonder: Where are the thronging masses, the propulsive force, the clanking noise, or at least a bit of the grime that patently distinguish the Big Apple from such better-mannered but not quite as interesting or important cities as, say, Toronto or Seattle?

Hopper was not, of course, trying to record the city he saw around him with faultless accuracy. He chose his subjects with care to begin with, then proceeded to take out, to reimagine, to clarify, to get to those aspects of a given scene—"a restaurant on the corner of Greenwich Avenue"—that seemed, to him, essential. And what he came up with in *Nighthawks* and elsewhere differed radically in content and tone from what other artists—and their number was legion—discovered in a city whose energy and ambition were such that in the years following the Civil War, New York had, as Lewis Mumford noted, already become an "imperial metropolis." By the end of World War II it would take over from Paris and London as the cultural and financial capital of the Western Hemisphere.

For the energy we can look to painters such as John Sloan or George Bellows, and to Hopper's unflaggingly enthusiastic instructor at the New York School of Art, Robert Henri. Henri encouraged his students to avoid the still life and classical motifs and to search instead for the unvarnished "truth" of life in downtown dives, tenements, waterfront alleyways, and Bowery bars. The point was not to condemn or idealize but to respond to the great democratic dynamic, what Thomas Bender has called the "barely controlled chaos" of workers of all kinds, immigrants and former farmhands vying to survive, tenements with screaming kids and bedecked by clotheslines, of people on the make. They were the masses, trying to figure a way up against enormous market forces they had no control over and perhaps only barely comprehended in a city too big and developing too quickly for any but the fast and keen to keep their bearings, and perhaps not even them: Who knows who would thrive, who fail? But who could fail to be stirred to creative heights by an epic human tapestry in the making? This, Henri insisted, was the subject, what must be painted. He emphasized the artist's duty to accept the "ugly" along with the "beautiful," recommended "virility" as more important than "technique," and inspired his students to what one impressed critic called an "echo of the significant American life around them."

Hopper respected Henri and took much of his attitude toward subject matter from him. He would likely never have painted a nondescript urban diner without having been exposed to Henri's ideas. But it was Bellows, who came to New York in 1904 by way of Ohio and was the same age as Hopper, as well as a classmate, who most passionately adhered to the spirit of Henri's teachings. He soon raised New York's lower reaches and himself to the apex of the art world with paintings like *Stag at Sharkey's* (1909) and *Both Members of This Club* (1909). These depict the quasi-illicit boxing matches (boxing was illegal at the time) that regularly took place at members-only establishments for gambling purposes. Sharkey's, run by an ex-boxer and criminal named Tom Sharkey, was on a well-worn circuit of casinos and betting parlors. The crowd at his popular club was a motley mix of poor and middle class and wealthy, slum denizens and slummers in search of an adventurous night out. In *Stag* they are united in their attention to the ring, for practical reasons: They want to know if they'll win or lose money. But they would pay close attention anyway, given Bellows's convincing presentation of ritualized violence.

Every muscle on the two boxers is strained. Their heads collide and their bodies shove against each other, a balance of opposing forces, ready to tumble forward if the other boxer stops pushing back as hard as he can. Bright red tints one's neck, the other's face. A right arm draws back for a punch. Everything is raw energy and motion—even the referee looks like he's giving all he's got as he reaches in to break them up—only one instant from a single bout on one night of many. There will be plenty of fight left over when the match is done, plenty of fights to come, just as virile, just as exciting, and the city will feed off this energy. This is the very pounding heart of the city, enough of a heart for everyone, after all, or at least for anyone with balls enough to grab on and ride: Their ambition will be realized.

In grand New York fashion, Bellows himself aggressively tilted toward success: Think Norman Mailer, Andy Warhol, think Julian Schnabel, a long line of serious talents and utter frauds for whom self-promotion was a necessary and therefore justified means of distinguishing themselves from all those other writers, painters, musicians, or whatnot. *Stag at Sharkey's* was shocking the way a Robert Mapplethorpe image of homosexual intercourse would prove shocking in the 1980s—just enough to force the public's attention in the artist's direction. For the same reason, one of the boxers in *Both Members of This Club* is black, hence the painting's title, which does not comment on or reprove so much as foreground the issue of race, as good a method as there was at the time to push buttons, create sensation. And so it did. If Hopper floundered in obscurity and matured late, Bellows found fame early and peaked early, his significant work done by his early thirties, after which he lost his edge like a cock rocker with an ebbing libido, and died early, of a ruptured appendix, in 1925.

But the energy Bellows captured in his youth found a new form and new style in modernist painters who celebrated the rise of a robust and ever-changing cityscape unlike any that came before, an unprecedented technological wonder. Painters like Joseph Stella, who regarded the Brooklyn Bridge—the subject of his stunning *The Voice of the City of New York Interpreted: The Bridge* (1920–22)—as an "APOTHEOSIS" of "the new civilization of AMERICA" (caps his). Painters like Georgia O'Keeffe, who, before her career-altering experience of the wide-open spaces of New Mexico in 1929, spent some ten years in the city, complementing her trademark vulvic flowers with gloriously phallic skyscrapers, the best known of which is *The Radiator Building—Night, New York, 1927* (1927).

Tall and dark against a velvet blue night sky shot through with beams of light, O'Keeffe's *Radiator Building* is bursting with electric life shining bright from a hundred-odd windows, from the vestibule on the bottom floor all the way up to the glowing crest at the top. Meanwhile, the white smoke that spews from the top of the not-quite-so-tall building beside it is not a drawback of progress but a spout of semen, life begetting greater life. Just as the city effectively channeled the virility and raw energy embodied by Bellows's boxers in *Stag* into epic erections of steel and concrete, so the Radiator Building itself, erected only a few years before O'Keeffe's painting, prepared the way for even taller and heavier buildings, buildings yet more assertive of the greatness of this city's rising destiny. Four years after O'Keeffe completed her painting, in 1931, the president and the governor of New York would together oversee the opening of that "ultimate monument to technological achievement" and "eighth wonder of the world," the Empire State Building. Not the prettiest building ever constructed by man, nor the most innovative, but the point was strength, mass, and unparalleled height.

Strength defined New York, became what the city meant to the common tourists, who, along with kings and presidents and millionaires and movie stars, regularly flocked to the observation deck on the eighty-sixth floor to look out over the home of Babe Ruth and the lesser-known but more significant Robert Moses, New York's visionary overlord. Between 1924 and 1968, Moses oversaw the expenditure of tax dollars—$27 billion, on parks, playgrounds, beaches, bridges, public housing projects, tunnels, highways, expressways, underpasses, overpasses, and sports stadiums, all allowing the city to function while accommodating the strivings and desires of miscellaneous millions.

Imagine for a moment the mighty Moses standing on the top of the tower on the 102nd floor of the Empire State Building with a phalanx of servile bureaucrats in tow, surveying his multiform achievements and calling them very good indeed—how far he stands in every way from the New York Hopper portrayed in works like *Automat* (1927). We hit the ground hard: no raw energy, no marvelous new civilization, no ambition, no triumph. Instead, a young woman sits with downcast eyes at a round table in a nameless Automat, with barely enough enthusiasm for life to lift the cup of coffee she holds in her right hand near a small empty plate that might have held a roll or sandwich. Behind her a darkened plate-glass window reflects nothing of the Automat's interior except for a line of lights along the ceiling. We see no crowds, only her, alone, in the center of this vast city. Why bother to remove hat and coat? She has not. She knew she would be alone, that the chair opposite would remain unoccupied. Perhaps this is why she chose an Automat. No need to underline her isolation with a perfunctory "hello" and "have a nice day" from a waiter. Better to put coins in a machine and avoid contact altogether. But even here she can't avoid the insulting irony of the homey bowl of bright red and yellow fruit on the windowsill.

If *Automat* serves as an acerbic counterpoint to a painting such as *Stag at Sharkey's, Radiator Building* might be usefully compared with Hopper's ominous *Approaching a City* (1946). The point of view is from a train. We do not see the train, nothing so lively, only rows of tracks leading into a darkened concrete tunnel with a high concrete wall to the right. Above the wall we see the top stories of a pair of small apartment buildings and the massive concrete bulk of a factory with tiny windows and a pair of smokestacks. Above the factory a bit of baby blue sky provides stark contrast with the sickly greenish yellows Hopper used for most of the rest of the painting. The feeling we get is not one of embarking on an adventure in which we will overcome obstacles, test ourselves, and (of course) pass with flying colors, but the nausea that might creep over us on being brought to a maximum-security prison.

A certain trepidation makes sense, however, in a city where we find a young woman as forlornly alone in an Automat as she might be in a prison cell—as it does in the street-corner diner in *Nighthawks,* which seems cut off, isolated. The diner itself is cut off, without any means of exit or entrance except perhaps the ugly ocher door behind the coffee urns with a tiny square window in it, a door that we might find in an institution, a hospital, or, indeed, a prison. Certainly we can see no signs bidding prospective patrons to enter or exit. That plate-glass window that curves around the corner seals in the three customers and server like plants inside a hothouse. Their visibility only emphasizes their separateness, while the diner and the street corner reproduce in miniature the divided and walled-off space of the extensive metropolis of which they are a part.

The customers and the server, while in the diner together, also seem cut off from one another, as if they have internalized the city's walls and are imprisoned in their own heads. The single male customer has no relation or interaction with the couple and the server, and the couple, while they sit together, are each on their own little planet, like a pair of unsynchronized eyeballs, one looking down, the other straight ahead. There is interaction between the man of the couple and the server, who look at each other. But this interaction appears forced, painful, the customer having said something out of the corner of his mouth, the server reacting with a strained grimace. Even a simple exchange of words seems to carry inordinate threat, as if they have reason to assume the worst of intentions in each other, as they would if they were in fact incarcerated.

John Carpenter's entertaining whim of a sci-fi movie, *Escape from New York,* does reimagine the city as a maximum-security prison. This may not have seemed such an outlandish possibility at the movie's release in 1981, following a decade of recession, crime waves, urban decay, and white flight. The easy thing to do would be just to build a fifty-foot containment wall around the place, mine the bridges, and send those few dangerous felons not already there, in! Which draws out the metaphor: It would not just be an ordinary prison, but a prison run by the inmates, democracy as anarchy, as if that tunnel in *Approaching a City* might also be a passage down to a twentieth-century version Hades, the City of Dis—hell. So has New York been portrayed in many a police show and comic book: old Gotham, too dark and full of odd recesses and secret passways ever to be brought to heel by the forces of law and order, except perhaps by a man who is half arachnid and shoots webs from his wrists or a man who dresses up as a bat. But even then there are enough cartoon villains out and about to keep your basic superhero with special access to the evil side of our collective psyche busy for decades.

New York as a criminal's playground is what we find in any case in Herbert Asbury's *Gangs of New York* (1928; made into a movie by Martin Scorsese in 2002, but read the book). Yellow journalism posing as history, *Gangs* portrays the Big Apple as little more than a rotten core. Manhattan with its impoverished, congested, and disease-ridden slums might have been an all-too-successful experiment in breeding homicidal thugs, who by and large ran the city from their filthy hovels, nickel whiskey joints, rigged casinos, and bordellos masquerading (but barely) as dance halls, from the years preceding the Civil War through the early decades of the twentieth century. The cops, meanwhile, when not outnumbered and outgunned, were on the take, and in any case the members of gangs like the Whyos and the Hudson Dusters murdered on behalf of City Hall when not murdering on their own behalf or just to keep things rowdy. Were the rare honest cop to arrest one, he would likely be released the next day by order of the mayor.

All of this adds up to a tellingly different New York from the one we find in, say, the mannered, tragic novels of Henry James and Edith Wharton, where the city becomes a stage set for failed dalliances and the occasional suicide among the polished but repressed well-to-do, and is a tellingly different New York from that of Robert Henri and George Bellows. Asbury's New York could contain the boxing match Bellows portrayed in *Stag at Sharkey's*, but the energy in Asbury is negative, the violence only violence, an obstacle to new civilization rather than the virility behind it. "Happily," however, he tells us in his introduction, the "refractory citizen" that *Gangs* chronicles "has now passed from the metropolitan scene," along with, presumably, the particular combination of "vice, poverty, and political corruption" that had produced him.

Not true. The era of Robert Moses and Hopper's *Nighthawks* was also the heyday of the legendary hit-man collective Murder Inc. and sustained plenty of gangs, many of them now Mafia. Meanwhile, another recorder of gangland atrocities was on the scene, Arthur "Weegee the Famous" Fellig, armed not with a pen but a camera.

He called himself Weegee after Ouija, the popular psychic board game, to advertise his alleged ability to predict the scene of a crime and arrive there before other photojournalists, a useful talent for a freelancer who made money only when the tabloids bought his pictures. He would later estimate that he had photographed some five thousand murder scenes. Sidewalk shots were common. One well-dressed man lies facedown in his own blood on concrete with a revolver a few feet away. In another photograph, a man's head rests just above the gutter beside a broken bottle, while three cops stand without interest (they've seen it often enough before) in a row behind him with a sign above them that reads "The Spot Bar and Grill." Newspapers cover yet another murder victim with only his shoes visible beneath the marquee of a theater showing a movie called *Joy of Living*. Weegee also caught the corpses of men killed in restaurants and bars and countless other miseries: tenement fires, car wrecks, bums in doorways, drunks passed out in diners and on park benches or piled like old coats in holding pens, bruised killers posing for mug shots, transvestite pickpockets in paddy wagons, homeless children, children under arrest—one, a sad-eyed teenager, for strangling a four-year-old girl.

He was a professional who had to work fast and efficiently (he used a police scanner and practically lived in his Chevy), and his black-and-white pictures tend to have a certain look: The background is darkened and cropped so as to bring the flash-lit subject to front and center, highlighting a corpse, say, and perhaps a few anxious bystanders, policemen, or paramedics who arrived too late. But Weegee's photographs make art out of what is essentially a craft. The compositions are direct but elegant, the outlines sharp, faces often caught with a startling clarity at the very moment when something about the precariousness of life has become all too evident. They glisten with anguish and, taken as a group, provide a powerful vision of the most modern of cities as a modern inferno, where anything but especially death—whether accidental or resulting from passion or ruthless calculation—can happen anywhere, on any corner.

But because Weegee captured the result rather than the cause, the corpse but not the killer, the tenants fleeing or huddled in the cold rather than the arsonist, and because the gritty night (he worked mostly at night) congeals around his parade of misfortune victims, we don't know whom or what to blame but the city itself. Despite the glory of the Radiator Building and the Empire State Building and Robert Moses's messianic efforts to single-handedly reclaim New York from its own chaos, the city nonetheless breeds violence. What can people do, crammed together in such conditions, but kill one another on occasion? They do kill and steal and destroy, but it's the city's fault. We can go further: Three photos of an old peddler getting sideswiped by a taxi—peddler raises himself from a doorway, peddler lies bloodied on street beside his cane and pencils, peddler receives last rites from a priest—might be a triptych for an altar to New York as a strange, unforgiving, and egregiously capricious deity.

Something similar is going on in Hopper's etching *Night Shadows* (1921). A lone man in hat and jacket walks along a deeply shadowed city street, his own black shadow behind him, and the straight black shadow of perhaps a tree or an unlit lamp-post cutting across his path at a sharp angle some fifteen feet ahead of him. An amazing effect, that shadow. After it passes him it hits a storefront to his right and climbs up over an awning before ballooning into a monstrous mass. The man is walking toward this shadow, which seems perhaps like a mistake. We see him do this from above, as if from an apartment window. But the perspective is too sinister to be that of a happenstance voyeur; rather, it's as if the city itself is looking down, without any kindness: "Where can you go? Where can you hide from me? I have you surrounded. . . ."

Nighthawks, for its part, has its share of impenetrable darknesses in the second-story windows of the building across the street from the diner (is somebody in there, hiding, lurking, do-ing . . . something?!?), in the stores beneath them, and in the shadows behind the diner, where a corpse might lie undiscovered until morning. Despite its lack of grime, the street corner is empty enough for a murder or two, perhaps involving one of the customers at the diner, for they have knowledge and understand-ing of those shadows, we realize. From those shadows they ar-rived, and into them they shall once again disappear when they leave. They partake of whatever the city and its populace may be capable of: whatever suffering, whatever crime.

The question arises then, whether you can emphasize what many people would say (correctly) is wrong with the city without also insisting on reform, like the late-nineteenth-century sociologist and photographer Jacob Riis did. His groundbreaking pictures of often terribly debased lives in the overflowing tenements of lower Manhattan (three families crammed together in a tiny basement apartment, etc.) were meant to shock viewers into a more acute awareness of their "brotherhood" with these poor folk, and into action. As was also the case with the communist-influenced social realist painters of the 1930s, who saw New York as an arena of avarice and gross injustice, and sought to portray the unacknowledged nobility of the laborers who assem-ble the products and maintain the services the rest of us effort-lessly enjoy. But even during the Great Depression Hopper himself remained far enough from left-wing sympathies to de-spise New Deal government activism. If there is oppression in the city, it derives from the masses, not the individual. And even this may smack too much of an agenda for a painter who refused to acknowledge that his art had any sociological content "what-soever."

Hopper would understand, one guesses, the caveat Asbury offers for *Gangs,* which, he tells us, "is not a sociological treatise, and makes no pretense of offering solutions." Nor does it attempt "to interpret or analyze." What then does Asbury's book offer, besides often dubious, sometimes openly mythic information? Well, if "guilty pleasure" can be construed as a reputable literary genre, then *Gangs* is a masterpiece. Asbury strikes a revealingly wistful note in the book's final sections: The gangs are not what they used to be; they're disappearing, they're gone. Weegee's photographs are also sensationalistic, even pornographic. We get a corpse, the fact of a crime, a tragic fire, an accident, but that is all. We cannot deduce any moral, do not need the story. The tabloids may have filled in the hoary details, provided the pro forma call for *something* to be done, but it was the excitement and floating fear produced by his pictures that sold copy.

Not that the scenes he captured did not move Weegee. He was from the slums himself, having emigrated from Austria in 1909, at the age of ten. He left school at fourteen to help support his family, and left home at eighteen for flophouses and whatever jobs he could scrounge up (including playing fiddle for silent movies and working as a hole puncher in a Life Savers factory). He photographed a world he knew all too well. Hopper was a true New Yorker in another sense, for he was one of many who came to the city to escape small-town provincialism and make something of himself. And he must have felt attached to the city on some level, because he stayed. But unlike Weegee's roving Chevy, for example, Hopper's apartment at 3 Washington Square might also have been a kind of retreat—in the city, yet separate. He remained there for decades, long after the hard years were behind him, and he could quite easily have afforded something nicer, roomier, and with perhaps fewer steps to climb from the street to get inside.

Hopper was in the city but not as someone who involved himself with the city's day-to-day workings and identified the city's fate with his own. He was more like a small-town artist wannabe, always seeming as if he had just arrived. By the time he created *Nighthawks*, however, he was no longer gawky—if he ever was— but apart, permanently. Hardly the most gregarious of people (his wife once commented that talking to him was "like dropping a stone in a well, except that it doesn't thump when it hits bottom"), Hopper was heir to an American Protestant (Puritanstyle) sense of isolation, the belief that each man must face God alone. He did not keep up with the religion of his youth, but that he saw people in the city as isolated, as cut off from one another as he was cut off from them, suggests this isolation never left him.

If Weegee's photographs are pornographic, Hopper's paintings keep New York slightly at bay. His paintings tease the viewer like a garter belt glimpsed beneath the pulled-up skirt of a woman getting out of a cab. Hopper's views of the city are just such glimpses, from sidewalks, from trains, and from the El, into offices, apartments, and restaurants; the viewer of *Nighthawks* gets a glimpse from the other side of a claustrophobic urban nightmare of vice and violence. For this very reason the painting exerts a seductive pull: There is the dizzying possibility of entering those shadows and getting away with anything, even murder; lawlessness—from a distance.

Jazz

The wild energy of New York City in the twentieth century may be something we cannot fully appreciate without also listening to the modern, highly improvisational version of jazz that rose from the clubs of Manhattan in the late 1940s and early 1950s.

Jazz is not just New York City, of course; jazz is America, individualism as an aesthetic principle, ever since Louis Armstrong's explosive trumpet took over the Dixieland sound of New Orleans and set the stage for the great soloists of the big New York–based swing bands of the 1930s. They in turn set the stage for the soloist to become the very center of jazz, and for the rise of postwar players such as, famously, Charlie Parker, who performed mostly in small combos of maybe five or six members. Each member was, ideally, a soloist, rejecting convention to improvise in a distinct style according to his own unique promptings and what was happening around him with the other players who responded in kind, thereby making music anyone might understand, feel, and find a kind of truth in.

There is a painterly equivalent of this in the work of abstract expressionist Jackson Pollock. Having arrived in New York by way of Wyoming and California in the early 1930s, he became the most touted artist in the country in 1949 (when Parker's innovations were also being touted) due to the promotions of *Nation* critic Clement Greenberg. Greenberg, a Marxist who saw art as historically determined and regarded pictorial representation as outmoded, latched on to Pollock as the new aesthetic frontier. A laudatory article in *Life* followed Greenberg's lead, and a year later a young German refugee named Hans Namuth made Pollock a living legend with an impressive series of photographs of the artist. We witness the very act of creation, just as we would while watching Charlie Parker perform. Pollock is intense, energetic, in the moment, on the very edge. He leans over a large canvas he has laid on the floor of his studio and waves his brush to release looping streams of pigment through the air, as if transferring to the paint itself the turbulent emotions he cannot and, for that matter, does not even want to control: Let gravity bring that paint down onto the canvas as it will; it is not up to me anymore!

If Hopper, on the other hand, once claimed to "improvise," he seems to have meant retouching paintings he had already planned out carefully with preliminary sketches. Indeed, the connection between Pollock and Parker—both brilliantly spontaneous and notoriously self-destructive, both dying early, only a year apart (Pollock at forty-four in 1956, Parker at thirty-four in 1955)—would seem to exclude entirely an artist as meticulous and restrained as Hopper. Yet there is something jazzy about *Nighthawks,* in the anarchic urban atmosphere, the sense that anything might happen, but also in the arrangement of four people who seem cut off from one another even though together they form an elegant tableau and do, necessarily, interact.

They are aware of one another, compose themselves accordingly, order and serve coffee, perhaps even wonder about one another: Call them a quartet, if you will, the diner a stage, ourselves an audience. They are famed for their subtlety, their performance made up of wayward glances, slight gestures, ominous murmurs, long pauses, apparently ordinary movements exposing an enormous amount of underlying tension. Cigarettes and coffee mugs substitute for instruments. You should see what this one guy can do with a glass of water! Or, if that's too much, allow that as they while away their evening at a Manhattan diner, a small combo likely plays in some other corner of the city, perhaps nearby at a club in the Village or uptown in Harlem.

Maybe they perform together regularly, or maybe this is an impromptu meet-up lasting a set or an evening that will or will not occur again. Either way they will make music together but remain musically separate, not absorbed into the performance as a whole even as they help create the whole, which is also specific to the circumstances of this late hour in this particular venue. Their music takes in the enthusiasm, or lack of enthusiasm, in the crowd, the cheers and the jeers of hecklers, drifting smoke, scrapes of chairs, conversation, and sounds leaking in from out-side: a subway rumble, a car horn, a shout, a scream. All must be navigated by the saxophone, trumpet, piano, bass, and drums, just as the people in *Nighthawks* seem both to belong to and to transcend the environment in which they find themselves at this moment.

"Now," as a Parker title has it, "is the time."

Now is the time in a broader sense as well, for jazz (which dates from the 1890s) is very much a modern art form, if only because spontaneous improvisation means more when it can be recorded for fans and fellow musicians. But also because the harmonic complexity, propulsive rhythms, and speed of a player like Char-lie Parker (who regularly performed at nearly twice the maxi-mum rate of metronomes of his day) is well fitted to the overwhelming energy and chaos of a city like New York, to the possibility that we might get lost there or drowned out, never seen amid the crowds or heard above the din. His unremitting creativity evokes a kind of euphoria, not because of the modern world, but despite it, and despite numerous personal problems—addictions, breakdowns, failed relationships, the death of a young son. His music is like weaving effortlessly through a rush-hour traffic jam in midtown. Which does make him ill suited for comparison to the less than obviously euphoric Hopper.

A more fruitful comparison might be made with Parker's pro-tégé, Miles Davis, and what critic Gary Giddins has described as "his predilection for the middle range, his measured lyricism, his hot-ice disposition." Davis had too long and varied a career for easy summation, but the ice side of his sound, the cool, standoff-ish tone that distinguished much of four decades' worth of per-formances, was established early on, shortly after he quit playing with Parker and organized the band that recorded *Birth of the Cool* in 1949 and 1950. Parker had brought Davis into hot jazz, as fiercely expressive as it was complex and fast. The initially unpopular but influential *Birth of the Cool* was Davis's foray in the opposite direction: He pared the music down, got rid of what he did not need, and forged an essential, signature style not so much lacking in emotional content as implying a vast reservoir of emotion just beneath the surface.

Part of the power of his playing is in what Davis does not do, the catharsis or out-and-out euphoria he does not allow the audience or himself. Always capable of an explosive flurry of notes, with a few here, a few there, he could plunge the listener into the depths. Often with his Harmon mute and the mouth of his trumpet up close to the microphone, he might be whispering. He makes a pause, silence itself, pregnant with what he must be holding back, what strength, what anger. Anger because whereas Parker is open, generous, Davis is self-contained, mournful, lonesome. While Parker says things are all right no matter how bad they seem, Davis says, Don't get too happy because as far as I am concerned something is most definitely not right, will never be right, and a whisper is as good as a shout because neither will make any difference.

Something similar happened with Hopper in moving away from his youthful flirtations with French impressionism and the emotive potential of broken-up brushstrokes and thick pigment. He began to favor a smoother image unified by employing what Hopper once referred to as "pretty simple" color schemes and just enough paint for a given effect, as if he were declaring himself the anti–van Gogh. Even in turning from impressionism toward American realism, he avoided the virtuoso, warts-and-all inclusiveness of Thomas Eakins in favor of a sparer style, less generous, less open, less about accepting life and more about getting to some essential knot, something not quite right in the way of things.

Flourishes, technical and artistic, are there (his complex use of light in *Nighthawks,* for example) but not shown off. He does not want us to notice his efforts. He wants us to see what he sees, which is why Greenberg—whose progressive aesthetic required an artist to wear his innovations on his sleeve, as did Pollock—could dismiss Hopper as "simply a bad painter." Hopper's emotions, as well as those of the people he portrays, are not subdued so much as strategically suppressed.

The city may be seductive in *Nighthawks,* to Hopper as well as to us, and this quality may reflect Hopper's desire to delve into those shadows to find lawlessness, to be rid of the stifling manners of small-town Victorian America and perhaps of all moral claims. But this desire remains muted, and keeping it and the self from which it springs muted is what constitutes *Nighthawks*'s perspective on the wild energy of New York City, making the painting an emblem of the mentality of cool.

Chapter Three

The End of the World
Came Sometime Yesterday

> I call you by name, my green, my fluent mundo.
> You will have stopped revolving except in crystal.
> —WALLACE STEVENS

As Americans, we vaunt our ability to stay ahead of what we call "the technology curve," to innovate and to invent and market the most cutting-edge devices. This is what keeps us, and will continue to keep us, at the head of the pack in the much discussed "globalized" economy. But we are also true believers in technology and in machines. We often mark progress by technology allowing us to do more, by machines increasingly able to manipulate reality in accordance with our needs and desires. We see before us a much happier future because of technology. We expect a new house, for example, to take advantage of silicon chips for total atmosphere control, and (the story goes) an oven where potatoes bake to tell the blender when to get started on the cold cucumber soup. New refrigerators might alert the grocer through a wireless Internet connection that we are just about out of milk and some more will be sent us without our having to be aware of the transaction, for payment, too, can be handled by machines. All of these advances will presumably let us do whatever else it is we want to do, garden, say, or paint, or invent more new technology.

But we are also well aware that technology robs something essential from our relationship to the world of air and water and soil we inhabit, and to ourselves as beings for whom, as Emerson once put it, nature is our "old home." The machines we invent become the framework of our environment; they replace nature and what might be called the natural order of life.

In the nineteenth century, for example, the passage of the sun across the sky marked time. This was nature's time or "God's time" and could vary by but a few odd minutes from town to town, but made, as it happens, a hash of train schedules, which were becoming more important to daily life and to business. Railroad executives (not any select body of scientists or chronologists, not any agency of the federal government) decided therefore to divide the country up into distinct time zones and declared the start of what they called standard time at noon on November 18, 1883, the year after Hopper was born. By the 1940s, when he painted *Nighthawks,* New York was as much a giant machine as the modernized house described previously as a big computer posing as shelter. Manhattan was almost totally constructed from layers of technology, from skyscrapers to elevated commuter trains to circuit-board street grid to a vast subterranean infrastructure of power lines, sewers, water mains, and fifty miles of iron pipes to carry steam heat throughout Manhattan. This is also another way that New York might be said to function as a kind of prison. This city cuts us off from our biological origins, from ourselves and from our natural responses to one another, creating a robotic, clockwork order that mutes the individual and encourages the city's massed, tightly fit inhabitants to behave in a more or less randomly licentious, randomly violent fashion.

Hopper was stubbornly refusing to react to the then very real threat of aerial bombardment in the days and weeks following Pearl Harbor when he made *Nighthawks,* but the painting does reflect an awareness of the wholesale mechanization of society that redefined time and made a city like New York possible. This was the same mechanization that allowed such a fantastic thing as factories to manufacture airplanes that in turn might fly over from someplace out in the ocean at high speed and drop explosive devices. One of these bombs might very well—who knew?—have scored a direct hit on Hopper's apartment building and put an end to whatever he was painting, and, not to mention, his life. Far more frightening bombs that could raze an entire urban center in a single apocalyptic blast were only a few years away.

In *Nighthawks* technology seems only incidental. It is present as a matter of course in the inclusion of a cash register, large coffee urns, smooth pavement laid down specifically to facilitate the driving of cars, and the unnaturally even glare of the fluorescent lighting. But it is also there in the way that glare accentuates the metallic blues and pale greens that Hopper used for the street and sidewalk, and in the precise geometry of the painting's composition. The clean lines of the diner's roof and window close in on the clean lines of the redbrick building beyond, uninterrupted by any decoration or even a scrap's worth of debris, as if to mimic the impersonal sense of utility behind the design of, say, a toaster.

With precision we have uniformity, repetition. Every toaster from the same given design is identical. The row of identical circular stool seats in the diner complements the row of same size, same shape windows in the building across the street. There is a complex mathematics of shadow and light throughout, which we get from no sun or full moon or stars. This is manufactured light, manufactured shadow, and makes the various, stand-alone components of this midcentury Manhattan corner feel enclosed, integrated, like specialized but interdependent assembly sites in an auto plant. This nameless, antiseptic diner would make a fine factory canteen: We are on the graveyard shift, giving part of our pay back to our employers for the food and caffeine we need to keep manufacturing more machines.

Massive government support of industry during the war years may be what finally lifted the United States out of the Great Depression and brought on the unprecedented wealth and material conveniences of the next fifty years. "The home front became one gigantic factory," as a recent history sums up the aftermath of Pearl Harbor. But beneath the gleaming surface of a present defined by an ever more advanced future lurked the fear that something may go horribly wrong, that, say, along with our toasters and blenders and television sets we will be unexpectedly atomized. More bizarrely, we fear we might even mechanize ourselves into obsolescence. This is the fear behind the *Matrix* trilogy (1999, 2003, 2003) and such movies as *The Terminator* (1984) and *Terminator 2: Judgment Day* (1991). The latter movies conjure a future in which machines have taken over and travel back in time to battle a humanity not yet aware enough of the folly of its dependence on technology to stop the machines from taking over.

Machines have already taken over, however, in Thomas Pynchon's wildly satiric World War II novel, *Gravity's Rainbow.*

The title refers to the downward trajectory of the V-2 rockets Germany fired at London and Antwerp in the fall of 1944 following "Brentschluss" (burnout), when, fuel gone, gravity took over. But it might also refer to the downside of modern technology in general. The V-2 was only the second successful long-range rocket (1942's smaller A-4, also German, came first) and as such became the basis for rockets that took men to the moon as well as for today's ICBMs and the Cold War's paralyzing threat of nuclear annihilation. Pynchon's protagonist, Lieutenant Tyrone Slothrop, U.S. Army, in Berlin after Germany's defeat, dons a rocket costume to avoid the Allied authorities, who, he has reason to believe, want him dead. He becomes known as "Rocketman," a kind of supremely impotent superhero. In a sense, after World War II, we all became "rocketmen," defined by a new machine that brought the United States and the USSR as close together as rival gangsters aiming .38 specials at each other along a dank alley, despite the enormous geographical and cultural gulf between the two countries. Rockets thereby determined politics, national boundaries, and the life and death of millions across the planet.

Rockets did not influence the outcome of World War II, however. They came too late and were still too unreliable, too difficult to aim. But for Pynchon, machines were already more important than any soldier's courage or any general's clever military strategy. Machines—tanks, submarines, fighters, bombers, battleships, etc.—made courage useless. They determined military strategy. World War II was not the cause but the culmination of our romance with machines and the profiteering of transnational corporations that produced them and did not rightly care which side triumphed. The only thing they cared about was what one of Pynchon's characters calls "the System," the engineering, manufacturing, and selling of ever more powerful machines and that it continues onward—as indeed it did.

The System meets not our ends but its own: "the politics was all just theatre, all just to keep people distracted" while "not only most of humanity, but most of the World, animal, vegetable, mineral, is laid waste. . . . Living inside the System is like riding across the country in a bus driven by a maniac bent on suicide. . . ." To say the "home front became one gigantic factory" after Pearl Harbor is to pretend that we had not long before given ourselves over to machines, that the West as an inextricably intertwined whole was not already one gigantic factory, requiring a war, and a really big war at that, to fully realize its capacity. Society was already well on the way to becoming a gigantic factory during Hopper's childhood. This may be the most profoundly disorienting of the many changes that occurred during Hopper's lifetime: The nineteenth century's fervor for applied science paying off in spades, the twentieth like a cloud-piercing steel monolith suddenly appearing in the worn and twisty path of a horse and buggy.

This would have been noticeable even in Nyack, of course, and dramatic, but more so in Manhattan (where Hopper moved at seventeen), which could not have grown as rapidly as it did without modern technology. It was in Manhattan in 1882 (the year of Hopper's birth) that Thomas Edison had overseen the completion of the first centralized power station on Pearl Street. Edison, in the spirit of the age, did this for the sake of progress but also to improve the market for his many devices, which, like the filament lamp (electric lightbulb, 1879) and the phonograph (1877), could not run without power. To Edison, inventions (one thousand patents during his lifetime) meant money: He had founded the first corporate-style laboratory (his "invention factory") in 1876. He would found the Edison General Electric Company in 1889 and buy out his nearest competitor in 1892 to create General Electric—which would eventually introduce the fluorescent lighting portrayed in *Nighthawks*.

A shockingly busy guy, Thomas Edison. When English photographer Eadweard Muybridge combined his 1878 invention, the zoopraxiscope, which used a series of photographs taken in rapid succession to reproduce and study the motion of animals, with Edison's phonograph for the first crude "talkie," Edison was not to be outdone. In 1891, he invented the kinetoscope, capable of showing fifteen seconds of motion imagery, but he failed to grasp the full commercial potential. A mistake: The Lumière brothers patented screen projection in Paris in 1895. By 1920 the United States alone had ten thousand movie theaters serving 10 million customers per week.

The goal was not just machines but reproducible machines that could be sold to the public, to businesses, to governments, and to armies. The goal was signature machines, machines that redefined daily life. The automobile was pretty much figured out by 1900, but it would be refined by Henry Ford's assembly line and Model T for mass consumption. The camera became widespread after one John W. Hyatt, looking for cheaper material than ivory for billiard balls, developed an early version of a magical goo known as plastic. He dubbed his plastic celluloid (1868), and George Eastman used it in film for the Kodak camera, which was introduced in 1888: "You press the button, we do the rest." Celluloid combined naturally occurring ingredients camphor and cellulose; a fully synthetic plastic, Bakelite, was patented in 1909.

We now produce billions of pounds of plastic annually in the United States alone. Plastic is the dream of capitalist technology: It can be made into almost anything. What doesn't contain plastic? What doesn't plastic contain? It is keypads, dashboards, casings, handles, knobs, switches, buttons, and dials: the ultimate buffer between us and what we'd prefer not to be too conscious of. But the new symbiosis between man and machine was and remains fully exposed in the humble bicycle, which became what we basically think of as a bicycle by 1885 and caught on quickly: Five years later there were ten thousand on the roads and three hundred twelve manufacturers. The leap from there to airplanes looks enormous, but the Wright brothers made bicycles in Cleveland before making the first manned flight (gliders excluded), 120 feet worth, in 1903.

The more you invent, the more you can invent, but also the more you need to invent. In the 1890s, cities increasingly congested with all their new factories and sweatshops and laborers and their families required taller buildings, such as Chicago's twenty-one-story Masonic Building (1892). Skyscrapers required more reliable elevators (invented back in 1854), made possible by the electric motor (1889) and a system of weights and pulleys perfected in 1905. This is all fine as long as you can keep up, except the cycle turns vicious at the onset of World War I, which marked a burgeoning awareness that technological progress also required increasingly efficient means of committing mass slaughter. Such is the lesson taught in battles where entire legions could be wiped out by a single Maxim gun—named after its inventor, Hiram S. Maxim, who greatly improved the machine gun back in 1883, from 33 to an astounding 666 rounds per minute.

Airplanes would also prove effective—Pearl Harbor being a case in point, Hiroshima being another—but not as effective in the long run as submarines, which came into their own in the 1890s. Now one is all you need: A single submarine fitted with a dozen nuclear missiles could decimate the very civilization that worked so hard and with such pride to bring machines such as the submarine to such an advanced state of development. What more severe indictment of technology could there be than the ability to kill so many strangers so easily? Strangers like, say, the customers and server in *Nighthawks,* where a scene from arguably the most advanced city of the twentieth century becomes a negative space, and a diner's electric glare is welcoming only against a backdrop as desolate as a graveyard. Hopper's unwillingness to grant technology its due, much less celebrate its triumphs (even as he captured revealingly modern details like the lighting in *Nighthawks*) is evidenced by what he did not paint.

Although based in New York, Hopper never portrayed those pinnacled skyscrapers that came to dominate the skyline in the 1920s and 1930s, or the skyline itself. He painted factories on occasion but usually off in the hazy distance, and with all the charm of tombstones. He painted trains but more often portrayed empty tracks running like open wounds through cities and otherwise tranquil towns. He avoided airplanes. He painted cars, but rarely, and never moving, always parked. His many streets are mainly vacant of all forms of transportation, including, ironically, the country road in his tersely titled *Gas* (1940), which portrays a small gas station with a Mobil sign hanging from a pole and a trio of bright red pumps diligently tended by a balding man in a vest and tie.

He is dwarfed by those pumps, this man; he is their servant of mere flesh and bone. They limit him, his life, while he embodies a loneliness and a hopelessness, of which he himself does not seem fully conscious. The dominance of technology over humanity in this painting is clearly connected to something else this man does not seem conscious of but that we can clearly see: nature. His back is to a thick forest of lush green trees across the road, an expanse of light blue sky above, and a tall curling wave of orange and yellow grass like a bed of flame. The station might be some remote wilderness outpost, except it is a business for cars that pass often enough to generate profit, and the man tending the pumps performs only those tasks he must to keep that business going. It makes no difference to him if that forest is on fire, or if it's about to be clear-cut and replaced by a parking lot, just so long as cars continue to pass and to run on gasoline.

The people in *Nighthawks,* meanwhile, could not look at a forest if they wanted to. If in his work as a whole Hopper elided or downplayed aspects of the modern world that displeased him, here he gives us not the slightest indication of nature. There is no plant life whatsoever, not a token, not a fake, no flower in a vase in a windowsill or a bowl of fruit. No prickly weeds poke up through cracks in the sidewalk. No stray cat struts or sooty pigeon skulks. Not a single cockroach, not a fly, is in evidence. And more: no moon, no stars appear, just what might be a sliver's worth of an overcast night or the darkened wall of another taller building, just above the Phillies cigar sign, in the center of the painting.

This is, of course, kind of odd. The need to be reminded that such things as grass and leaves still exist, and are more than tasteful ornaments, can become acute in New York, now and in 1942. But way back in 1844, William Cullen Bryant, already fearing that massive development would obliterate all signs of Manhattan's pastoral past, used his position as editor of the *New York Evening Post* to campaign for what would eventually become Central Park, an 840-acre swath of greenery in the gray sprawl of the city. This gem of urban planning was revitalized in the 1930s, when Robert Moses made visiting Central Park easier and more comfortable, adding playgrounds, a cafeteria in the zoo, and evicting a small herd that still grazed in an area known as the Sheep Meadow. In fact, Moses, when not destroying entire neighborhoods to make room for an expressway, was planting some two million trees throughout the metropolitan area.

That not one of these trees, not a single bird or rat, finds its way into *Nighthawks* evokes a striking peculiarity: that it became more possible for more people, and more valued by more people, during the twentieth century than at any previous period, to have no particular awareness of our relationship to the earth. They might have no contact with either untended wilds or plowed and planted soil. They no longer needed to know, say, that cheese comes from milk and milk comes from cows, or that clothing is made from the hair and the hides of animals. They might even wear only clothing from factories, made entirely of synthetic fabrics like rayon (introduced in 1884) and nylon (1935), eat only prepared meals, go from air-conditioning (c. 1920) to air-conditioning, and from car to pavement to office to car to apartment.

This is not bad, but a triumph, some might say. But desolation means something essential is absent, something that would otherwise suggest joy, beauty, a reason to hope. And what is finally desolate about *Nighthawks* may be precisely the absence of nature. This is especially significant for a nation that began with the serendipitous "discovery" of an entire continent of wilderness; the idea from early on had been not just to exploit the resources available but to cultivate the land for the benefit of all the citizens of God's Earth.

"Can you think that America shall be nothing but *Miery Places and Marshes,* given to salt?" asked Puritan leader Cotton Mather in his *Theosophus Americana* (1710). The answer is, of course, no. In America, "the Lord will create a New Heaven and new Earth."

Theosophus Americana was written especially for the merchants of Boston. The more produce they sold, the more land that would be cultivated, which was what must be done to prepare for the thousand-year reign of Christ prophesied in the Book of Revelation, and the remaking of the world as a "watered Garden and an Eden." The language was less biblical, but the meaning much the same, when James Wilson, a signer of the Declaration of Independence and delegate to the Constitutional Convention, spoke in Boston on Independence Day, 1788. Wilson enthusiastically exclaimed that "an enrapturing prospect opens on the UNITED STATES! Placid HUSBANDRY walks in front, attended by the *venerable plough*," and went on to celebrate the manifest accomplishments of commercial cities such as Boston and New York along with those of the nation's farms.

But the farms defined America. Although he was no stranger to the attractions of urban life, Thomas Jefferson's ideal for the republic he had helped to found was nonetheless a dominant political base comprised of gentlemen farmers and plantation owners. They are, he wrote, "tied to their country & wedded to its liberty with most lasting bonds," and therefore make "the most vigorous, the most independent, and the most virtuous" of citizens. He pursued this ideal for himself with the construction of his hilltop estate, Monticello, which combined gorgeous vistas of forest and river with a thirty-two-room mansion. He pursued it for the populace at large with the Louisiana Purchase—some 830,000 square miles of territory from the French—in 1803. He then launched a *Star Trek*–like "Voyage of Discovery," under the leadership of Meriwether Lewis and William Clark, to explore all this new undeveloped land.

What Lewis and Clark found was often idyllic. The "face of the country," Lewis wrote at one point, "was covered with herds of Buffaloe, Elk & Antelopes," who "are so gentle that we pass near them while feeding without appearing to excite alarm among them." Idyllic also meant ready to use. When journalist

John L. O'Sullivan coined the term "manifest destiny" in 1845, he was saying that God intended the continent to be "over-spread" so the "multiplying millions" might enjoy "free development." This included the century-long transformation of what Washington Irving once admiringly called "boundless and fertile wastes" into ranch and pasture and the "amber waves of grain" sung of in "America the Beautiful." Of course, there would be many a city and town, too, but they would not deplete nature's bounty. Yet in the mid-nineteenth century, thinkers like Emerson lauded not farms but the wilderness, as if anticipating the danger of too much cultivation. Still, while he might write of the "great and crescive self, rooted in absolute nature" or compare a walk through a forest to attending church, Emerson never devalued civilization: "oak and elm shall gladly serve us," as he put it, "though we sit in chairs of ivory on carpets of silk." And Whitman could celebrate "the garden the world anew ascending," even as he admired "the vast trackless spaces" soon to be covered with "the foremost people, arts, institutions, known."

But the balance would shift, and nature would grow more and more distant as those institutions multiplied and industry developed. The real precursor to our own more anxious awareness of nature is Emerson's more radical friend, Henry David Thoreau. His 1854 diatribe, *Walden,* scathingly denounces allegedly "civilized men" more worried about damage to their fashionable pantaloons than to the legs the pantaloons cover. But Thoreau also attacks those who cultivate the land, who are, say, concerned with the upkeep of a farm they had the "misfortune" to inherit and that demands "excessive toil." They have lost touch with true nature and with deeper truth, with God, as has even the salt-of-the-earth-style laborer, like "the teamster on the highway." "Does any divinity stir within him?" The answer is no, the lowly sap's "highest duty" being (laughably) "to fodder and water his horses!"

The longer answer is to avoid town and farm both, get back to nature and use only what you need, to retreat, as Thoreau did to a small cabin off Walden Pond outside Concord, Massachusetts. There he leisurely watched the loon play upon the water, the partridge lead her brood past his window, observed a hunter skin a fox, and in general relished the natural world in an unblemished state. In doing so he recovered for himself an unblemished state of physical and mental well-being; his bitterness dissipated. He was reenergized, retuned, made hopeful, forward-looking—a new man. The almost absurd self-assurance and optimism of the book's final sections would be pompous and patronizing if Thoreau's prose wasn't so zingy, so unabashed: "There is not one of my readers who has yet lived a full human life," he proclaims. "These may be but the spring months of the race."

Not surprisingly, Thoreau-like retreats were popular during the turbocharged progress of the late nineteenth and early twentieth century, anticipating the like of Edward Abbey. Later to be credited as the originator of today's quasi-terrorist group Earth First!, Abbey became the new Thoreau with the publication of *Desert Solitaire* (1968), his sardonic account of being a ranger at Arches National Park and his disgust with abetting the intrusion on nature by what he called "industrial tourism." Thoreau arguably anticipated as well the transformation of a small farm in upstate New York into one big back-to-nature rock-and-roll party with some half a million participants at the legendary open-air festival known as Woodstock. "We've got to get ourselves," the well-worn anthem bearing the same name puts it, "back to the garden."

There is some Thoreau in us today when we look to what we

think of as unblemished nature to improve ourselves and society. We become vegetarian to harm the earth less, or vegan to harm the earth even less. We recycle, at least, or buy certified "organic" foodstuffs free of pesticide, herbicide, preservative—of anything artificial. And there was Thoreau, too, as guiding light, leading the way for such late-nineteenth-century writers as the bestselling John Burroughs, who promoted nature appreciation as an antidote to increasingly loud, fast-paced, nerve-wracked urban miasmas of factory smoke and tobacco fumes. In 1920, Hopper's former classmate at the New York School of Art, Rockwell Kent, published *Wilderness,* a description of his adventures as a homesteader in the wilds of Alaska and his newfound awareness of "cosmic nature." Hopper himself admired Henry Beston. Beston's *The Outermost House* (1928) described a year of solitude on the coast at Cape Cod and preceded Hopper's own decision, in 1934, to design and build a simple, shingled house with a sunlit studio on an isolated Cape Cod hillside near the tiny former whaling village of Truro. He and his wife, Jo, spent half the year there every year afterward.

Overlooking the Massachusetts Bay, what has become known as the Hopper House at Truro was a more permanent extension of a long-term interest in nature. Throughout his travels and sojourns across the country, Hopper had recorded the mountains and sunsets and fields and woods he encountered in sketches and watercolors, some of which he incorporated into major works in oil. "My aim in painting," he said, "has always been the most exact transcription possible of my most intimate impressions of nature."* Such statements (he made many similar ones) seem

---

*This quote, from Hopper's "Notes on Painting," published in the catalog for his 1933 retrospective at MOMA, continues: "If this end is unattainable, so, it can be said, is perfection in any other ideal of painting or in any other of man's activities."

odd, however, for nature was primarily used as background or only subtly present in many of his paintings—a bit of blue sky here, a few branches there—and some of his subjects, like *Nighthawks* (and see also *Drug Store* [1927]) excluded nature entirely. But like Emerson, he was aware of nature's significance to all human activity, even when it was absent. If in *Nighthawks* Hopper demonstrates a facility for capturing artificial light and shadow, this derives from a hard-won ability to portray sunlight streaming through an apartment or train window or glancing off the side of a building like the mansion in *House by the Railroad*.

The expressive vitality of Hopper's sunlight remains one of his best-known achievements. But he regarded his interest in sunlight as evidence that he himself was "not very human," and nature is often portrayed in his work as no longer within the scope of human endeavor. A series of paintings completed on Mohegan Island between 1916 and 1919 show uninviting crags and cliffs along a rocky coast with no people, no boats: not only uncultivated but beyond cultivation. The small farms and barns that he painted later might be about the deterioration through neglect of Jefferson's hoped-for republic of virtuous farmers. Though set against green, rolling hills, they evince no practical purpose—as if we used to grow food but no longer. Rural roads festooned with telephone poles lead off to nowhere in particular. And in Hopper's paintings there is no sense of welcome, of nature beckoning us forward for a closer look, and no sense that we might want a closer look. In *Western Motel* (1957), a broad sunlit mountain shows through a lobby window beyond the hood of a car and strip of pavement; the motel's purpose might be to provide a view rather than be a temporary shelter from which we might explore further. In fact, Hopper painted many of his landscapes from within cars and trains. By 1960, he had stopped bothering with even that much: "I don't work from nature anymore. I find I get more of myself by working in the studio." Hopper's nature is nature in the machine age: nature at a remove; nature seen from a parked car (or while whizzing by); postcard views of nature from a prescribed itinerary; nature, finally, as idea, as dream of nature. But we may wonder if the people in *Nighthawks* so much as dream of nature.

Lewis Mumford once maintained that in even "the stoniest pavement of the city there are cracks. And out of the bleakest soil, between these cracks, a few blades of grass will grow . . ." Not in *Nighthawks,* where the sidewalks have no cracks. Technology has taken over nature completely in this scene, a perception that today is supported by, for example, cyberpunk novelist Bruce Sterling. In a *Wired* magazine opinion piece, Sterling argues for more bioengineered crops: "Designer plants make deserts bloom, detoxify ruined soils," etc., all of which will be necessary to "eliminate malnutrition, and abolish hunger for a future population of 10 billion or so." But in *Nighthawks* remedies are beside the point. Nature is only what is absent, including food.

The people in the diner don't seem especially interested in eating, and the diner shows little evidence of serving anything to eat. There are salt-and-pepper shakers and napkin dispensers, but dirty plates from recently departed customers do not lie out upon the counter. The kitchen must be off behind the ocher door, because we see no grill where hamburgers might sizzle, no steam rising from a pot of hot chili or chowder. The woman does hold a bit of sandwich, but she looks at it without appetite, mouth closed, as if wondering how it came to be in her hand, and what exactly is she supposed to do with this thing called "sandwich," again? What the customers do want, and all have, is that diner staple, the cup of coffee, though whether they plan on drinking the coffee, or just ordered it as an excuse to be there, is another question.

This plays off the emptiness of the apartment windows and empty storefronts across the street, where there is no sign of habitation. The absence of nature, of even food, makes *Nighthawks* seem an image of humanity winding down: This is all that's left, a few joyless stragglers, some scattered others, keeping up appearances as best they can—out of habit perhaps. Soon they, too, will be gone, and in an otherwise empty diner only the fluorescent lighting will remain, powered by a generator that refuses to quit.

The masterful sci-fi flick *Blade Runner* (1982, but I'm going by the far superior director's cut, released in 1991)* opens with a panoramic night shot of Los Angeles in the year 2019: black, electric, endless. The effect is as if the entire American continent were turned into one gigantic Manhattan without parks, without trees. The pet animals we encounter later in the movie are bio-engineered fakes. And by then we have guessed that the earth is barely habitable, due, we assume, to overdevelopment. Most of the tenants of all those high-rises have relocated to "off-world colonies" where, according to announcements broadcast through the city, they gain "a chance to begin again in a golden land of opportunity and adventure."

Staying behind may nonetheless be the right choice. Even the

---

*A recent capsule review in *The New Yorker* (August 30, 2004) compares the sci-fi flick *I, Robot* (2004) to *Blade Runner* and remarks on "moody lighting in the manner of Edward Hopper." This is more than coincidental: The lighting in *Blade Runner,* which takes place almost entirely at night, is also Hopperesque and is especially reminiscent of *Nighthawks.*

bioengineered humans, or "replicants," used as slave labor in outer space head for Earth when they escape, though when they do they are killed, or "retired," by a "blade runner" like the movie's weary hero, Rick Deckard. His challenge is to distinguish between renegade replicants and real (i.e., natural) human beings. He uses a battery of questions designed to provoke an emotional response. But the replicants' emotions have been enhanced by the manufacturer, Tyrell Corporation. "Commerce is our goal here at Tyrell," as Tyrell himself tells Deckard, " 'More human than human' is our motto." He has been giving replicants prerecorded memories: virtual childhoods add psychological complexity. Some don't know that they are replicants.

This presents a problem for Deckard. Less difference in emotional response between replicants and humans makes retiring replicants, which he was sick of already, more like murder. Then two more problems present themselves. He falls in love with one of the new replicants and cannot bring himself to kill her. And he cannot know for sure that he himself is not a replicant with prerecorded memories. At the movie's conclusion we find out that he is.

He has to be told. Hauntingly, there is no other way. When it's all we've got, technology acts like a hall of mirrors. Seeing and experiencing only our own inventions, we lose orientation, have no external fact, i.e., nature, to so much as reassure ourselves that we exist. We might as well be trapped on a TV stage set. Reality itself comes to seem manufactured, provisional, "postmodern." Or postreal, which is what gives *Nighthawks* its end-of-the-world quality.

But *Blade Runner* pulls a neat little trick: The replicant whom Deckard falls in love with smokes cigarettes. This makes her seem more human: Can we imagine a car engine, or, more to the point, a computer, smoking? *Wanting* to smoke? Having what we call a vice? If one did, we would know artificial intelligence is not so artificial anymore. That could, in fact, be a test—not of being human exactly but of possessing the mechanical equivalent of a self.

Note the cigarette between the fingers of the man facing us in *Nighthawks*—can you see it there? That small yet potent detail? And note also that his cigarette is not him, but external, something he wants and can hold on to, to remind himself (and us) that he is . . . alive.

That Cigarette

If America is a garden in the making, tobacco is the noxious weed that we can't seem to eradicate, and has been ever since Columbus first discovered tobacco here in 1492. But tobacco became especially virulent in the form of the cigarette in the late nineteenth century, following the invention, by one James Albert Bonsack of Virginia, of a machine that soon allowed the Duke factory in Durham, North Carolina, to produce some 4 million "little white slavers" per day.

There was no shortage of Cassandras. *The New York Times* denounced cigarettes back in 1884, warning that the country's morals would soon be no better than Spain's due to the cigarette habit. By the early twentieth century, doctors were linking damage to lungs, brain, spinal cord, and heart to cigarettes. Anticigarette campaigns were launched, anticigarette groups and foundations formed, and city- and state-wide antismoking ordinances passed, banning the sale of cigarettes to minors, banning their sale altogether, banning them, period. In 1904, New York City Board of Education member Charles Hubbel called smoking the worst "habit or vice that can be named." In 1911, Dr. Charles Pease of the Non-Smokers Protection League of America, spoke for many when he proclaimed his "constitutional right" to breathe "fresh and pure air" without sucking down secondhand smoke. Henry Ford led a number of businessmen and factory owners in refusing to hire cigarette smokers, whom he thought untrustworthy.

But cigarettes calmed the nerves of soldiers during the slaughters of World War I and calmed their nerves again during the slaughters of World War II. And not just soldiers. Perhaps cigarettes were too reliable a way to relax, too portable, fit too conveniently into the jagged rhythms of the machine age, smoothed out the dislocations, punctuated the long workdays. Perhaps they gave too many people something to do with their hands during moments of idleness, stretches of boredom, were something to put between themselves and the strangers that crowded their cities, between themselves and the smells and dirt of the cities. Perhaps cigarettes were simply something they could control, an addiction they chose, on some level, to indulge. Perhaps the righteous denunciations of cigarettes had an effect opposite from the one intended, giving them an attractive, forbidden aura that lent sizzle to the movies of the 1930s and 1940s, not to mention the movies of today, with cigarettes once again being subject to bans following countless studies completed over the past several decades confirming beyond a doubt that they are indeed very, very unhealthy.

The generally abstemious Hopper was a smoker. Cigarettes (and cigars) appear in many of his paintings, but more intriguing is the cigarette he himself holds in a photograph taken in November 1941 by Arnold Newman, who was doing a series of portraits of well-known artists. It is intriguing because the cigarette is unlit, a prop, chosen, according to Newman, by Hopper, who must have been in a theatrical mood. In other photographs he appears uncomfortable, dismayed, or simply stares or glowers directly at the camera. But in the portrait with the cigarette, Hopper is dressed in a black suit before a large blank canvas, brow set, mouth with the shadow of a disapproving frown; he doesn't appear to notice or care that he's being photographed, and keeps the hand with jutting cigarette poised as if he may take a puff or may not—What's it to you? He is in total command, a gangster about to order the execution of a rival, or a corporate executive who might unflinchingly terminate the employment of half his staff.

About a month later, Hopper would be using himself as the model for the man facing us and holding a cigarette with the same hand (left) between the same two fingers in *Nighthawks*. That cigarette lends subtle but significant emphasis to his forward-leaning posture, to whatever he has said to the server. He may have only ordered food, after all, or made a casual comment out of the corner of his mouth, but the server's grimace does imply the broaching of a less agreeable subject.

A dangerous vice, but for this very reason smoking suggests a willingness to take a risk. His cigarette helps to make the man facing us the dramatic focus of *Nighthawks,* the one who, despite the desolate setting, speaks to instigate change, to get a response, however sour, just as Hopper risked starting a major painting only days after the attack on Pearl Harbor, when he could not know for sure whether twentieth-century technology had defeated nature. Perhaps the end of the world had already begun.

When Freedom Means
You Don't Know Who You Are

The necessity of producing food lay behind talk of a "land of plenty" in the eighteenth century and the celebrated transformation of "boundless, fertile wastes" into "amber waves of grain" in the nineteenth. Hunger would presumably be abolished in the "watered Garden" happily anticipated by Cotton Mather back in 1710, at least for the faithful. Thoreau's two-year sojourn at Walden Pond depended on the notion of subsistence, that nature would not only provide but do so willingly enough to allow our philosopher the "leisure" to develop "true integrity." (Actually, nature got help from Thoreau's mother, who brought him dinners; from Emerson, financially; and from friends with whom Thoreau had occasion to dine.) Taking the festival's promoters by surprise, the enormous crowd encamped at Woodstock required a militarylike supply line of food and drink, without which they would have starved (and left a much different impression on the culture than one of peaceful togetherness and free love).

But diners like the diner portrayed in *Nighthawks* are about more than food. Austrian artist Gottfried Helnwein was onto something with *Boulevard of Broken Dreams*. This popular copy of *Nighthawks* replaces Hopper's anonymous customers and server with dead legends of twentieth-century culture: The couple become an ecstatic Marilyn Monroe and a smoking, scowling Humphrey Bogart (but he enjoyed scowling); the man with his back to us becomes James Dean, his face turned and at least not unhappy; and the server becomes a youthful Elvis Presley, looking happy as a lark. Where else would such tragic but beloved idols be in the afterlife but the heavenly equivalent of a diner? Diners are not just places to eat, and they are not places where we go only to eat. They are a kind of sanctuary from the hustle and bustle of business and survival, from the vastness of the American continent, of American society, and from our personal anxieties and cares. They are where we get out of our cars and abandon for a brief period the sacrosanct privacy of our houses, apartments, our kitchens and dining tables. In diners we let our paths through life cross with those of a random assortment of others, knowing that we will find a seat, be welcomed and be served, so long as we have money for fried eggs and toast—or at least a cup of hot coffee.

Diners provide a particular vision of what it means to be American, to be free. They are casual: Shirt and shoes required, but the shirt can be a torn rock T, the shoes scuffed or a worn pair of sneakers, and the sunglasses, the Stetson, the baseball cap, can come off or stay on. Diners should be open late, and the ideal diner should be open 24/7, ready to accommodate any schedule or lack of schedule. They should offer a breakfast of pancakes and sausage for dinner, meat loaf and mashed potatoes at 3 A.M., and an endless supply of coffee no matter the time, though cup after cup be requested until the customer is too wired not to get up, pay the bill, and exit.

They do not cater to idiosyncratic tastes and requests, as a better, more expensive restaurant might. You get what you get in a diner. But because they are so standardized, so predictable, with a menu that varies surprisingly little from one to another across the country, they are almost subversively democratic. In diners, something approaching a classless, equal society actually occurs. Everyone is treated exactly the same, gets called "honey" by the bosomy waitress in the pink uniform with the laminated name tag (this waitress, goddess of diners, often goes by the name Madge or Flo and promises to "get those hash browns started"). No one—rich or poor, fundamentalist or atheist, liberal or conservative, gay or straight, married or divorced, ex-con, unemployed, or bank manager, prostitute or police officer—doesn't belong. Where else do presidential candidates go during primary season to meet a cross section of the public, to demonstrate their commonness, but to a diner? You might meet or at least sit near anyone, even a world-class painter like Edward Hopper, who ate many a meal at cheap restaurants and went to diners for too many cups of coffee during long afternoons after giving up trying to paint for the day.

Hopper would have understood the cheap restaurant he portrayed in *Nighthawks* as a sanctuary, a place to get away from nagging cares and concerns, from the home that had grown stale, from a feeling of failure and a sense that he was not doing all that he could do. He would have understood that the customers in *Nighthawks* might be anyone, escaping for a while from the cool greens and blues and dark shadows he painted in the street outside, and that those two large silver coffee urns offer a sense of security: One reliable source of warmth and comfort will remain in ample supply. The fluorescent light in the diner may not be sunshine; it may be too blank, too uniform, but it is light nonetheless. The diner itself may not be the most attractive or the most homey, but the bright jade green windowsill forms a boundary between inside and outside, refuge and exposure. It allows the customers, whatever their lives may be like outside the diner, however troubled or troubling, simply to be someone at a counter, like so many others throughout the city and across the country.

Hopper's diner is part of a lineage of diners that includes the small diner in Arizona where the heroine of the movie *Alice Doesn't Live Here Anymore* (1974) gets a job as a waitress. Alice initially hates the job and the diner, despises her coworkers, and has no interest in the customers. She and her twelve-year-old son are trying to get to California, where she dreams of restarting a singing career that she abandoned when she married her recently deceased (and abusive and unlamented) husband. She has no money, no real future, knows no one, stays in cheap motels, takes up waitressing only to make enough to keep going west, and only wants to perform her duties and be left alone.

But the diner breaks down her wall of privacy. A loud, foul-mouthed fellow waitress turns out to have the proverbial heart of gold. The gruff and crusty cook/manager is willing to let them discuss Alice's personal problems in the women's room for an hour while his business goes haywire and not fire them. And one of the regular customers is a divorced man with a ranch and an artistic sensibility who seals Alice's happy fate by falling in love with her. The diner gives her the family she doesn't have in an otherwise dreary and friendless Southwest. The movie became the basis for a long-running mid-1970s sitcom, which omitted the difficulties that led up to her finding a place for herself in the diner but retained the sanctuary, the camaraderie, and added a laugh track.

There is also the diner in writer-director Barry Levinson's movie *Diner* (1982), in which a group of young men in Baltimore in 1959 make the transition to adulthood, to women, marriage, children, jobs. Meanwhile, the country as a whole teeters on the cusp of the radical sixties, when everything they are not sure about will be thrown into question. The Fells Point Diner is where they can hang out, eat, smoke, drink coffee, and talk and argue about whatever they want: Sinatra or Mathis, who's the better singer? They drop their guard, are free to be themselves, and stay as long as they like, all through the night. As they themselves are beginning to suspect, the rest of their lives will involve compromise, disappointment and pain, but, as one says to another, "There will always be the diner."

There are many more such diners. They spring up, often unexpectedly, in movies and TV shows and novels, all variations on the diner of pop American myth, diner as miniature utopia: diner upon a hill. In *The Sopranos,* Tony Soprano meets his psychologist in a diner. She has been seeing patients while holed up in a cheap hotel for her safety, and they need to air things out. The result is not satisfactory. She's had it with treating a mob boss. But the diner is where they can drop the strictures of their professional roles and talk honestly, where she can be a frightened woman rather than a doctor yet know that this sometimes-vicious gangster will not harm her. The 1990s hit sitcom *Seinfeld* is, notoriously, "about nothing." The characters behave poorly, glean no insights, gain no special satisfactions from their actions. They would probably be intolerable if they did not continue their snipes and groans, put-downs and whining in public, especially in the diner scenes, which, in this writer's recollection, occur about once per episode. That they are openly themselves in the diner and feel no need to dissemble, to whisper, proves that all the fuss is indeed "about nothing." And who would not want to be there with them, excitedly discussing nothing, as safe from reality as people can possibly be to simply, purely, wholly . . . enjoy their coffee?

But if it is a version of the diner of pop American myth, there is something unsettling about the sanctuary provided by the diner in *Nighthawks.* The jade green boundary may be there, but the window itself is too large, keeps too much of the diner visible to the street, too much of the street visible from within the diner, while at the top of the window nothing comes between the inner light and the outer dark. They are jarringly juxtaposed. The outer dark leaps right in, shadowing most of the man with his back to us and the left shoulder of the man facing us, the one who has said something the server doesn't like. He has brought some trouble into the diner, along with his cigarette. But at least he is interacting with the server, and as one-half of a couple, he is, on some level, a social being who may be negotiated with, whatever he has said. In contrast, we will never see the face of the man with his back to us; however long we look at him, however careful an examination we make; he will never be more than a hat and a jacket, an ear, a hand gripping a glass. Although out in public, he remains utterly, resolutely private.

It is he who undermines any sense of community, reminds us that everyone in the diner remains more or less closed off from others. The customers, the server, ourselves—were we to enter—are not together, but are people who only happen to be in this particular diner at this particular time.

The man with his back to us makes the diner itself—otherwise so recognizable—as a common diner—unfamiliar, uneasy, and unsafe. We look in from outside, see him sitting off on his own at the corner of the counter, as if outcast even within a diner, and think twice about entering. That anyone is welcome means *anyone,* including, say, Frank Chambers, the amoral drifter who narrates James M. Cain's classic pulp novel *The Postman Always Rings Twice* (1934) and one day happens to enter the Twin Oaks Tavern, "a roadside sandwich joint, like a million others."

Inside, he orders orange juice and cornflakes for lunch, then, having no money, allows the unsuspecting older man who owns the diner to give him a job. But our hero spies the owner's young wife, no beauty but her "lips stuck out in a way that made me want to mash them in for her." Frank soon has her planning to murder her husband, and after succeeding on the second try, they take over the diner, spiff it up, and improve business. That Frank is caught and sent to the electric chair hardly solves the dilemma the novel presents: The place where we might go to relax, to eat, has an open door, and anyone might walk in. Or, more broadly, in a democracy like ours: How do we tell the difference between an amiable stranger and a clever psychopath? What type of person will we meet next?

Might it be the likes of Dix Handley, from John Huston's classic film noir *The Asphalt Jungle* (1951)? He wanders through an unnamed Midwestern city made up of dilapidated brownstones, dank alleys, and hulking warehouses—"If you want fresh air, don't look for it in this town!"—until he arrives at a squat, dingy diner with AMERICAN FOOD written across the top of one side and HOME COOKING across another. Upon entering, he immediately hands the man behind the counter, Gus, a gun that Gus hides in the register before two policemen who have been following Dix enter and arrest him. Or might it be cabbie Travis Bickle of Martin Scorsese's *Taxi Driver* (1976)? He convinces a blond beauty named Betsy to meet him at a diner on Columbus Circle for "coffee and pie." Then he scandalizes her by taking her on a date to a Times Square porn theater and attempts to assassinate the presidential candidate for whom she volunteers. Or might it be Pumpkin and Honeybunch, a young couple sitting smoking and drinking coffee in a booth of a large, crowded diner in the opening scene of Quentin Tarantino's *Pulp Fiction* (1994)?

They are, we soon discover, discussing whether to rob a liquor store, where whoever's behind the register has likely been robbed so often that he may keep a shotgun with him and be angry enough to use it. On the other hand, no one expects a robbery in a restaurant, least of all the customers. "One minute they're having a Denver omelette, next minute someone's sticking a gun in their face," says Pumpkin. Why not this restaurant? "I'm ready," says Honeybunch. "Let's do it!" They kiss, produce pistols, rise, and Honeybunch screams: "Any one of you fucking pricks moves and I'll execute every last one of you!"

Hopper admired a similarly threatening diner scene from Hemingway's short story "The Killers." A pair of big-city hit men shows up one day at a small diner in a Midwestern town called Summit, where, we're given to understand, there's nothing to do, and little of note ever occurs. They order eggs after being told it's twenty minutes too early for dinner, then blithely reveal to George, the manager, and Nick Adams, the only other customer, that they are there to murder a man named Ole Anderson who comes in for dinner every night at six o'clock. They will murder him when he arrives. They do not know him, have never seen him before, and he does not know them. They are doing a job, which also entails taking Nick into the kitchen and tying him up with Sam, the cook. However, when Anderson does not show up, they release Nick and Sam, kill no one—"You got a lot of luck," one of them tells George—and leave. Nick goes to the boardinghouse where Anderson lives to warn him, but finds him resigned to his coming death. "I got in wrong," he says. "There ain't anything to do."

That Hopper admired this story upon reading it in *Scribner's* in 1927, going so far as to write a letter (a rarity for Hopper, who disliked writing) applauding the magazine for publishing an exception to the "vast sea of sugar-coated mush that makes up most of our fiction," is not surprising. It is as much a slice of life as a Hopper painting, as narrowly and intently focused, as dry in tone and economical in means, as dependent for effect on what it leaves out, which, in the case of "The Killers," could fill a novel and did fill out two feature-length movies that expanded on the story (both titled *The Killers* and released in 1946 and 1964). We never learn who the hit men work for, or what Anderson, an ex-boxer, did to anger their employer, or anything specific about George or Sam or about the story's protagonist, Nick Adams. They don't know that the two unfamiliar customers are killers until the killers tell them, just as we do not know who the customers in *Nighthawks* are—or, really, anything at all definite about them.

We don't feel that they are, but they could be locals who have made the establishment into a comfortable second home— comfortable to those, anyway, who are used to it, who find its apparent desolation appealingly offbeat. The seeming contretemps between the server and the man facing us might be a minor and quickly forgotten spat between old acquaintances. Locals or not, the customers could be respectable citizens. The man facing us might be an accountant in town for business and to check out the nightlife, while the woman beside him might be a proper love interest (although they have no rings, are not married) or an improper love interest or a looser type looking for a good time with a tourist—not spotless but hardly vicious. The man with his back to us might be nothing more sinister than a lawyer after a long day of work, his cup of coffee just the thing to keep him awake for some well-earned entertainment—taking in a show, hearing some music. They could all be bohemians, artists from the Village, eccentric but mostly law-abiding. Good people down on their luck. Good people up on their luck. However, they could just as well be grifters, junkies, gangsters, or ex-convicts looking for a score.

The woman could be contemplating her role in an upcoming crime as she distractedly considers her bit of sandwich, while the man beside her utters a terse threat or makes the server a proposition—part of the take if he hands over whatever cash is in the diner. The man's outfit—fedora, jacket, shirt, and tie, all typical of the period—certainly tells us nothing. And we know nothing about the identically garbed man with his back to us, who sits on the corner as if capable of behavior that sets him apart from humanity—cold-blooded murder for pay, for pleasure, or whatever evil or destructive or simply unpalatable practices we might think up for him.

But then what place would be worthy of the name sanctuary if it was not available to the worst among us—the serial rapist along with the Boy Scout? *Nighthawks* is arguably a truer, if more disturbing, representation of the diner as a kind of sanctuary than more saccharine (what Hopper might call "sugar-coated") versions. But what does a sanctuary, where we might meet a killer on the prowl, provide sanctuary from, exactly?

Diners originated in Providence, Rhode Island, in the 1870s. A newspaper salesman named Walter Scott noticed a need for after-hours food service for workers on the late shift and anyone else obliged or inclined for whatever reason to stay out after 8 P.M., when all the restaurants in Providence would close. Having hitched a wooden wagon to a horse named Patient Dick, he roved the town through the night selling what would become and remain basic diner fare: sandwiches, hard-boiled eggs, pie, and coffee, all homemade, all priced at a nickel. Competition— larger wagons, wagons that stayed in one place, and wagons with indoor seating (mainly stools) in case of rain—soon followed, and spread from town to town in the Northeast. In 1891, Charles Palmer of Worcester, Massachusetts, found it worthwhile to patent a wagon with a kitchen and dining area designed for mass production.

By the 1920s, diners had evolved into self-contained restaurants, factory-made and measured for easy delivery to whatever location the buyer thought would be profitable. The buyer was either an individual or company; the diner in question was either a single business or part of a small chain. There were do-it-yourself mom-and-pop diners as well, made from buses, houses, garages, and from scratch. There were detached diners, like the restaurant in *Nighthawks,* whose plate-glass windows (as opposed to a row of smaller windows) mean it was not factory made, though the polished wood stools and counter, the coffee urns, and the server's uniform all say "diner." There were diners set in the ground floor of large buildings, along waterfronts, and on busy street corners. They appeared in a wide variety of sizes and shapes but tended—especially the prefab models—to be long and narrow and boxy. They often looked, not incidentally, like railroad dining cars. They were called "cars" in the industry and were transported by rail during the 1930s, and later on by

Mack truck. Their means of delivery seems appropriate enough, for these cheap, convenient eateries—first known as "lunch wagons" or "night lunch wagons" and then as diners—that proliferated through cities and towns, and in the late 1920s began dotting the sides of the new highways snaking their way across the country, were well suited to the mobility and pace of the machine age.

There were some twenty-five million privately owned automobiles in America by the time *Nighthawks* was painted, and diners were entering a heyday that would last through the 1950s. Adjunct to hotels, motels, boardinghouses, bus and train stations, early and late newspaper editions, snappy lunch breaks and dinners on the run, diners were part of a powerful and productive and energetic society always working, always on the move, night and day. They helped to build a great yet engagingly informal nation, where people came and went according to their needs and dreams but were hospitable, unified, and eating the same food—always the pies, the burgers, the coffee, the fries—in an atmosphere that remained the same from region to region. But diners were also about dislocation and anonymity, about no longer making a firm distinction between night and day, dinner and breakfast, between one region's history and customs and another's. Diners served people who were passing through without making firm connections, people not tied down to any one location, any one neighborhood, any one job, to a regular evening meal with the family, but who might wish they were tied down, more stable, connected. Instead diners were tracked along various nodes in what might be termed the network of transience that crisscrossed the United States during the twentieth century.

Hopper never moved from his Washington Square apartment. We might call him territorial, but he took many a lengthy road trip through the country—at least once per year—staying when he did so at cheap chain motels and motor courts. In his art he was almost perversely obsessed with establishments that temporarily hosted people; he depicted people sitting reading or just looking at nothing in particular in hotel lobbies and hotel rooms, as well as train compartments, Automats, and cafeterias. These people do not interact; they are alone, waiting until it is time to get up and go elsewhere. The establishments in which they find themselves are impersonal, nondescript. They are distinctly uncozy. They are strictly, stringently, utilitarian.

We don't necessarily feel sorry for, say, the solitary woman in the wide-brimmed hat paging through a magazine in *Compartment C, Car 293* (1938). But as the painting's title suggests, we do feel that she is shrouded in a modern kind of isolation. The setting erases her identity. She is nothing more than a woman in a wide-brimmed hat paging through a magazine. We may feel sorry for the solitary young woman sitting in her slip reading a letter in *Hotel Room* (1931). She is bent forward, forlorn, but her bland white environs are notably unworthy of personal emotion, of her sorrow. And we may be haunted, as if by ghosts, looking at the couple in *Hotel by a Railroad* (1952).

They wait together, this couple, in a hotel room, the man standing and smoking before a window through which we see only another wing of the hotel, a large, blank gray building, and a stretch of rust red railroad track. The man is nicely dressed in slacks, a shirt, and vest. His hair is well kempt, his mustache neatly trimmed. But the woman sits in an armchair reading a book wearing only a pink slip. She is not going anywhere anytime soon, and neither is he, we guess, though he might be trying to look as if he's got plans of some kind. Both of them have gray hair. They are too old to be nowhere. What are they doing in this hotel room? And how long will they be there? Did they come from someplace definite or just from another such room, traveling by train from hotel to hotel, in some twilight zone comprised entirely of temporary accommodations? There is a deep melancholy in the painting, a sense that they are stuck in a state of transit, that they will never be anywhere but in transit. In some sense, we are all only temporary, in transit from birth to death, so the only thing they are waiting for, whether they realize it or not, is their eventual dissolution.

Not only them. Transience defines the culture as a whole and bleeds into Hopper paintings even when it is not such an obvious theme. In his many apartment scenes, people stand or sit without anything in particular to do, their dwellings as nondescript as a room at a Holiday Inn. What keeps them there? Why them and not someone else? Why there and not somewhere else? In his paintings of bland office interiors, the workers seem less permanent than their desks and file cabinets. They just happen to have jobs with this or that business with such and such duties attached to their employment, opening that envelope, examining these papers. They might continue to perform these duties for thirty years or cease to perform them the day after tomorrow, when they will be replaced by others who will perform them with the same sense of doing what they are doing because they are not doing something else. What, finally, is their relationship to a given office except that this is where they got a job when they needed a job, a job that does not provide them an identity so much as deny them one?

In this sense, precisely because he is so trenchantly anonymous, the man with his back to us in *Nighthawks* is the archetypal diner customer. He is what we all become as we wait in a bus station; or wonder exactly how we ended up sitting in an office unable to remember what it is we were doing just a second ago; or cross the threshold into a diner and make the most normal, most unrevealing of orders: "Coffee, please." But the diner in *Nighthawks* takes this anonymity to an extreme. Most diners evince some attempt to distinguish them from other restaurants to provide a setting with a semblance of uniqueness, of personality, in which the customers might share. But here we find no throwaway decorations on the walls, no handwritten signs advertising the "special," or neon signs saying EATS or BEST COFFEE HERE, no claims the food is homemade—no signs at all. There's not even a name, however generic—"Stella's Hot Grill" or "The Red Robin" or "Twin Oaks Tavern." The diner in *Nighthawks* exhibits a sense of transience—that the people in this diner might be anyone or no one at all, that they are, for the present, without ties, utterly anonymous—almost as a selling point. Come on in, leave your life behind and get lost. You are lost in any case, these days, so accept it, make homelessness your home, namelessness your name.

Anonymity itself becomes a kind of sanctuary. We no longer worry about retaining the sense of personal identity, the connections, the ties that a mechanized, all-too-mobile society undermines. In fact, we discover a dizzying freedom upon letting it all go. Just as we have no idea who the man with his back to us is, no one has any idea who we are, what we may or may not be capable of, as we sit there at the counter, sipping our coffee. We might be anyone.

That we might be anyone suggests that we might become anyone, leave our old selves behind for someone new and better. In the opening scene of *Pulp Fiction,* the young couple, Pumpkin and Honeybunch, take advantage of the diner's restful anonymity to reflect on their recent activities and change course from robbing liquor stores to robbing restaurants—the very diner they are sitting in, in fact. But they soon discover a more complete change—giving up robbery entirely—is possible. In the movie's final scene (which, due to the looped narrative structure of *Pulp Fiction*, is a continuation of the first scene), another customer, a gangster named Jules, easily takes away Pumpkin's pistol, produces his own, larger pistol, and aims it at Pumpkin. Jules would, he explains, normally kill Pumpkin without thinking much about it, except he is going through what he calls "a transitional period."

His transitional period is a response to a recent near-death experience, but it engenders a dramatic decision made while Jules was "right there eating that muffin." He will cease being a gangster and instead "walk the earth, from place to place, seeking adventure." Jules "will still be Jules," he explains, but now he will be the good person he always could have been. A diner, with its impersonal atmosphere, is both a surprising and appropriate place for such a transformation, which lies at the very heart of what we think of as being American: the chance to make, or remake, personal destiny. The prostitute might reform, turn lady, marry a millionaire; the kid from the projects become a pro basketball player, a lawyer, or president; the pimply high school outcast become a rock star.

But the desolate setting of the diner in *Nighthawks* doesn't offer much promise; instead, it suggests transformation downward. The lawyer might become an amoral drifter who seduces a wife into murdering her husband. The man facing us, who could be a law-abiding accountant, might become a thuggish crook. And the server might react sourly to this man's proposal to rob the place where he works, but then, thinking over how little his job means to him, decide to take a chance rather than stay where he is for another thirty years. Given the chance, we ourselves might behave with the irrevocable abandon of, say, the protagonist of Tom Waits's song "Frank's Wild Years," who one day for no better reason than he doesn't like Carlos, his wife's blind Chihuahua, abandons his wife, "a spent piece of used jet trash." Worse, he lights their house on fire and watches it burn while "parked across the street, laughing," then "puts on a Top 40 station." That there is nothing to stop us from doing so is more frighteningly (and excitingly) evident in a diner than elsewhere.

An even more frightening possibility is that the desolation surrounding the diner in *Nighthawks* might take up permanent residence within us, and that the ability to be anyone and do anything could finally mean being no one, doing nothing. In *Pulp Fiction,* fellow gangster Vincent angrily tells Jules he is not transforming into some new, improved version of Jules; he is leaving what position he has in society, however morally compromised, and becoming "a bum. Without a job, a residence, or legal tender, that's what you're going to be, a fucking bum."

In the David Lynch movie *Mulholland Dr.* (2001), a normal-looking, clean-cut, clean-shaven man in a suit meets a friend, another normal-looking, clean-cut, clean-shaven man, in a booth at the Sunset Boulevard site of a Los Angeles diner chain called Winkies. He tells his friend that he has twice dreamed about Winkies, "this Winkies," as he says. In the dream, they are both where they are now, but it is "not day or night, kind of half night" and "I'm scared . . . and you're scared." He realizes, in the dream, that "there is a man, in the back of this place, he's the one who is doing this." The two friends pay their bill and go out back to exorcize this fearsome dream, but they discover the man from the dream is actually there, with a blackened face, greasy hair, and rotten yellow teeth: A demon? A bum? Both?

Upon seeing him, the man who had the dream drops dead. He has met himself as he might look if he had no job, no money, no home, if he suddenly lost all claims to his identity and had to exist in a twilit netherworld where he might live behind a diner rather than meet friends inside of it.

In *Nighthawks*, the diner gives us sanctuary, but only by putting us on the very edge of just such a netherworld. This is why food is not so important as those cups of coffee that stand out, white as they are, against the mahogany countertop, beckoning us to enter and to linger there on that edge, to teeter.

Those Cups of Coffee

Three customers, three cups of coffee. Coffee was the drink of the machine age, not just a morning bridge from the vagaries of sleep to the sharp focus of the day but oil for a body fueled by red meat. Factory laborers who did not have time or money for a proper lunch drank coffee to keep awake and cut their appetites. Like cigarettes, coffee comforted soldiers during World Wars I and II.

Coffee became the choice drink of Revolutionary patriots, who, following the Boston Tea Party in 1773, abandoned their previous preference for tea. It also provided comfort for Union soldiers during the Civil War. (However, coffee was too scarce and expensive in the destitute South to be made available to Confederate soldiers.) By the latter half of the nineteenth century, domestic consumption had taken off, and Americans were drinking six times as much coffee per capita as Europeans.

Apparently we needed more stimulation for working harder. Hungry and impatient, we drank coffee by the ton as we invented and mass-produced our machines, smoked our cigars, and ate our steaks. We got coffee in our stomachs first thing in the morning before work and drank coffee—cheap, watered-down coffee, recycled ground coffee, coffee adulterated with chicory, instant coffee (an American invention, introduced in 1910), coffee from vending machines (the first, the Kwik Kafe, again American, was introduced in 1947)—all day long. We drank coffee at dinner and coffee through the evening, when our craving for new and varied experience, our need to explore the very society we were creating with the help of coffee, remained unsated and we were not yet ready to slide into sleep.

Coffee had its detractors. Divine revelation led Mormon Church founder Joseph Smith to ban his followers from consuming coffee and all other beverages containing caffeine, along with tobacco and alcohol. But concerns were more usually derived from that peculiarly American, quasi-religious, and decidedly puritanical obsession: good health. Complaints that coffee wracked the nerves, enervated even as it energized, led future breakfast cereal magnate C. W. Post to hawk a grain-based coffee alternative, Postum, back in 1896. He made a fortune and kept coffee traders on the defensive for decades with aggressive, anticoffee ad campaigns. Unlike cigarettes, however, coffee has not been solidly linked to serious ill effects. It is also the acceptable vice, the fallback, not prized for its specific attributes or supposed benefits, but for being there. It is what's available, adjunct of speed and achievement, but also of weariness, anomie, and idleness. Step into the hamburger joint, the deli, cafeteria, Automat, corner café, the diner behind the hotel by the railroad tracks and there will be coffee to get you through. Whoever you are, whatever you're up to, that's what you need—a cup of coffee. Even today, the preferred sanctuary is not the diner or the fast-food restaurant, not the chain family restaurant, McDonald's, or Denny's, but the coffeehouse.

There is always a coffeehouse, often many, competing with the local branch of the evil empire of coffeehouses, Starbucks. It is where we go when there is no place to go, to have a pastry or muffin or the new eggs and sausage, with coffee the mainstay, liquid warmth. We sip it while paging through a stray newspaper, which we peruse not because of any interest in the content but because content of some kind seems necessary to keep the brain from pondering too closely the question of why something more pressing is not engaging our attention. Coffee, meanwhile, is the anchor; it keeps the person as a whole from floating away, as in *Nighthawks*. Without their coffee, the customers would have no excuse to linger. They would have to leave the diner, to go . . . where?

Chapter Five

Wayward Lust, Part 1:

Hard-core *Nighthawks*

The veriest schoolgirl of today knows as much as the midwife of 1885.
—H. L. MENCKEN

We know little for certain about the customers in *Nighthawks* except that they are people who happen to have found in this diner on this particular night a convenient shelter and a cup of coffee. Yet we can surmise significant bits of information, including something about the relationship between the man facing us and the woman at his side.

Their postures—both lean forward, elbows on the counter, the line of her shoulders inclined slightly downward toward him, even the way their coffee cups are placed beside their bent elbows on the far side of each of them—suggest a kind of casual intimacy. She especially, with her reddish brown hair and tight burgundy shirt, her eye shadow, her rich red-lipsticked lips, has a warm sexual presence, and he does not seem the least surprised by this. Whether they have already consummated or will soon consummate their relationship, they are definitely a couple, these two; they have arrived at the diner together and will likely leave together.

But they are not married or engaged, not formally, for they wear no rings. Their relationship is an illicit one, and while their hands overlap due to the painting's perspective, they do not touch. In this nameless, out-of-the-way diner, the type of place that it would seem might embolden them to touch in public—even here that might be taking things a little too far.

America's long-term conflict over sexual matters is notorious and has not disappeared. The biggest political scandal in decades was not political at all, involving as it did an adulterous blow job in the Oval Office, yet it resulted in a vote for impeachment against President Clinton. More recently, the accidentally-on-purpose exposure of singer Janet Jackson's breast—specifically her nipple, as the rest of women's breasts are on display pretty regularly in the mass media—presumably scandalized the hundreds of millions of viewers of Super Bowl XXXVIII, and became a reference point for America's declining morals, or excessive prudery, for months.

This briefly viewed but now legendary nipple also gave the FCC an opportunity to claim a stance of righteous indignation. It has since cracked down on taboo network TV depictions of slow caressing and male actors' hairy butts. This has come to pass despite pornography—in which the excitement of seeing a nipple or several hundred nipples fades before almost bizarrely extended shots of penetration (vaginal, anal, oral)—having been readily available in neighborhood video shops for more than twenty years, and in movies and peep shows at adult bookstores since the early 1970s.

The contradiction does not suggest repression as much as a

kind of schizoid culture in which the many rebellions against restrictions on sexuality have liberated behavior and expression without actually dislodging a heavy prohibition. We have been through the promiscuity of the Jazz Age, when F. Scott Fitzgerald noted that "none of their Victorian mothers had any idea how casually their daughters were accustomed to be kissed" ("kissed" likely a polite euphemism we would dispense with today). Moreover, we have witnessed the free-love ethic of the sixties, when promiscuity was not so much indulged as mandated. The recent popularity of the soft-core HBO sitcom *Sex and the City* excited no great wonder, no mass protest. Virginity today is often an embarrassment rather than an honor, and a large number of lovers is a sign of prowess rather than depravity. However, Americans still argue obsessively over whether we should mention even the existence of condoms to high school students, who can see erotic display every day on MTV. Some of us still regularly decry the fall of a once loftily innocent national psyche into a "sick" pit of "degeneracy" (the quoted terms come from former Speaker of the House Newt Gingrich).

Meanwhile, those who regard liberation as a less than harmless, life-affirming celebration of pleasure and the body quickly brand anyone who might suggest otherwise "puritanical." The term is meant to bring to mind those rigid, hypocritical seventeenth-century religious leaders who supposedly hated sex. They were the type who readily believed that a bunch of girls made hysterical with what was only puberty gone haywire—due, precisely, to repression—were possessed. When the girls blamed alleged witches for their condition, the so-called witches were promptly hung.

But this use of the term "puritanical," like this sex-based version of the Salem witch trials—exemplified by Arthur Miller's play *The Crucible* (1953)—gives an imprecise impression of the

Puritans. They were morally rigid and seem to have had a special problem with masturbation, for the same reason that many people have a problem with marijuana: It leads to harder stuff. Harder stuff for the Puritans included sodomy, i.e., same-sex relations, as well as bestiality, which for them exposed the truth about lust—that it made us no better than brute animals. The punishment for such activity could be whipping or the stocks, or it could be death. But still, Puritan leader John Winthrop—whose "city upon a hill" rhetoric was so successfully re-employed by Ronald Reagan in the 1980s—could hardly have hated sex. He fathered sixteen children with four wives in his lifetime. More generally, the Puritans enjoyed writing erotic love poetry (so long as it concerned relations between a married couple), while their more spiritual effusions were rife with explicit language: Ejaculation was a favorite metaphor for prayer. Also, when two young people intended to get married, they would be allowed "bundling"—sleeping together to get used to intimacy—with the caveat that they not have sex quite yet, though accepting that they probably would. The Puritans were not antisex, that is, or even antidesire, though they did believe that sex must be practiced for procreation and to solidify the bonds of family.

What we mean by "puritanical" is more often something like the nearly pathological prudery of the Victorian era. Such prudery dominated the culture when Hopper was growing up, especially among the churchgoing middle class of small towns, such as Nyack, if not in big cities, such as New York. In lower Manhattan, bordellos and clubs, where women danced a lewd cancan for the drinking crowd, actually became so common in the years after the Civil War as to earn one neighborhood the intriguing sobriquet Satan's Circus (doubtless a designation of immense value to businessmen who depended on the cash of curious wayfarers). Even in New York, however, the chorus for reform was strong and strident by the 1870s, when the country as a whole underwent a wave of repression. The middle class in particular emphasized the importance of abstinence to such a degree that "bundling" would have provoked scandal, as would erotic poetry, and they granted a shocking amount of authority to such single-minded crusaders as Alexander Comstock. Head of the New York Society for the Suppression of Vice, Comstock was for decades the righteous scourge of daring publishers, artists who presumed nudes a suitable and established subject for serious painting, and even those museums and colleges that might exhibit classical artworks he deemed to be smut.

Although he was a child of the Victorian era, Hopper accepted the term puritan in relation to himself and his art. He even encouraged the identification when he named a painting of a stolid pair of clapboard houses, reminiscent of the one in which he grew up, *Two Puritans*. Hopper would as late as middle age seek out and read Harvard-based philosopher George Santayana's 1936 novel *The Last Puritan* as soon as it became available, as if made anxious by the opportunity to discover something about who he was. The title refers to the protagonist, Oliver Alden, also a child of the late nineteenth century, through whom Santayana attempted to dissect closely what he took to be the basic (repressed) American character. Santayana made much, for example, of Oliver's mother's refusal to come into physical contact with her son for so much as an occasional hug by the time he reached five years old and the effect this had on him as an adult. Like Hopper, Santayana was confounding the Puritans with the "puritanical" Victorians.

But insofar as he did confound the Victorians with the Puritans, this makes Hopper only more of what we think of as American by bringing him closer to what has become our collective understanding of why we are so conflicted about sex. This understanding is not completely unjustified: Our morally rigid Puritan roots arguably granted the prudery of the Victorian era greater significance than it might otherwise have had. We confound them because they compounded each other. Together, they brought our attitudes about sex to a critical point, which helps explain why Santayana does not hesitate to call his fictional Victorian a Puritan, and also makes him a direct descendant of the Pilgrims who arrived on the *Mayflower.* Oliver is the hapless inheritor of an impossibly harsh sensibility with which he does not exactly sympathize. For him, Santayana explains, the spirit (mind, morality, reason) is divorced from the body to the infinite detriment of the latter. "Sensuality" is "disgusting," the physical appetite only "the endless fire of life always devouring itself." As we discover in the book's first chapter, to give in to lust, to "have" a woman without marriage as Oliver's father, Peter, once did, is to prove oneself on the wrong side of "the evident designs of Providence," i.e., among the damned.

When Peter Alden confesses his youthful peccadillo to his older brother, Nathaniel, a man so severely "abstemious" he never so much as leaves his house except to check on his "financial affairs" or attend church, he hopes for some forgiveness. But Nathaniel's response is immediate and irrevocable: "He walked out of the room" and "never saw his brother Peter again."

A man like Nathaniel would understand that the couple in *Nighthawks* are fornicators or are in danger of fornication, as would Peter—though without so severe a judgment. The Last Puritan himself, Oliver, was a disbeliever who saw the limits of his uncle Nathaniel's restricted outlook but nonetheless shared that outlook. He would be aware that his disgust with the couple's apparent relationship was contingent upon his upbringing but would experience disgust nonetheless. Because he would coldly regard intimacy as a distracting "nuisance" that would compromise his intellectual integrity, he would not feel an erotic pull from the couple or from *Nighthawks.*

This is not quite the case with Hopper. Though reserved and circumspect, he seems to have been one for whom taboos are in themselves exciting. As a young man in Paris, Hopper was fascinated by the loose behavior of pre-Lenten celebrants, the "girls with bare necks and short skirts trying to escape the confetti" as he put it in a letter home. He also sketched the prostitutes who openly plied their trade in the streets and cafés of the city, emphasizing their big round breasts and buttocks, their thick makeup and high-heeled shoes.

New York City must have held a similarly erotic fascination for Hopper: all those people; all those activities taking place behind the closed doors and drawn blinds of all those apartments; all those women walking up and down the streets, riding in the subway, the buses, the El. He must have, as Santayana says of Peter Alden, "felt a canine impulse to run down the side alleys, to explore the unsavory recesses hidden there behind corners." Or at least he must have contemplated the possibilities offered by a city so full of vitality but with so many shadowy recesses, so enticing in its architectural jumble. Its very size and density gives it a mysterious, gothic atmosphere that alone might inspire sexual fantasies of a decidedly taboo character.

That it did, for Hopper, is evidenced by such paintings as *Night Windows* (1928), where in a lit apartment with wide open windows, a woman in a pink slip bends over, bare legs in full view as she performs some household chore. Point of view is key: She is being observed by an unseen voyeur from an apartment a floor or so higher than hers, looking out from his window, from darkness. The subject of the painting is less the woman spied than the voyeur spying; his secret, inchoate desire, his potential for deviant behavior. *Office at Night,* meanwhile, painted in

1940, the year before he began *Nighthawks,* was inspired, Hopper said, by "dark glimpses" from the El train "of office interiors that were so fleeting as to leave fresh and vivid impressions." In this case, the "fresh and vivid" impression, because it was "fleeting" (a suspicious formula), is a pale man sitting at a desk in a bare office fretfully staring at a piece of paper while his notably voluptuous, dark-haired secretary stands at a file cabinet. She is turned toward him with tilted head and lidded eyes, intent to seduce. Hopper originally gave the painting the dirty-old-man title, *Time and a Half for Over Time, Etc.*

Add to the erotic frisson of city life the anonymity of people sitting in a diner late at night on an otherwise empty corner, and the couple in *Nighthawks* shows Hopper seeking out a context in which he might elide repression to toy at least with the possibility of illicit sex.

We might, then, grant *Nighthawks* an admittedly tentative place in a wider art movement, an attempt to break toward a more open expression of sexual desire, alongside, say, work by the photographer Alfred Stieglitz. Though eighteen years Hopper's senior, Stieglitz—from a cultivated, upper-class family—was much more able to take part in the license of the postwar era, famously having an affair with his younger protégée, painter Georgia O'Keeffe (born in 1887, five years Hopper's junior). He eventually married her, and also, significantly, brought the emphatically sexual side of their relationship out into the public (or at least the public that comprised the art world) with a series of gorgeously composed black-and-white nude photos that he took of O'Keeffe. These were honestly, unashamedly erotic: O'Keeffe's hand poised upon bare flesh above her exposed breasts (*Breasts and Hand,* 1918); and her marvelous body, from above her knees to beneath her shoulders (*Torso,* 1919). They formed a response to what Stieglitz saw as an obstruction to the true potential of *Spiritual America,* the title he gave to a 1923 closeup of the harnessed haunches of a gelding.

Stieglitz and O'Keeffe were doing their part in readying the culture for release from the asylum it had been all too easily remanded to by such neurotic inquisitors as Comstock. So were writers such as Henry Miller and his sometime lover, Anaïs Nin, who published erotic short stories and kept a diary that detailed her sexual exploits, including sleeping with her own father: "We burned away all the prejudices." Miller's novels contain explicit descriptions of illicit sexual activities—affairs, one-night stands, threesomes, trysts with prostitutes—loosely based on his actual experiences, with himself as protagonist. He used degrading terms like "prick" and "cunt"—the latter referring to either a woman or her sex organ, as if there were no difference between the two. He included offhand references to illegal abortions and comic riffs on venereal disease. All this was not to enhance the taboo quality of the writing but to obviate any taboos against sex—the hard, physical fact of it.

The so-called obscene is mainly a problem for "prudes, bigots, and other psychopaths," as Miller put it in 1944. His groundbreaking first book, *Tropic of Cancer,* published in France in 1934, was promptly banned in the United States and remained unpublished here until the early 1960s. That was when the sexual realm suddenly seemed as large and open a territory as the Louisiana Purchase. Artists like Miller and Stieglitz and O'Keeffe (with her paintings of phallic skyscrapers, vulval flowers, and her erotic modeling, she had been a sex symbol for the intellectual class since the mid-1920s) were the Lewis and Clarks to whom one turned as guides for a culture in the midst of a political and spiritual, and also commercial, revolution.

In the 1960s, there was the optimism of the hippies regarding free love, that it really was a choice between opening up oneself to the infinite potential of the libido or to violence, which was defined as an outlet for people who had turned their backs on sex. "Make love, not war"—as if had only the right people had been in charge, Vietnam could have been a sweaty, harmless orgy. Such idealism only fueled the profits of the porn industry, which had entered the mainstream, tentatively, in the 1950s. Then cheaply printed G-string and pasties magazines, such as *Titter* and *Wink,* were increasingly popular, as were movie shorts of dancing women with titles such as "Tease-O-Rama." America's first high-end sex magazine, *Playboy,* hit newsstands in 1953. The 1960s pushed the limits with pseudo-documentaries about nudists, along with soft-core exploitation flicks with timid but inviting titles such as *The Mermaids of Tiburon* (1962) and *The Playpen* (1967). Imports, often Swedish, showed sex with a patina of scientific/educational value or combined explicit scenes with lefty politics, most famously in *I Am Curious (Yellow)* (1967). But hard-core porn as out-and-out entertainment exploded in 1972. That was the year of the mainstream release and acceptance of *Deep Throat,* about a woman who can get satisfaction only from a sword-swallowing style of fellatio because her clitoris is not where it should be, but down in her throat. Silly and poorly made, it garnered critical praise and earned a reported $100 million at the box office.

Hard-core porn is a satirical thrust at the pretensions of civilization; it presumes that all those activities we think so significant are merely distractions from what too many people refuse to admit is the greatest and most honest pleasure available: a good fuck. But porn is also an assertion of the misery of repression, and the happiness that can be derived from the unleashed libido. All shame and strictures are void in porn; erections always last and always renew and beautiful women are always ready and willing and looking for orgasm and every fantasy will be fulfilled and fulfilled again and then again. Every locale—from office to hotel room to suburban backyard to stairwell to hospital to car to factory floor—is but a setting for sex, so why not a diner, a diner like the diner in *Nighthawks*? Has anyone done this? If Hopper's painting toys with the possibility of illicit sex, then we might see it as a still from a remarkably ambitious porn movie that describes the increasing liberation of sexual behavior across the twentieth century.

In 1900, the couple facing us would be unambiguously scandalous, even damned. In 1925, they might be charged-up Jazz Age hipsters. In 1933, they might be Bonnie and Clyde, outlaw lovers on the run. But when we get to 1975, the man might not be making the server grimace with an insult or by suggesting a robbery but by asking if the server finds the woman attractive. The server, confused at first, soon realizes what is implied; he has some qualms about the propriety of the offer but quickly gets over them—doesn't everyone but the most unredeemable of hypocrites? He and the couple and the man with his back to us are all soon buck naked and show no sign of wondering why they are suddenly using the countertop for a round of thoroughly uninhibited, unrestricted sex. They indulge every variation. The sex goes on and on, for what seems like far too long, in a numbingly mechanical way. But we are mesmerized nonetheless, right up to the triple-cum-shot finale.

These cum shots would be external, as they always are in hard-core porn. They prove that actual sex has actually occurred. But more important, they demonstrate that this was not about procreation, not about family, or any kind of personal commitment; this was only about sex. Might we say that hard-core porn is rigid in its insistence that there is nothing else going on but sex, asocial, amoral, emotionless—and therefore perfect—sex?

Hopper's paintings and his personal life certainly show Hopper himself at least taking steps in this direction. We find this in his fascination with prostitutes and in the erotic tension of paintings such as *Night Windows* and *Office at Night:* In the darkness of one and in the fretfulness of the man in the other, repression is the source of the trouble. He may or may not have ever gone so far as to approach the prostitutes of Paris or New York. In any case, he remained relatively inexperienced regarding sex, even in his early forties, when he married Jo, who was herself still a virgin at age forty. But after he started a relationship with Jo, Hopper's art matured almost overnight. Sex may have been what allowed him to get over his own reluctance to paint in a style that was entirely his own and that fully engaged the world around him. He finally became himself, one might say.

And in addition to the casually elegant sketches he made of Jo lounging nude around their apartment—stretched out on the bed with an open book, for example—Hopper now had Jo as model for all the women in his paintings. This seems to have instigated a form of role-playing fantasy, as if to experience illicit sexuality without actually betraying each other, which they never did. Jo could be a voluptuous secretary about to seduce her pent-up boss. She could be a woman in a pink slip parading herself, as if unwittingly, in a well-lit apartment before wide-open windows with Hopper as the voyeur who she imagines must be present, watching and desiring from within his own darkened apartment.

She could be the woman in a tight burgundy shirt with a bared neck and orange hair sitting in a diner late at night, just as Hopper could (and did) pose for the man sitting beside her.

But the Hoppers' actual sex life was not especially satisfying, at least not according to Jo. She complained in her journal of his unwillingness to worry over her pleasure in bed, that he treated her like a "dog." To draw a straight line from problems of intimacy to the bouts of violence that marred the Hoppers' marriage might be going too far. But Jo also complained of Hopper's "sadism," and her understandable sense of neglect seems to have been a major cause of the screaming fights that led to Hopper beating Jo, and Jo scratching and biting back as best she could— behavior they apparently kept up for decades, until they were simply too old for it.

This helps explain why the eroticism of *Nighthawks* is not liberating, like that in the work of Stieglitz—whose "favorite word," according to one confidante, was "affirmation"—or like that of Miller, who granted licentiousness a charmingly heedless quality. Rather, it remains repressed, tainted, in the emptiness of the scene where they cannot quite bring themselves to touch each other. They do not openly regard one another, either; there is a distinct absence of affection.

Hopper himself remained conflicted. On one hand, he was caught looking toward a sexual abandon he could not quite accept. On the other, his abuse of his wife and his creation of semipornographic scenarios with her for his paintings suggest that for him, even married intimacy was as fraught with a sense of doing wrong as, say, an appointment with a prostitute or an adulterous affair.

The Victorians made such an issue out of sex that it has become one of our great obsessions, but we can trace our conflict over sex back to the Puritans. If they sought to contain sex within a rigidly moral, family-supporting, procreation-encouraging order, the Puritans were also radical nonconformists and outcasts. They ended up in America because they thought they could greatly improve society by shedding old church hierarchies, displays, and ceremonies, and establishing a more direct relationship between God and each individual worshipper. Thus they were rigidly moral: You wouldn't want to encounter Him alone without the cleanest of conscience.

By emphasizing the individual, the Puritans helped to pave the way for the political freedoms framed by the Declaration of Independence and the Constitution and for our assumed right to seek unique destinies and decide moral truths for ourselves. This right influenced sexual behavior from early on, or so it would seem, given the attitudes that took hold during the early-nineteenth-century religious ferment known as the Second Great Awakening, which encouraged a variety of decidedly nonconformist responses to lust. These went from the total renunciation of sex by the Rappites and the Shakers, to revisiting Old Testament–style polygamy among the Mormons, to such provocations as the "complex marriage" entered into by members of the Oneida Community. The latter was founded in 1847 in upstate New York by an unordained preacher named John Humphrey Noyes, who was all about sexual pleasure as a means toward spiritual "perfection" but felt monogamy attached us to other human beings rather than God. He advised his followers that the "marriage supper of the Lamb is a feast at which *every dish is free to every guest*. Exclusiveness, jealousy, quarreling, have no place there. . . ."

But while the Second Great Awakening resulted in a variety of sexual experiments, these were, after all, small groups— cults—and a stringent, quasi-Puritan attitude toward sex remained in effect. The Oneida Community, barely tolerated during its thirty-year existence, was finally forced to disband in the late 1870s, and Noyes himself abandoned the United States for Canada. Mormonism is currently the country's fastest growing religion, but at its founding, Mormons were considered freaks and pariahs. They were hounded west until they settled in Utah, which was refused admission to the Union until Mormons officially renounced polygamy, in 1890. Nathaniel Hawthorne, at the end of his fictional revision of the seventeenth century, *The Scarlet Letter* (1850), made his adulterous Puritan, Hester Prynne, wish for a "new truth" to "establish the whole relation between man and woman on a surer ground of mutual happiness." Still, he left her "stained with sin" and "bowed down with shame." And such an otherwise trenchant nonconformist as Emerson did not so much as stoop to consider illicit sex or promiscuity in his essay "Love" (1841), but cast a cold eye upon even those sensual yearnings that spurred young couples to marry. This "base affection," as he called it, was only something to be gotten over as their relationship matured and they learned to "admire true strokes of character . . . discourses and actions," thereby becoming "pure and hallowed."

Emerson, at least, admits that physical attraction is an unavoidable fact and serves a good purpose. He does not evince the type of pathology Santayana gave his emblematic Victorian/Last Puritan, utterly unable as he is to deal with sexual desire. But Emerson's view would not have displeased the Puritans or such contemporary moralists as William J. Bennett, the former cabinet member and author of a series of sermonizing bestsellers including *The Broken Hearth: Reversing the Moral Collapse of the American Family* (2001). Bennett is a bit pathological in his focus on popular entertainers (it bothers him greatly that singer Melissa Etheridge is a lesbian with a kid), in his bland self-assurance, and in his intolerance. Yet Bennett, like the Puritans, doesn't so much denounce lust as promote legally sanctioned monogamy to buttress "traditional" families over such alternatives as homosexuality, open marriage, wife swapping, cohabitation, etc., all of which he myopically traces to the "liberationist critique" of the 1960s and blames for the "social carnage" of divorce and child neglect in the ensuing decades.

While Emerson must have been pretty certain that on this issue at least, he would be met with considerable agreement, Bennett might as well be throwing punches at a tidal wave: Today even the Oneida Community seems quaint and redundant. This is partly a synergistic effect of modern communications technology—the constant, unstoppable dissemination of sexual imagery and other expressions of license—plus the capitalist verity: "sex sells." However, it is also due to our having gone so very far in the twentieth century—and so very quickly. *The Marriage Revolt* (1915), a well-selling selection of essays by sociologists who explain why the institution was outmoded, provides an intellectual gloss for what was already a trend. By 1923, the year Hopper married, the divorce rate was an astounding fifteen times that of the 1870s, which alone suggests the decreasing importance of lifelong commitment to another human being, of family and the sacred vows taken by man and woman. Increasing importance went to "base affection," to individual fulfillment, to following one's particular lust, however wayward and no matter where it may lead. So one might leave wife or husband, have affairs, as did Henry Miller, who left a wife and young daughter for a promiscuous dime-a-dance girl he met in a Broadway dance hall. We might explore homosexuality, or bisexuality, as did Georgia O'Keeffe, who outdid and greatly upset the unfaithful Alfred Stieglitz by taking up with another woman (actually two women, then another man). We might masturbate alone, have multiple partners, spend our evenings at meat-market-style singles bars or S-M clubs, or fetishize latex—all fine so long as all participants are free and willing.

But even though Bennett's arguments won't have a serious impact on mass behavior, they do keep very much alive the sense that the prevalence of sex in the culture is wrong and becoming more so. To put it another way, Bennett and those who support such calls for restraint still provide us with the gold standard by which we judge behavior, both of others and ourselves. What we end up with is not quite liberation, and is more like an ever greater conflict. We keep marriage and monogamy as the highest values, even while we deny that marriage and monogamy are anything more than a personal choice. And, as if to make matters worse, we present ourselves with a Pandora's box of other choices through the media, through pornography, through a detailed dissection of the indiscretions of errant schoolteachers and pedophile priests and Hollywood stars and even, in the cases of Bill Clinton and John F. Kennedy's legendary voracious sexual appetite, of presidents.

Hopper's Pandora's box wasn't opened by the prostitutes of Paris, though it was in Paris that he first seems to have encountered the temptations of the flesh on public display. Paris was foreign, different, and Hopper's letters home contain broadly conceived distinctions between France and America. It was twentieth-century America that left traditional morals behind and no longer made an unyielding distinction between his own marriage and an illicit affair. And it was Manhattan, at once so modern and so desolate, where a couple like that in *Nighthawks* are in lust with each other because there is nothing else in their surroundings, in the nameless diner where they sit, in the artificial light inside or the shadows along the empty street outside, for them to care about. Lust is not fulfillment. Lust is what's left.

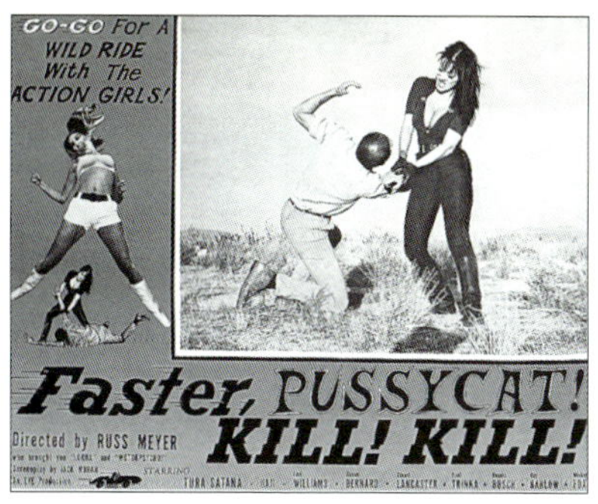

Faster, Pussycat! Kill! Kill!
COURTESY EVE PRODUCTIONS, INC./
PHOTOFEST

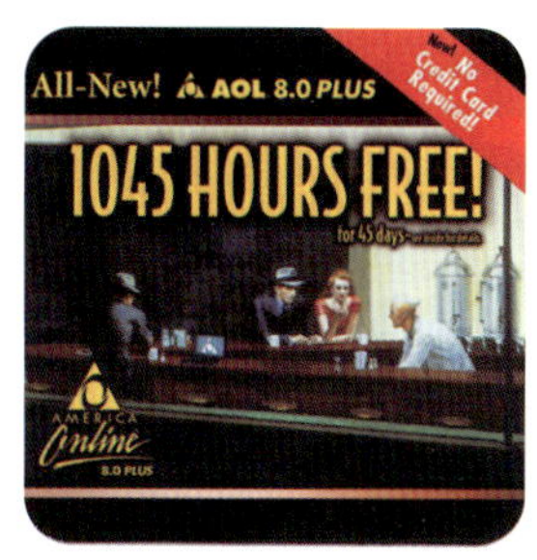

Free start-up disc from AOL. COURTESY AMERICA ONLINE, INC.

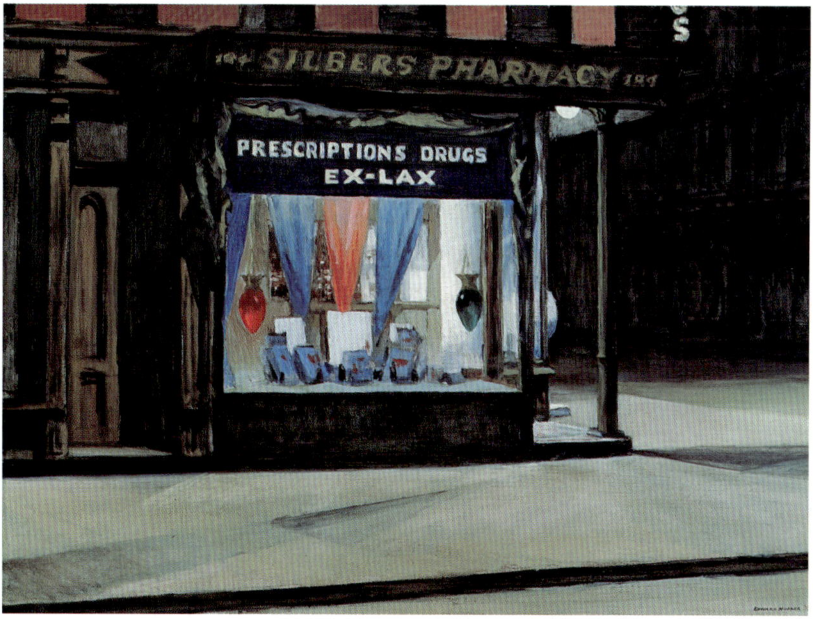

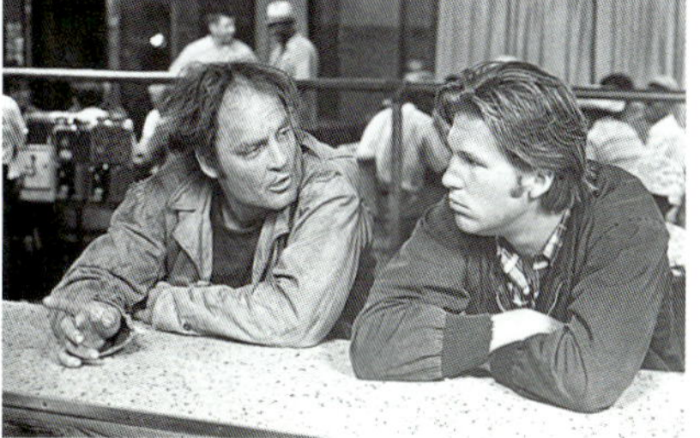

Drug Store EDWARD HOPPER, 1927. MUSEUM OF FINE ARTS, BOSTON. PHOTOGRAPH © 2004 MUSEUM OF FINE ARTS, BOSTON

Fat City
COURTESY COLUMBIA PICTURES/
PHOTOFEST

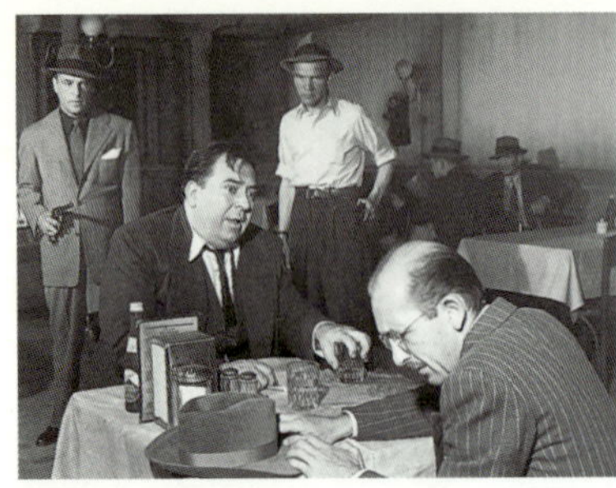

Force of Evil
COURTESY ENTERPRISE PRODUCTIONS,
INC./PHOTOFEST

New York Movie
EDWARD HOPPER, 1939.
THE MUSEUM OF MODERN ART/LICENSED
BY SCALA/ART RESOURCE, N.Y.

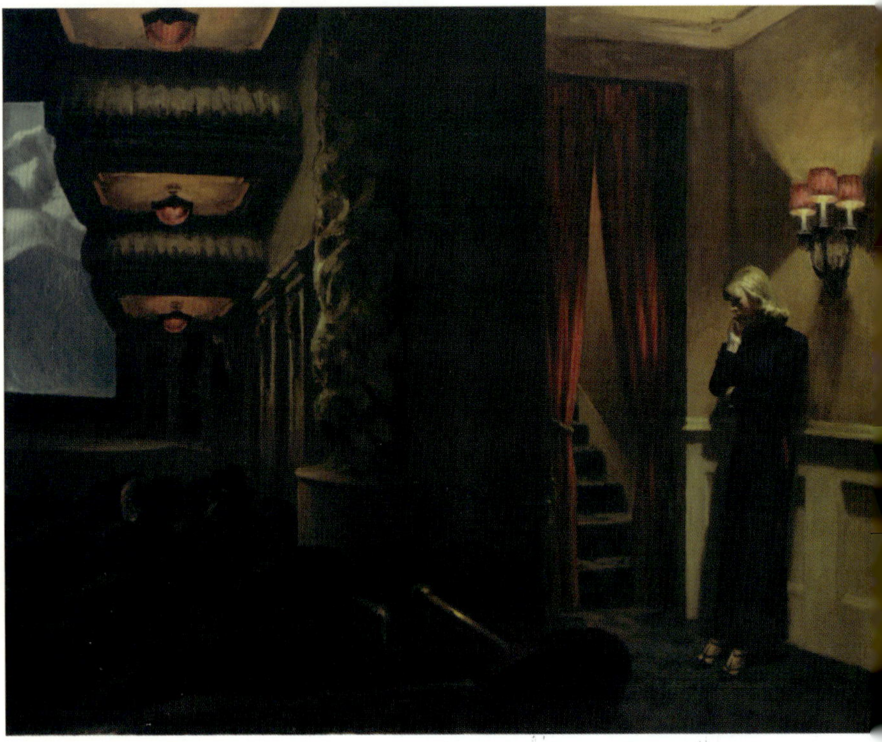

Pickup on South Street
COURTESY TWENTIETH
CENTURY–FOX/PHOTOFEST

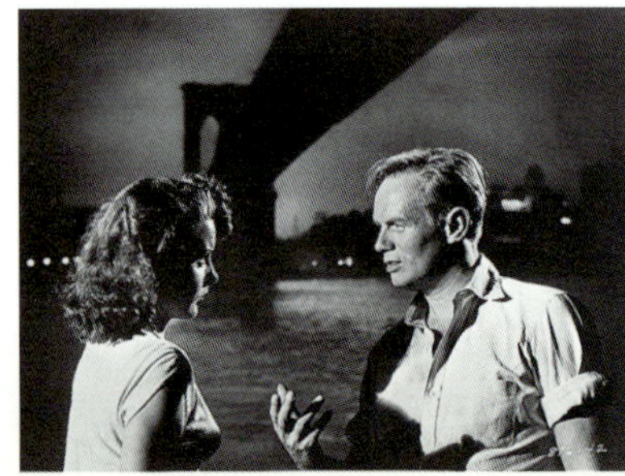

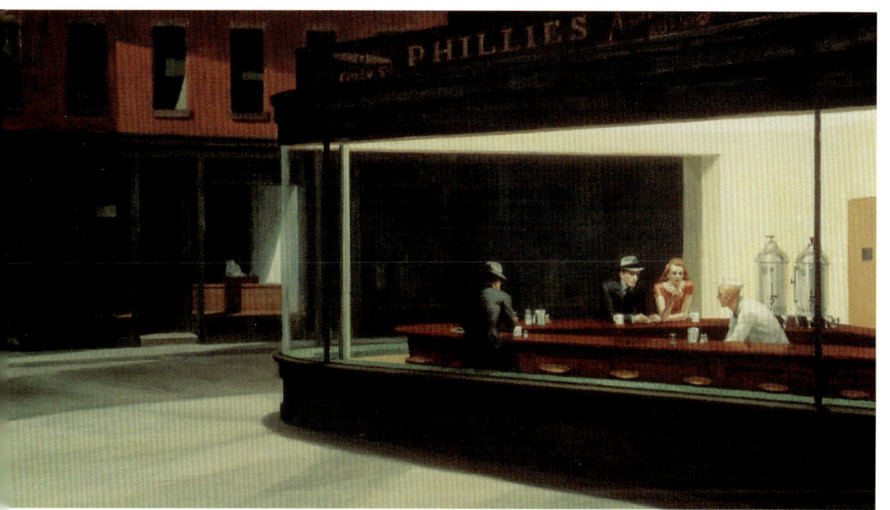

Nighthawks EDWARD HOPPER, 1942.
FRIENDS OF AMERICAN ART COLLECTION, THE ART INSTITUTE OF CHICAGO

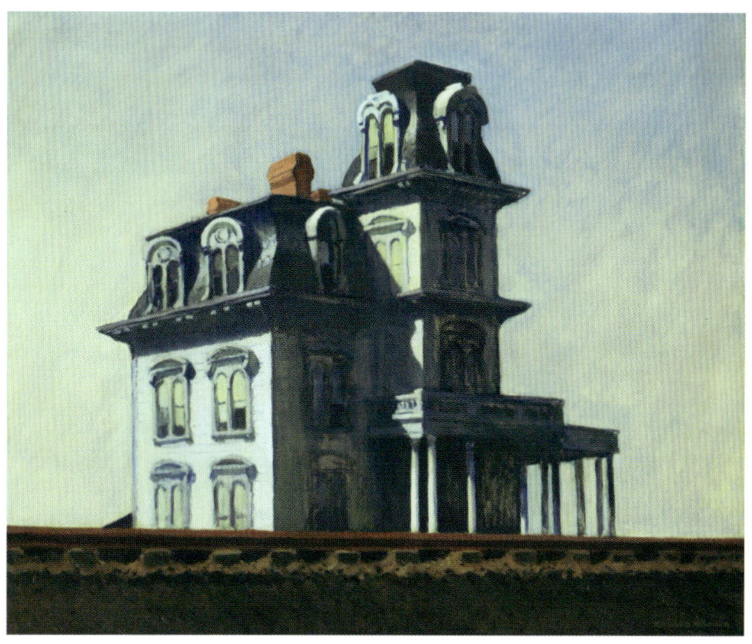

House by the Railroad EDWARD HOPPER, 1925.
THE MUSEUM OF MODERN ART/LICENSED BY SCALA/ART RESOURCE, N.Y.

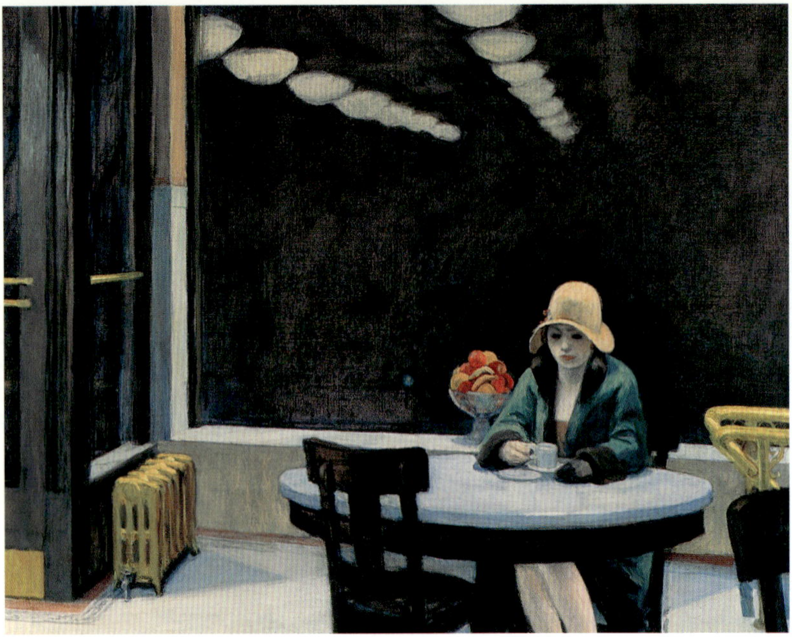

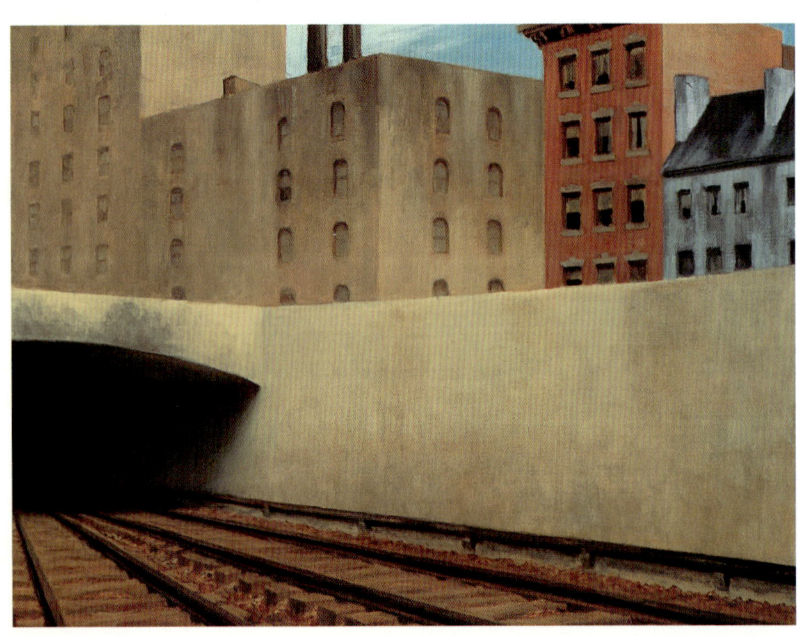

Automat   EDWARD HOPPER, 1927.
DES MOINES ART CENTER PERMANENT COLLECTIONS

Approaching a City   EDWARD HOPPER, 1946.
THE PHILLIPS COLLECTION, WASHINGTON, D.C.

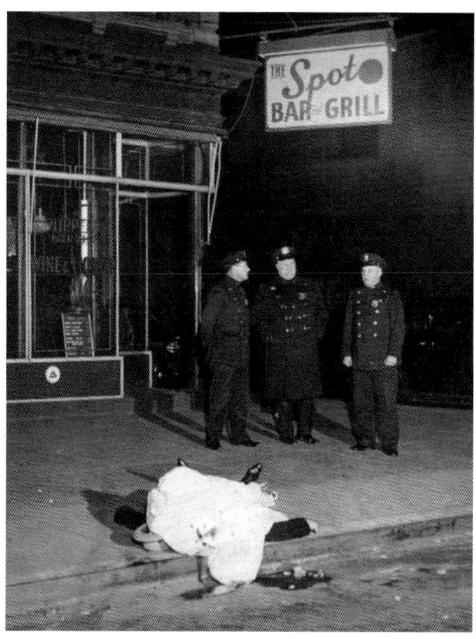

On the Spot WEEGEE
(ARTHUR FELLIG), 1940.
HULTON ARCHIVES/GETTY
IMAGES

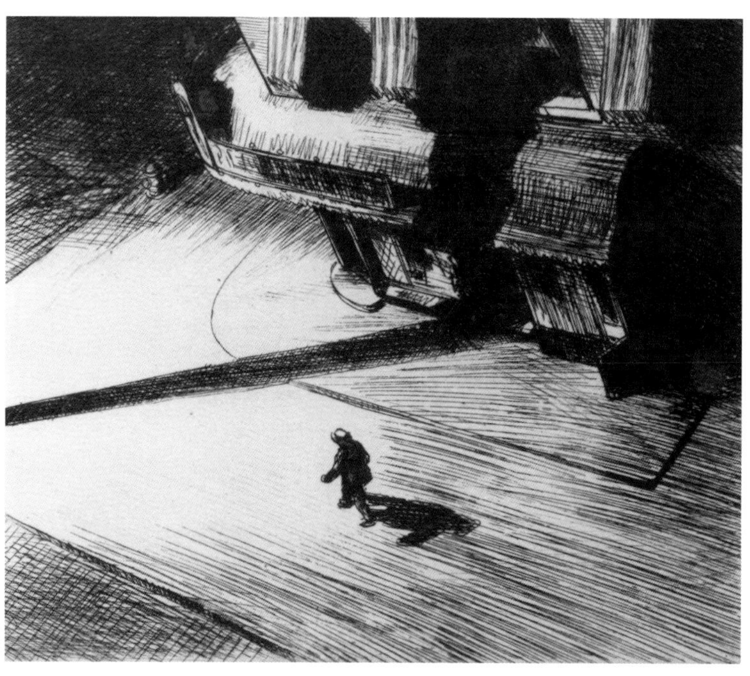

Night Shadows EDWARD HOPPER, 1921.
COLLECTION OF WHITNEY MUSEUM OF AMERICAN ART.
PHOTO CREDIT: ART RESOURCE, N.Y.

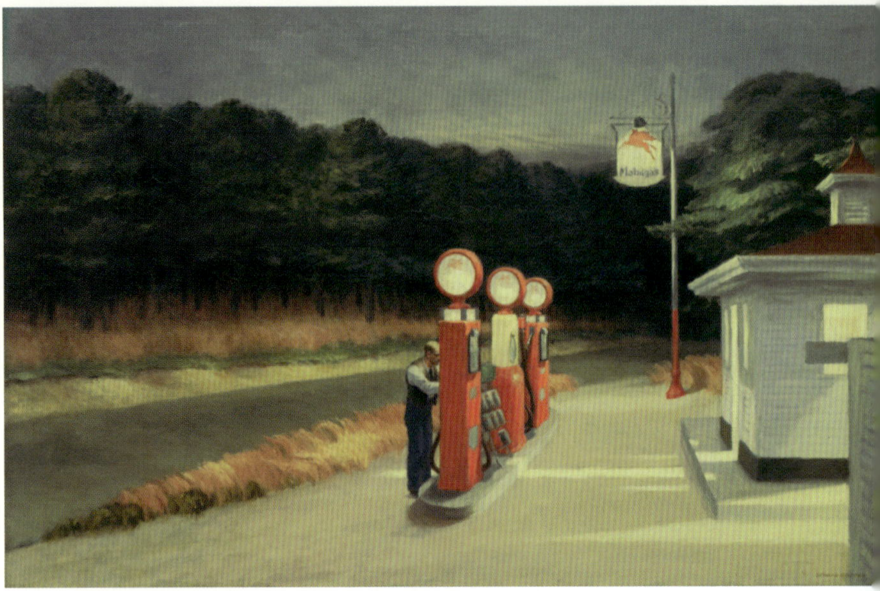

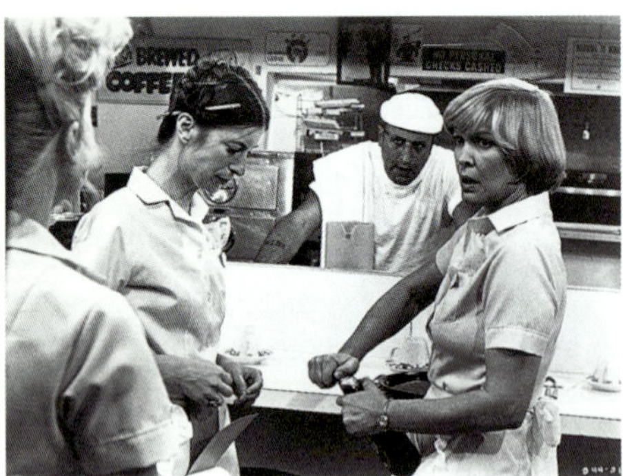

Gas   EDWARD HOPPER, 1940.
THE MUSEUM OF MODERN ART/
LICENSED BY SCALA/ART
RESOURCE, N.Y

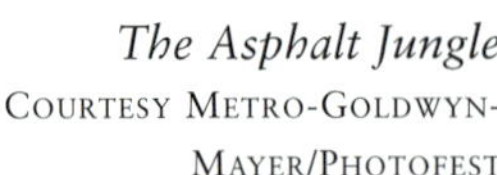

Alice Doesn't Live Here Anymore
COURTESY WARNER BROS. INC./
PHOTOFEST

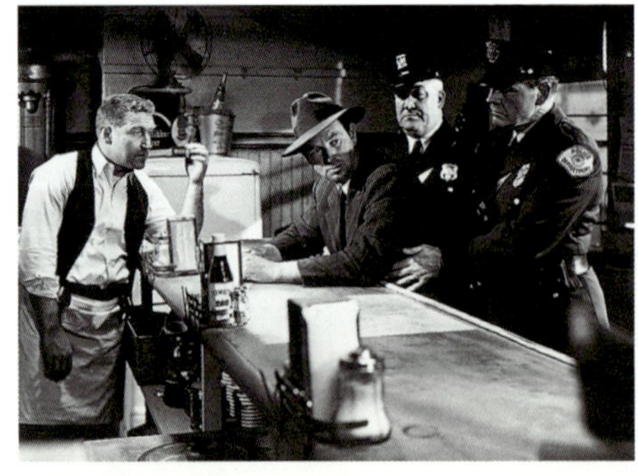

The Asphalt Jungle
COURTESY METRO-GOLDWYN-
MAYER/PHOTOFEST

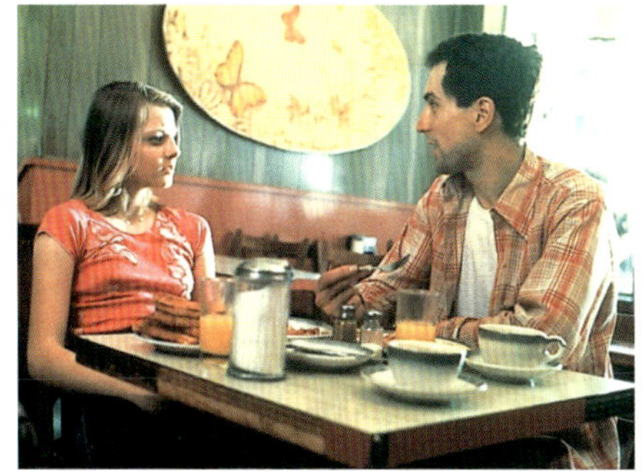

Taxi Driver
Courtesy Columbia Pictures/
Photofest

Pulp Fiction
Courtesy Miramax
Films/Photofest

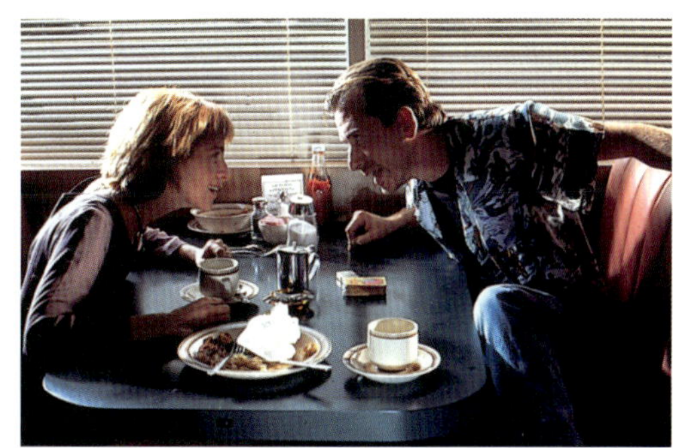

Office at Night
Edward Hopper, 1940.
Collection Walker Art Center,
Minneapolis, M.N.

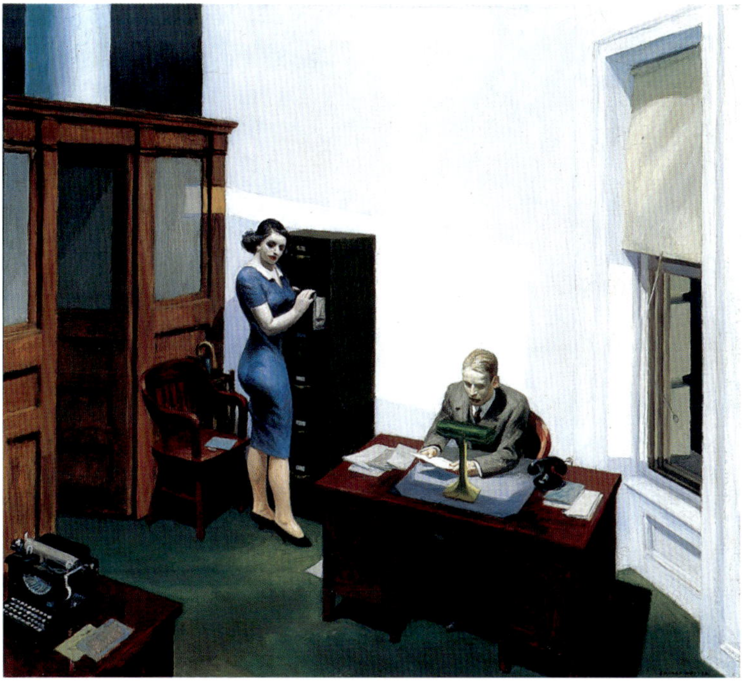

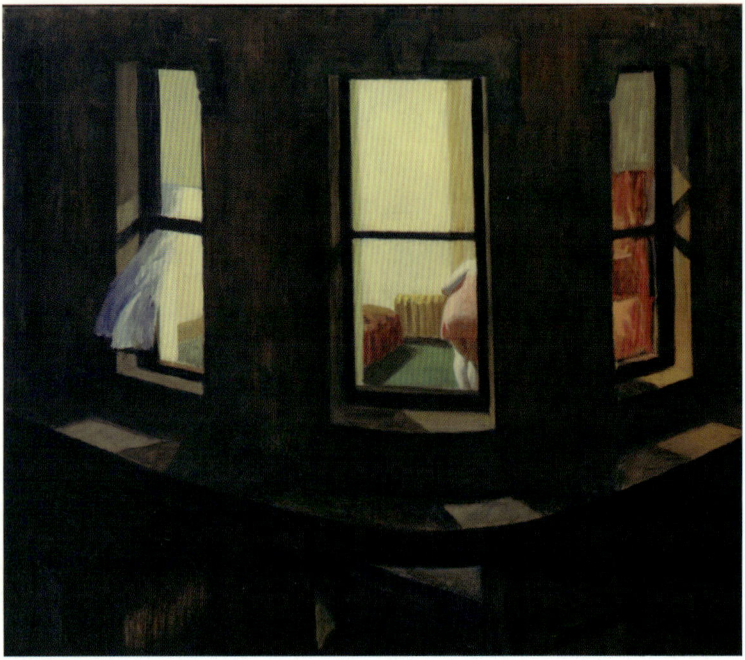

Night Windows EDWARD HOPPER, 1928.
THE MUSEUM OF MODERN ART/LICENSED BY SCALA/ART RESOURCE, N.Y.

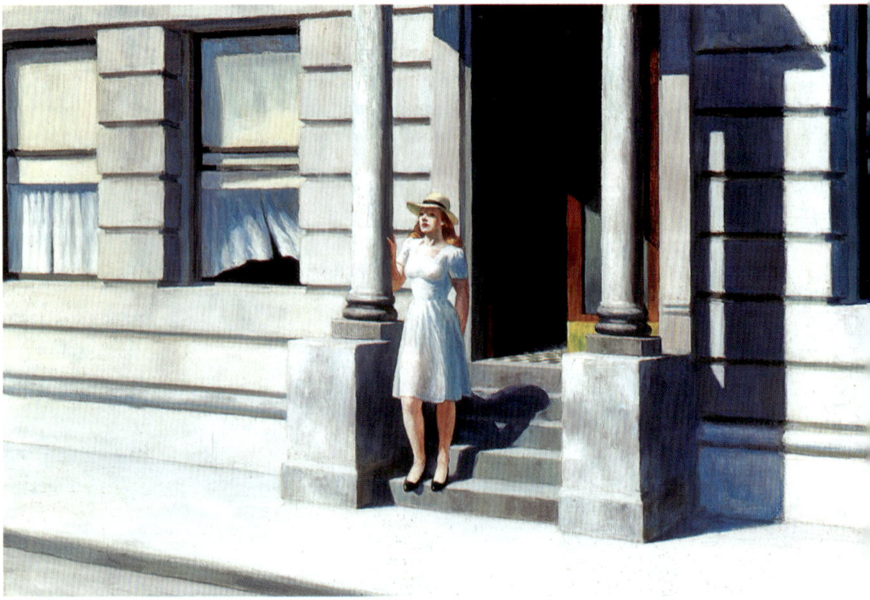

Summertime EDWARD HOPPER, 1943. DELAWARE ART MUSEUM

Blues

Blues music draws on African traditions that managed to survive generations of slavery, but was born sometime in the early part of the twentieth century. With its toots and hoots and unmelodic squawks, its heavy repetitions and clickety-clack rhythms, blues is, like Hopper's paintings, very much a reaction to the machine age, to its loneliness, alienation, profanity, and its focus on sex.

"I love the way you walk," sings John Lee Hooker in "Dimples" (1956), "I'm crazy 'bout your walk" in "Boom Boom" (1962); and "Big Legs, tight skirt / About to drive me out of my mind," in "Big Legs, Tight Skirt" (1965). Commentators have noted that while black gospel music celebrates mercy and grace and the promised life to come in the hereafter, blues deals with the pleasures and pains of life here on earth. In this sense blues might be—like Stieglitz's nude photographs of O'Keeffe and Henry Miller's dirty novels—a corrective to an American religious tradition that unlike Hinduism, say, or European Catholicism, emphasizes the mental over the physical.

The pre-Lenten festivities of Catholics in Paris gave Hopper a heady whiff of open, public sexuality. The Catholic Church, notoriously sex repressive, nonetheless makes a sensual appeal even during masses conducted amid the glow of sunlight through stained glass and the spicy smell of incense on a gold-bedecked altar before a skinny, androgynous Christ on a cross often bearing an expression that combines physical pain with a writhing ecstasy. The Vatican may have insisted on putting fig leafs on the gorgeous male nudes that Michelangelo painted on the vaulted ceiling of the Sistine Chapel, but even with their genitals covered, these figures celebrated the whole person. It is hard to think of a parallel in American Protestantism, which tends to reject the sensual components of worship as idolatry.

Blues, for its part, did bring sensuality and sex into popular music in a way that drove rock and roll, inspired lewd hip shakes from Elvis Presley, and helped lead the 1960s toward an optimistic reappraisal of lust. Just as rock and roll was for many the devil's music, so blues is often about not just sex but illicit sex, affairs and betrayals, and often takes an antagonistic attitude toward religion. One of Hooker's most powerful songs is one of desperation and disbelief, "Burning Hell," from 1946, in which he goes to the church and asks one Deacon Jones to pray for him but concludes that "I don't believe / In no Heaven" or "in no burning Hell." This may be the price he had to pay to sing about lust elsewhere. Damnation itself seems to be the price paid in the lyrics of probably the greatest of blues singers, Robert Johnson.

Little is known about Johnson and much conjectured, including that he died young, poisoned by a woman he was having an affair with, who was jealous of another woman with whom he was having an affair. More extravagantly, it was said that he learned to play guitar as well as he did and to write such powerful songs by selling his soul to Satan. Certainly his songs portray a man possessed, who identifies the evil he finds within himself with lust, which overwhelms his good intentions and his capacity for love, as in "Kind Hearted Woman Blues" (recorded in 1936): "Got a kind hearted woman, do anything in this world for me / But these evil-hearted women / Man, they will not let me be." And lust tempts him to violence: "If she gets unruly," he signs in "32-20 Blues" (recorded in 1936), "and thinks she don't wan' do," then I'll "take my 32-20" shotgun "and cut her half in two." In "Me and the Devil Blues" (recorded in 1937), Satan makes a personal appearance, arriving at the singer's door, and is not unexpected: "I said 'Hello Satan, I believe it's time to go." The next verse: "I'm goin' to beat my woman until I get satisfied."

Lust leads Johnson away from religion, but religion remains the prism through which he views lust. Does he beat his woman because he blames her? Hopper abused Jo: She had him, so to speak, by the balls, and Hopper, like Johnson, conjures a world in which sex cannot be separated from an overall sense of despair. The couple in *Nighthawks* will be drawn together by lust and then thrown back on the emptiness of their surroundings, where they will have little else to do but find themselves in the grips of lust again. They are caught in a loop. Violence is perhaps the only alternative they have. If they do go so far as to touch, inflicting wounds may be as appropriate as a caress.

When lust blurs into violence, it blurs into violence against the object of lust: against women for inciting lust, for not satisfying or for satisfying it all too readily, for simply being women. Hopper's conflicted attitudes about sex were also about his wife as a woman, and about how he saw women in general. . . .

Chapter Six

Wayward Lust, Part 2:
Wicked Women and
Weak-Willed Men

When I was about ten feet from her, at the edge of the sump, she showed
me all her sharp little teeth and brought the gun up and started to hiss.
—RAYMOND CHANDLER

Unlike, say, in Europe, female nipples in America are always almost being exposed but not quite, not without a summons, an R
rating, or a "not for sale to minors" notice. But this seeming coy-
ness only underlines the ubiquity of lust-inducing displays of
women in movies, on billboards and magazine covers, on television, in sitcoms and commercials, undulating in music videos,
and out on the street. This is not, after all, the late-nineteenth
century of Hopper's childhood, when proper Victorian ladies
wore layers of clothing (*long* clothing: to the ankles, to the
wrists) and would keep their bodies covered even while out

swimming in a pond. And it is not the early years of the twentieth century, either, when a mere "slit skirt" could provoke not only scandal but arrest, and the mayor of Boston could score political points by personally seeing to the removal of an image of a "show girl" from a store window.

Laws prohibiting the wearing of slit skirts and semitranslucent "X-ray" skirts were at best holding measures that would already seem archaic by the end of World War I, when mores and manners were in enough disarray to allow for the rise of the flapper of the 1920s, who dispensed with the layers and wore tight-fitting tubelike dresses that clung to their figures. They also used elastic straps to flatten their breasts, and they bobbed their hair for an androgynous look that reflected a newfound equality with men. Women had been granted the vote in 1920, by which time they constituted one-third of the workforce, up from one-fifth in the 1890s. They could indulge in vices like drinking—illegally yet publicly, in speakeasies, along with the men—and smoking cigarettes, which was unacceptable for women prior to the 1910s. And they felt free for the first time to pursue their more earthy desires.

By the 1930s, with Hollywood stars such as platinum blond Jean Harlow in movies such as *Bombshell* (1933), and the bawdy, full-figured comedienne Mae West—"Is that a gun in your pocket, or are you just glad to see me?"—proved that a woman could be both openly feminine—all lips, breasts, hips and legs—and sexually experienced. In an earlier age, this would have been merely whorish and not fit for public consumption, but it was now somewhat whorish and fit for public consumption. Or almost. West made money but was harried, censored, and her movies were condemned.

But by the 1940s, pinups were a popular commercial art form. Well-known beauties such as Rita Hayworth and leggy

Betty Grable and the Varga Girls (the airy creations of illustrator Alberto Varga) could be scantily dressed and not whorish at all but clean, somehow innocent. Varga Girls in particular were presented stretched out against a white, spotless background, often in translucent, ribbonlike garments, as if floating in ether, with a kind of angelic poise. They were included in every issue of *Esquire* magazine and sent overseas to buttress the morale of GIs. They were the immediate predecessors of *Playboy* magazine founder Hugh Hefner's multimillion-dollar innovation, introduced in the July 1955 issue: the absolutely normal Girl Next Door, whom your average reader might "meet at a party, at the grocery store, or at work."

She was no whore. She was not even a professional model; she was an amateur, chosen from countless submissions by Hefner himself. More to the point, she was quite nice, friendly, happy, and willing to pose for a national audience with few or no clothes on, no harm done. To admire her body counted as no sin or unwonted perversion, but was a healthy, open-minded pleasure. Not to everyone, of course. There remained many people not so sophisticated as Hugh Hefner who still found such fare offensive, and some of the more daring purveyors of pornography were subject to police raids, confiscations, and, on occasion, arrest. But to its readers, *Playboy* served as a "primer" for what was expectantly implied would be a wonderfully satisfying sex life, whether monogamous or involving a series of fun-loving women—from right next door!—and helped to introduce a new era of society as a whole. Those old, absurd Victorian values were being declared outmoded and joyless and even strangely immoral.

The pinups, Varga girls, and Hefner's monthly Girl Next Door were heralds of the bare-legged, braless hippie chick of the 1960s, who was ideally as unthreatening as a pinup, as independent as a flapper, and as sexually assured as Mae West. They were heralds of Jane Fonda in the soft-core sci-fi romp *Barbarella* (1968), floating around nude and entirely content in her fur-lined space capsule when not saving the "Loving Union of the Universe" from "neurotic instability" and "archaic insecurity." And they were heralds of today's mainstream porn queens, like bestselling autobiographer and sometime TV commentator Jenna Jameson. The woman in *Nighthawks* is also such a herald, simply for appearing out at night in public in a tight burgundy shirt that reveals her neck and the soft outlines of her collarbone and her long smooth arms almost up to the shoulder.

She is, like a pinup, on display. Like a Girl Next Door, she is discovered in the most mundane of settings yet is sexual, erotic. The painting's invitation to wayward lust comes from nowhere but the curve of her lipsticked lips, her sultry eye shadow, her good looks: high cheekbones, symmetrical features, nicely rounded face, and long, rich-toned, orange-brown hair.

The history of sex in twentieth-century America is the history of the progressive liberation of women and of the public display of women's bodies (men's bodies we do not find as intriguing). From one perspective, this makes the history of sex also the history of voyeurism, of what women let men see and what men get to see in their entertainment and out on the town, always with a question hanging in the air: Should we be seeing what we are seeing? Is it okay? Hopper likely had his first good look at female anatomy as a kind of voyeur while sketching nude models at the New York School of Art, which he entered at seventeen in 1900. The experience apparently made a long-term impression on both his art and his libido.

We are always either peering in windows at women in Hopper

paintings, as with *Night Windows,* or the women are near windows so that someone else might be peering in at them. They are often fully or partially undressed, or they have the top buttons of their dress or shirt undone, as does the secretary in *Office at Night.* There's a lot of cleavage, a lot of heels, a lot of shapely legs on view in Hopper: His women are women without doubt, with large—sometimes almost unbelievably large—breasts and wide, child-bearing hips. He was fascinated by the brute physical fact of women, that they exist and are different from men, which is exactly the type of fascination that lies behind a striptease. Hopper's most overtly prurient painting is, in fact, of a striptease, and was based on sketches he made at the Republic Theater on Broadway and Forty-second Street, where the striptease as an act was first introduced, to a lot of fuss and condemnation, in the early 1930s. In *Girlie Show* (1941), a woman in a light blue G-string and sparkly blue heels prances across a murkily lit stage while holding behind her a light blue wrap she has just removed, uncovering a pair of large and (somewhat disconcertingly) buoyant breasts with big pink nipples.

There is an obvious parallel between this painting and Hopper's sketches of nude models in art school. The painting is the version that anticipates sexual arousal; it is why the woman is there at all, why she has an audience; at the same time, it is dirty, wrong: Why else the taunting, piecemeal removal of attire? Yet most of Hopper's versions of voyeurism take place in the course of common daily experience, while waiting in a hotel lobby, while exploring the countryside, or while wandering through the streets of the city. His *Summertime* (1943), in which a woman lingers at the bottom of the front steps of a New York apartment building, is (in its way) perhaps even more revealing of conflicted desire than *Girlie Show.*

She is young, the woman in *Summertime,* and sunlit, and

wears a soft, tan, wide-brimmed hat and a white dress that suggests virginal innocence, as if any lust would be on the part of the dirty-minded male, unprovoked by her purer self. But she also has reddish hair that goes well with the thick layer of red lipstick, and is beautiful, voluptuous, with breasts as big and round as melons. What is more: Her left nipple is visibly pushing out against the fabric of the white dress, which is nearly transparent. We can make out the shape and fleshy hue of her right thigh all the way to her panty line. She is a voyeur's ideal prey, and the painting suggests that when Hopper meandered through Manhattan looking for subjects to paint, he was motivated also by a meandering lust, to gaze at women, strange women, modern women, remarkably uninhibited women, women like the woman in *Nighthawks.*

This is perhaps why the woman in *Nighthawks* forms the visual center of the painting. The gray hats and blue suits of her companion and the man with his back to us go better with the cool greens and blues and dark shadows of the street outside, as if that is where they belong, while the white uniform of the server effaces him, as such uniforms are meant to do. But her colors harmonize well with the mahogany countertop, the yellow walls, and take full advantage of the diner's fluorescent lighting.

She overwhelms them and us: We are outside looking in, through that plate-glass window, seeing, first and foremost, her. Which means we are wondering about her or should be. The woman in *Summertime* is either a surprisingly naïve virgin or all too self-aware. But the *Nighthawks* woman's more frankly seductive appearance might actually redeem an otherwise bleak scene, in the way that *Playboy* would redeem male desire for the entire nation. Or perhaps it suggests the very opposite, indicating how wrong (say, decadent) a direction the country has taken.

Voyeurism is the essential modern vice in *The Immoral Mr. Teas* (1959), one of the first nudie flicks, which earned a million dollars at the box office on a twenty-five-thousand-dollar-investment, inspired a slew of copycats, and abetted the rise of the adult film industry. Produced and directed by former *Playboy* photographer Russ Meyer, the movie follows the titular hero on his rounds as he pursues his single, obsessive avocation, ogling women, and while doing so mimics evolving levels of public tolerance, which encourage him in his quest. First, we get cleavage and tight, unbuttoned shirt shots of female pedestrians, a secretary at a dentist's office, and a waitress who serves Mr. Teas coffee at his favorite luncheonette. Then, on a trip to the beach, we get women in bikinis; then a topless woman posing for *Playboy*-style photographs, but with her nipples inconveniently blocked from Mr. Teas's view by palm fronds; then, at a secluded pond, full-on shots of actual women's actual breasts (!), nipples included (!!); and then, finally, in Mr. Teas's fantasies, fully nude women, albeit seen from behind (!!!).

That Mr. Teas must finally have recourse to fantasies suggests a problem, and there is a problem. For he is no updated Don Juan with a snazzy bachelor pad where, as Hugh Hefner once put it, he might "enjoy mixing up cocktails and an hors d'oeuvre or two, putting a little mood music on the stereo, and inviting in a female acquaintance for a quiet discussion on Picasso, Nietzsche, jazz, etc." He is not, that is, the suave sophisticate who might effortlessly impress and bed your basic Girl Next Door. Mr. Teas *is* "modern man," as the movie's mock documentary–style voice-over helpfully informs us, but in *Mr. Teas* that means being caught up in the "mad impetuous, driving bustle of the big city" and taking "more potent pills" for "larger stomachaches." Worse, Mr. Teas is but a lowly bike messenger clownishly garbed in a white boater and orange jumpsuit with a drearily predictable routine (once more we see Mr. Teas leave his house, board a bus, retrieve his little red bicycle, pedal his way through blaring traffic, etc.). Ogling women is his single pleasure, but because he does not so much as strike up a conversation with any of them (they barely notice his existence), he ends up "stranded in a vast desert of masculine frustration." His fantasies are like trying to slake an ever-worsening thirst with a picture of a water fountain.

Mr. Teas's predicament is a joke, to be sure: What in one scene appears to be a beckoning prostitute—finally! he'll get laid!—turns out to be a sort of black market laundress who irons his orange jumpsuit for him. But the joke is also on the movie's audience, who find themselves in the exact same predicament: unable to do anything but look and look some more.

The real joke, or irony, here is that the very same commitment to technology and industry that made movies possible also created such hopelessly bland, prefab urban environments as the one inhabited by Mr. Teas. The modern world makes the illusions provided by such movies as *The Immoral Mr. Teas,* as well as by the mechanically reproduced color pictures in a magazine such as *Playboy,* all the more necessary, and ogling women we will never meet all the greater a temptation. In the same way, the reason we do a double take when passing by the woman in Hopper's *Summertime* is that she stands out against the dull gray of the building behind her and the sidewalk beneath her like some exotic flower poking up through a crack in a parking lot. Similarly, the woman in *Nighthawks* stands out against her surroundings. They both provide us with something to look at, like a pinup of a woman in a polka-dot bikini frolicking on a beach might provide a pleasant distraction for an overworked husband

and father, or a GI needing to believe in something besides killing enemies determined to kill him, or just a lowly everyman with the usual, lowly everyman desires.

Yet the woman in *Summertime* is expressionless, distant, not warm or inviting. And we cannot quite separate the woman in *Nighthawks* from her bleak surroundings. Neither can she, it seems: Unlike pinups and *Playboy* models, she does not smile, does not seem especially friendly, does not seem nice, innocent, or happy. She seems indifferent, resigned. She is where she is. She participates in the play of desire and being desired because this is the role available to her, what she can and even must do whether she likes it or not, because she is a modern woman in a modern city. In such a place, there is no escape from the very bleakness pinups would distract us from, so why bother smiling? She is instead the antipinup: She drags those confident, beautiful women down from the bright ether and onto the shadowed streets, from beach to pavement, from animal-skin rug to a stool in a nameless, nondescript diner. And she drags us from the snazzy bachelor pads of our fantasies out into the night, where we meander, where our lust is raw, where we will stare at her from afar, through a plate-glass window, whether she smiles or not, whether she is nice or not.

This is not quite the same thing as saying she is somehow more real or more realistic than a happy pinup, a Girl Next Door. Or that she is only an unhappy pinup, a less than hopeful Girl Next Door. Or even that Hopper is condemning himself, or us, for lusting after her. But it does suggest that for Hopper, the cleaned-up, no-harm-done version of female sexuality was not convincing.

Following *Mr. Teas,* Russ Meyer made a career for himself as the "King of the D-Cup." He became a soft-core director who could be counted on to cast almost cartoonishly voluptuous actresses who were both fun to look at and too spectacularly well endowed for the audience to forget exactly what *Playboy* sought to deny: that we were being shown not sex or women but a performance about sex, about women. The voluptuous, well-rounded endowments of the women Hopper painted around the time he painted *Nighthawks*—the secretary in *Office at Night,* the stripper in *Girlie Show,* the young woman in *Summertime*—also suggest that we are seeing something self-conscious, a comment on the subject, rather than a direct transcription, of desire. And if Hopper's women are not perhaps as voluptuous, as well rounded, in their endowments as Russ Meyer women, they are not exactly like pinups, either.

Pinups were all about prominent breasts, prominent hips, but they were sleeker, more geometrical, more machine age, almost as if the ideal female figure should be reducible to a series of interlocking triangles. Wide shoulders and large, distinct, pointy breasts slanted down to a wasp waist before slanting back out to the hips then tapering down again along long legs that might be made to seem longer with lined stockings and heels. The heels also formed a point (or points, if the feet were apart) that completed the thin triangle (or triangles) framed by the lower hips and legs.

This look—often topped off by the modishly triangular hairstyle worn by the woman in *Nighthawks*—resulted from a kind of technological innovation. In the late 1930s, the long since dispensed with Victorian-style whalebone-reinforced corset was on the verge of a comeback, along with a version of the figure much admired and sought after in the late nineteenth century, known then as the "Grecian S." The smooth upper loop covered the breasts, the bottom loop the bustle-enhanced buttocks, with a pinched waist in between. The whole ensemble pitched slightly forward, so a fashionable lady might seem about to topple over as she, with frilly hat, tiny parasol, platform shoes, and practiced dexterity, strolled along Fifth Avenue. But the corset's comeback was, luckily perhaps, intercepted by the introduction of the more comfortable and less restrictive bra and separate girdle. The result was both a throwback and something new, made yet newer, more angular, by shoulder pads in jackets and blouses and by stiff cones stuffed in the bra to better define the breasts.

But while Hopper was a careful observer of female clothing and style (his women always look contemporary), the figures he gave them tend to recall the corset. What he seems to have been doing, consciously or not, is playing out the evolution of modern dress and the modern lack of inhibition using the conservative Victorian matrons of his youth. These women were the moral center of the household, raising the children and keeping the home in order while the men went to work, which may be why the culture fixated on women's bodies while chucking off Victorian-era restrictions on sexual display. If *women* appeared in salacious states of undress—with a smile no less—then we knew lust had gotten up from the gutter, taken a shower, and entered the parlor. Lust had become acceptable, with all that might imply (details, that is, to be worked out in the course of the century).

This moral role of women would have been strengthened in Hopper's own household because of the standing his mother, Elizabeth Griffiths Hopper, had in the community as the dutiful granddaughter of the minister who founded the church the Hoppers attended. She was also the financial center of the household, providing the house itself (built by the grandfather who founded the church), and the inheritance that kept Hopper's father's failures from adversely affecting the family fortunes. As if all this wasn't enough, Elizabeth had dabbled in fine art in her youth.

She was the one who encouraged Hopper to pursue his interest in painting, never imagining that he would use his talent and schooling to portray women of whom she would surely disapprove.

Yet Hopper himself only emphasized the contrast between his mother's moral values and his own prurience, between the virginal white of the young woman's dress in *Summertime* and what it exposes of the woman's body, as well as the contrast between motherhood itself and sex. Strikingly, despite the apparent fitness of his female figures for childbearing and nursing, the childless Hopper included very few children in his work, the rare exception being an etching, *The Lonely House* (1923), in which two little girls are seen searching the ground along the bare side wall of a three-story town house. The girls look tiny, bereft, abandoned to some meager amusement. In *New York Pavements* (1924), he did include a baby stroller being pushed by a nursemaid in funereal black past a large concrete building. In this haunting image, the stroller is only partly visible, shown from a skewed perspective, and entering the scene from the bottom left. In both *The Lonely House* and *New York Pavements* we get a sense that the modern world is an unwelcoming place indeed for the very young.

They have left motherhood behind and taken on a merely erotic interest, Hopper's women, or, more precisely, modern women in Hopper's portrayal of them. The secretary in *Office at Night* might as well be wearing a corset, given her smooth, round, S-shaped figure; she could be one of the upper-class ladies late-nineteenth-century artist Mary Cassatt portrayed in their carriages, at afternoon teas, on picnics, with infants in their arms, toddlers at their knees. But she is in the twentieth century—can vote, smoke, drink, and drive, works in an office, leaves the top buttons of her dress undone, wears underwear so tight we can discern the halves of her buttocks, and considers seducing her boss. Which raises the question: How will he, the boss, say no to her, given a choice between that piece of paper he's staring at and her quite considerable charms?

Camille Paglia, defending pornography, once wrote, "in this mechanized technological world of steel and glass, the fires of sex have to be stoked," meaning that industrialization requires a certain recompense in sexual display to make it tolerable, to keep our natural urges functional. To which one might respond, well, fine, but that particular tigress out of her cage, what's to keep her from eating us for dinner? A woman lingering on the front steps of an apartment building in a translucent white dress may distract us only momentarily, give our blood a little boost. Then again, she might lure us inside, destroy our marriage, make us abandon our families, and give us nothing but fleeting pleasures in return. Long-held beliefs might dissipate like mist in the wind when a stripper bares her big breasts and big pink nipples before us, replacing the dictates of God with the pull of desire.

And where do we find ourselves but out late at night, meandering, seeking desolation and emptiness, a place where morals have no hold, until we spot a woman with rich red lips and bare neck and arms sitting in some diner, a woman from who knows where, of what depth of depravity. We don't care. We are entranced.

From this perspective, the pinup is a monster formed from the ashes of an entire social order, a dominant lifestyle, a way of looking at and being in the world. Or she is but a suspiciously saccharine fake by which we delude ourselves that we have gained greater liberty, understanding, sophistication, and pleasure. But no: We are instead in the grips of one of America's most enduring popular myths, the femme fatale, that swervy seductress who shows up in countless pulp novels and B movies in the 1930s and 1940s. She is there to confront the hero and lead him astray, using her charms, her shapeliness, her breasts and hips, to get him to steal, lie, cheat, to commit murder, to allow her to commit murder for money, for love, but truly because she has what they all know they should not want but do.

She is the dark female force invading the realm of men, taking jobs and gaining a political voice while becoming sexier, looser, more available: irresistible. She is nascent in the gender-bending misbehavior of the flapper. In Howard Hawk's *Scarface* (1932, but set in the 1920s), the flapper sister of the gangster antihero seduces his number-two man by dancing like a viper in heat. Scarface will later kill the man for sleeping with his sister, who will herself die with Scarface in the movie's climatic shootout, as is somehow appropriate, for she's a bit too sexy—too aggressively so, the erotic equivalent of her brother's anarchic violence.

But the femme fatale proper is all woman and erases any distinction between sex and violence. She is the curvaceous diner owner's wife in James M. Cain's novel *The Postman Always Rings Twice* (adapted to film in 1946 and again in 1981), whose alluring "pout" alone provides the motive for the shiftless drifter Frank to help murder her husband. She is Mrs. Phyllis Nirdlinger, who ensnares the sober, successful, and respected insurance agent Walter Huff by wearing "a white sailor suit, with a blouse that pulled tight over her hips, and white shoes and stockings." She gets him to trick her husband into taking out a policy on his life, then to kill the husband while making it look like an accident, before betraying Huff with her stepdaughter's boyfriend and then shooting him, in Cain's *Double Indemnity* (1943; filmed in 1944).

The femme fatale is the natural enemy of such ultramacho figures as Raymond Chandler's hard-boiled private detective Philip Marlowe. She is the spoiled rich psychopath Carmen Sternwood, who murders men who refuse to have sex with her in Chandler's *The Big Sleep* (1939; adapted to film starring Humphrey Bogart, in 1946; and again in 1981, starring Robert Mitchum). She is the absurdly wealthy Mrs. Grayle, a.k.a., Velma, who'll murder anyone who might give away her tawdry past as a showgirl and consort of gangsters—she had "nice legs" back then and was "generous with 'em"—in Chandler's *Farewell My Lovely* (1940; adapted to film, starring Robert Mitchum, in 1975). She is Brigid O'Shaughnessy, a.k.a., Miss Wonderly, who gunned down private detective Sam Spade's partner and would likely gun Sam down if she thought it would help her. But he falls for her and keeps falling, even after he realizes she's a coldhearted murderess, even while he makes the phone call to the police that will send her to the electric chair, in Dashiell Hammett's *The Maltese Falcon* (1929, adapted to film several times, most famously starring Humphrey Bogart in 1941). She is Sharon Stone's cool rich blond bisexual who goes around without bra or panties and stabs men at the point of climax with an ice pick in *Basic Instinct* (1992). And she is, quite recently, Beatrix Kiddo, a.k.a, Black Mamba, the supermodel-gorgeous international assassin on an epic and epically bloody trail of vengeance in *Kill Bill, Vol. 1* (2003) and *Kill Bill, Vol. 2* (2004).

That the cleaner allure of the pinup only served to mask the dark force of the femme fatale might be demonstrated by the legendary career of Bettie Page. Her body earned her the sobriquet "Queen of the Curves," while her broad smile and healthy good looks made her the top model of the 1950s, seen most prominently in a scanty Santa suit in the December 1955 centerfold of

Playboy. But Bettie Page also posed for Irving Klaw, owner of Movie Star News, a film still, poster, and pinup store on East Fourteenth Street in Manhattan, where he also ran a discreet mail-order catalog business for bondage pictures. Mainly lesbian scenarios, these pictures were not explicit. Nipples remain covered and the girls rarely so much as touch one another. The excitement is provided by whips, ropes, hairbrush spankings, chains, studded leather, severe to terrified facial expressions, and makeshift dungeons. In this murky domain we may find Bettie trussed and gagged and suspended in midair or curled up in an armchair with a look of utter disdain and a cat-o'-nine-tails in hand, expecting abject worship from men no better than swine for daring to approach her.

The femme fatale is the woman in *Nighthawks,* deceiving us entirely with her charms, as if we in our fear and our desire detected a slight but revealing bemusement playing at the corners of those luscious lips at how easy it is to manipulate the male libido. What passes for allure is but a trick of the makeup, the artificial lighting, the chance harmony between her coloring and the mahogany countertop in a diner where she only bides her time. Soon she will be further liberated by a society too foolish to understand the danger, too stricken to notice the looming tint of dried blood on the brick buildings across the street. Sitting there, not caring what her companion may have said to anger the server, whether he may or may not commit a crime, pull a gun— whatever happens, happens—she is but a social-evolutionary beat away from getting up and going out and actively seeking men to destroy. She may then enjoy the absolute lack of restraint suggested by the wonderfully named actress Tura Satana in the Russ Meyer movie *Faster Pussycat! Kill! Kill!* (1966).

Satana plays Varla, the homicidal, knife-wielding leader of a trio of voluptuous go-go girls who, in their off-hours, cruise the California desert in foreign sports coupes and do whatever else makes them "feel good."

In the movie, these girls are pitted against a sour wheelchair-bound old man and his two sons, the old man a caricature of a member of Hopper's generation who clings to outdated Victorian values. On women: "They let them smoke, vote, and drive, even put them in pants, so what do you get? A democrat for president!" On trains: "Huff and puff and belch your smoke and kill and maim and run off, unpunished!" (He ended up in a wheelchair after he fell while helping a girl onto a platform at a train station.) We may reasonably deduce from the dilapidated ranch in an otherwise uninhabited scrub where he stubbornly resides, that the twentieth century as a whole similarly meets with the old man's stern disapproval. For him, the license of the 1960s (which included the advent of go-go dancing) portends not miniskirts, the frug, and idyllic free love, but a loss of any moral orientation whatsoever.

The old man is correct in this movie, which opens with a parody of a panicky public service announcement that speaks to his worst fears: "Ladies and gentlemen, welcome to violence, the word and the act. While violence cloaks itself in a plethora of disguises, its favorite mantle remains sex," or, more precisely, a "new breed" of women. If "the softness is there, the unmistakable smell of female, the surface shiny and silken, the body yielding yet wanton," this only serves an unprecedented rapacity recently unleashed upon the nation and already "operating at any level, any time, anywhere, with anybody." Cut to the go-go dancers gyrating frenziedly in a nightclub, then to male faces in the audience contorted with lust. But while the camera teases us with the wild curves of the dancers' voluptuous bodies, and the characters leer at one another, their breathy dialogue littered with double entendres, *Faster Pussycat* eschews nudity. None of a variety of couplings will be consummated before the jumpy plot, which involves the go-go dancers' attempt to steal money hidden at the ranch, interrupts them. We are headed not toward an orgy but toward a bloodbath instigated not by the old man with his handy shotgun but by the dancers themselves, who stab one another (fatal infighting: they are truly lawless) and, appropriately, wield a trendy machine, one of their foreign sports coupes, against the old man, crushing him in his wheelchair.

His death is also the death of Victorianism in general, the whole archaic, neurotic, insecure demonization of the body and sex, which is, after all, perfectly natural, perfectly okay, one of God's gifts—if you happen to believe in God. And with the death of the old man so, too, goes his vision of woman as threat, as femme fatale, as sexual dominator, as punisher, as killer. Varla herself dies in the movie's very last scene, run down by a pinup-style bikini-clad girl driving a large pickup truck.

Faster Pussycat is camp because it deals with a conflict that the movie itself demonstrates is no longer relevant: We really can sit back and enjoy the marvelous bodies of Meyer's actresses, whether as desirables or as comic effects or both, we are allowed to now. We still did not know what we would be allowed to enjoy when *Nighthawks* was painted, of course, but this does not necessarily make how the woman is portrayed there a statement against modern sexual display. Rather, we might see her as modern woman during an especially fearsome intermediate period. She arrives long after a slit skirt was cause for scandal, and long before a sexually liberated woman such as Jane Fonda might defend us from the "positronic ray" in the spoof *Barbarella*—"the American girl triumphing by her innocence," wrote Pauline

Kael—as well as try to help end the actual brutality of war in Vietnam.

The woman in *Nighthawks* stands out because she is in the process of emerging from beneath the shroud of the past. That she combines elements of the pinup and of the femme fatale in a single unified image may begin to explain the mind-set behind the violence of Hopper's marriage, while making his portrayal of her more potent, precisely because it is so painfully conflicted.

Crumb

By the 1960s, voluptuous women, like the women Hopper painted, like the women in *Mr. Teas* and *Faster Pussycat,* were out-of-date, their overlarge breasts and hips as much a sign of women's oppression as the corset, and as antiquated as the notion that lust and damnation had anything to do with each other. The 1960s ideal was more along the lines of the slender, perky Fonda, the boyish Audrey Hepburn, coat hanger–skinny supermodel Twiggy, and the slim and limber Marilyn Chambers, who was the clean-cut fixture of Ivory soap ads before starring in the early hard-core feature *Behind the Green Door* (1972).

However, none of these women fit the ideal of underground "comix" artist Robert Crumb, though he found his niche in hippie-central Haight-Ashbury in the mid-1960s. He did a cover for a Janis Joplin album, and attributes his often surreal style to the use of the quintessential 1960s drug, LSD. Crumb's women instead hearken back to the curvaceous models in the cheap 1950s pasties-and-a-G-string magazines he collects, but are often exaggerated to an almost monstrous degree, as if to realize some timeless archetype of pure femaleness. For Crumb, this means big muscled legs beneath enormous buttocks and enormous breasts with enormous nipples that he will—if the woman in question is wearing a top—with a connoisseur's flourish, show pushing out against the always tight-fitting fabric. Such creatures would doubtless overcome the mostly scrawny, shorter men who chase them if they themselves weren't too horny to resist the explicitly detailed (spread labia, penetration, gobs of semen, fellatio, etc.) rounds of lust, lust satisfied, and lust reawakened. Crumb dramatizes all this against a backdrop cluttered with power lines, telephone poles, trashed appliances, antennae, signs and more signs, cracked concrete abutments, junk cars, barbed wire, and smog-belching factories.

These backdrops are so Hopperesque in their keenly observed homeliness and their tragic sense of a better past lost to a technophiliac present that a direct influence might be supposed. Crumb is Hopper meets *Hustler*. And while Crumb is at least partly true to a 1960s cultural orientation, he shares none of the era's optimism. He does seem to unabashedly relish lust and to think of lust, and the display of women's bodies, as an escape from the twentieth-century wasteland of machinery and rampant commercialism. He also seems intent on overturning any neo-puritanical condemnation of sexual expression (like that, for example, which clouds much feminism), and refuses to censor his subject matter in any way, including bestiality, coprophagy, and incest. But he portrays the relations between men and women as irresolvable turmoil and frustration, hence a strip about removing the head of a woman (the voluptuous Demon Girl) so one Flakey Foont can enjoy her body without hassle.

In another strip, *All-Meat Comics* (1969), Crumb takes lust to an ungovernable, all-consuming extreme: All our surroundings, all our things, all our machines, have been transformed into flesh, as if the entire world were one big naked woman in heat. "It's fun to crash in all-meat cars!" Every aspect of the flesh, including blood and shit, is celebrated and made erotic: "Shitting is a pleasure! Go baby go!" he writes over an image of buttocks protruding from an ocean of feces. A legion of stiff penises on the march and a bundle of big breasts lead to a drawing of Crumb himself eagerly jerking himself off. In the last panel, a giant, fully sated penis lies on a darkened city street: "Whew!" And that's it, finally: masturbation material. As Crumb dolefully admits in *Anal Antics* (1971), "More sick humor that serves no purpose."

The promise of a bright new arcadia based on free love was just that, masturbation material. And that darker vision of lust, as the wellspring of a more thoroughgoing iniquity, with women as the source of lust, is still with us. We have come far, as a culture, by way of accommodating desire. We have women dressed as provocatively as prostitutes for a trip to the dentist or the grocery store, while mechanically reproduced images of pretty, scantily clad women are used to interest us in everything from beer to toothpaste to rifles. We have "adults only" magazines and DVDs, providing such gaping images of women's vaginas and rectums that we might think we cannot possibly go any further. But still, a proudly religious attorney general might feel a need to drape the decidedly nonprurient statue of Justice, whose bare breasts appeared behind him during newscasts. Still, the brief on-purpose-by-accident exposure of Janet Jackson's nipple on live TV can inspire two hundred thousand viewers to take the trouble to file complaints with the FCC and cause a spate of national soul-searching.

More than two months later, in the April 12, 2004, edition of *The New York Times,* op-ed columnist Nicholas D. Kristof saw fit to note how "Europeans are bewildered that Americans can feel more threatened by Janet Jackson's breast than by unregulated handguns." Well, that is because with a gun the difference is who's holding it and in what state of mind, while if a naked nipple isn't nourishing an infant, it may bring men to such desperate straits that they will use a gun to do wrong. For despite liberation, we remain conflicted, perhaps even more painfully so—we can no longer avoid the issue, it is everywhere, always. And we remain stuck outside the diner in *Nighthawks*, staring in at that woman, excited, tempted, perhaps even hopeful, but not getting any closer, not going inside, because we are scared, too, that we will never come back out.

Chapter Seven

Cheap Cigars and Ex-Lax

> Floodlit, Liberty looked less like a muse than ever, and more like a
> gargantuan neon logo: MEAT-O-MAT BEEF PATTIES, writ in flame.
>
> —Nik Cohn

If Americans are conflicted about sex, they are much less so about money, the need to sell something—a product, a service, or yourself at a job interview—to make and accumulate money, and the measuring of self-worth by how much made, how much accumulated. This not only means vast amounts of labor and creative energy are expended on advertising, but that even what are not advertisements—magazines, books, CD covers, and movies, not to mention résumés, political speeches, etc.—look and act like advertisements, attempts to grab people's attention, to sell. And what more efficient means of grabbing the attention of people conflicted about sex than with sex, particularly those scantily clad female figures that help sell everything from beer to cars to tampons. They appear within the advertisements them-selves, or they redirect our attention toward whatever is being advertised—computers, travel, cologne—within a magazine such as *Stuff* bearing a near-naked model on the cover, or between raunchy rap videos. Or they illustrate an article about Brazil, or vitamin D, or an exposé on prostitution in Bangkok. But they are there, or nearby, or coming soon. They are oil for the free-market engine.

Thus does one value subsume another. If, as the adage has it, "sex sells," this may not quite trump a sense that indecency is loose and at-large in contemporary culture. But it does make it difficult to see how restraint could prevail when the making of money is not only at stake, but is the stake, what we are, finally, obliged to do. The domestic porn industry, for example, grossed an estimated $10 billion in 2005, which kind of makes it a fait accompli, however many of us find porn offensive. Porn, in fact, may be the ultimate reduction of the modern capitalist formula: Sexual imagery not only is associated with a given product, but is the product, as if porn is selling the advertisement itself. And some of the nastier tropes in porn, those as much about abasement as lust, seem contrived in any case mainly to support the notion that people will, after all, do anything for money. Many of the scantily clad female figures used in advertisements and elsewhere, meanwhile, seem too clean, too polished, too perfect to be about sex. These women might themselves be products. They are about having enough money to attract such a creature, not for sex but for display, like cruising to the grocery store in a shiny Cadillac SUV.

Money is the key, for us, finally, not sex, and advertising with or without scantily clad female figures is money porn, and is ubiquitous. A mindless torrent of brand names and slogans and facile scenarios suggesting superhuman satisfaction through a mere purchase flows from so many sources and forces its way into our consciousness in so many places at so many times that it would be a task to even begin to make a sufficient list (television, billboards, T-shirts, shop windows, leaflets, trucks, and on and on). This is a relatively recent phenomenon. The twentieth century hardly saw the invention of advertising. But it did see the rapid rise, in its first few decades, of the number of companies hawking inventions that required advertising to obtain the public's interest and to distinguish a given invention from a slew of other, often confusingly similar, inventions. Henry Ford may have figured out how to manufacture an inexpensive yet reliable automobile, but how to let your basic American working-class everyman know that, if he purchased a Model T, he would be able to "enjoy with his family the blessing of hours of pleasure in God's open country"? Ford had to get the message out to the masses. So he and others like him increasingly invested their dollars in advertising: from some $7 million per year in the mid-1860s, when magazines still relegated advertisements to their back pages, to some $3.4 billion, an astounding 3 percent of gross national product, in 1929 alone.

By the time Hopper painted *Nighthawks,* it can safely be said, the advertisement for Phillies, with which he topped the diner—"Only 5¢," "America's No. 1 Cigar"—was both thoroughly unremarkable and an essential aspect of how the country looked. The product advertised—a cheap cigar—was thoroughly unremarkable as well yet is redolent of certain assumptions about money that helped bring about a culture largely defined by advertising.

This is in part because when we think of a cigar, we most likely do not think of a cheap cigar—a Phillies, or a Dutch Masters—though they are available at just about every gas station and convenience mart, any more than we think of Night Train when we think of wine. For cigars, like wine, are not supposed to be cheap. They are supposed to be expensive. The grade of tobacco used in cigars is supposed to matter. So is how various grades of tobacco are blended together, and the way the cigar is rolled, by hand, by someone who is experienced in what is considered a traditional and venerable (if somewhat lowly) craft. The person smoking the cigar is supposed to care that he's smoking a cigar, a unique item, a special item, as opposed to a cigarette, which is exactly the same as every other cigarette of the same brand. He should have a developed palate, be able to distinguish one type of cigar from another and judge the relative quality of any particular cigar, or what amounts to the same thing, have enough money to give the impression that he can make such distinctions, such fine judgments.

For what we associate with cigars is money, success. We think of people who have lots of money and are very successful, whether in sports (Michael Jordan), entertainment (Arnold Schwarzenegger), or most especially in business. We associate cigars with a large desk in a large office boasting a spectacular view of the surrounding metropolis, or with playing golf beneath temperate but sunny skies, or relaxing after dinner in an exclusive upscale restaurant with a snifter of brandy, say, or cognac.

The association between cigars and money goes back to the late-nineteen century. Cigarettes, formerly rolled by hand like cigars (Polish cigarette rollers were actually imported to New York City to keep up with demand), were suddenly manufactured by machine, making them cheaper, and put in packs of twenty, making them more convenient than cigars. Cigars, on the other hand, which took longer to smoke, were a kind of leisure activity. They were already, following the Civil War, the choice form of tobacco use (over pipes, cigarettes, and snuff) among the college educated and the up-and-coming.

Cigars then became identified with those who had already come up: recent and former generals and statesmen such as Ulysses S. Grant and Henry Clay, and stupendously wealthy barons of industry such as steel and railroad magnate J. Pierpont Morgan. Morgan not only bought the very best cigars but had them custom rolled, at $1.25 apiece. This was when the average cigar—often bought not by the wealthy but by those who wanted to partake of wealth, however tangentially—cost three cents, still a lot at the time for a single nonessential item consumed upon use.

Cigars symbolized the notion that becoming rich was the American dream, that by making and selling and improving industry and becoming richer and richer, a given individual helped himself and also, as Adam Smith claimed in *Wealth of Nations* (1776), helped society as a whole. Wealth was a happy result of progress, capitalist self-interest the wellspring of a true meritocracy, an idea that lent some currency to a faddish doctrine called social Darwinism, championed most prominently by Yale professor William Graham Sumner. Capitalism may be ruthless, Sumner argued, but that ruthlessness is healthy and ensures that the fittest survive, i.e., rise to the top, while the unfit get out of the way or help out as best they can. But men like Morgan, a staunch Episcopalian who gave generously to charity, were more inclined to regard their position and the position of others like them as an indication of hard work and character. They did not rise to the top because they were ruthless but because they were good, a position closer to that described, if scornfully, by German sociologist Max Weber in *The Protestant Ethic and the Spirit of Capitalism* (1904).

Weber traced America's acceptance and even celebration of a

wealthy elite to the Puritans. They believed in imposing God's rigid laws on their fellow men, but they also believed in predestination, that all man's activities and all history is foreknown and already laid down by divine will. God bestowed grace upon some and not upon others, chose some to rise and some to fall—those who rise being the heaven-bound elect and those who fall being preterit or left behind, bound for damnation.

One way the elect knew that they were elect was by dint of their virtue, particularly their dedication to hard work, but another was by receiving the material rewards of hard work. As John Winthrop put it to fellow believers while sailing for America aboard the *Arbella* in 1630, the "Almightie" has "so disposed" that "some must be rich, some poore, some highe and eminent in power and dignitie; others mean and in subjection." Winthrop's sentiments may seem horribly stern, but they are reproduced today. We find them in President George W. Bush's notion that God chose him for the White House, in massive tax cuts favoring the wealthy, and in our acceptance of such tax cuts. They help explain a more general alliance between right-wing religious fundamentalists and right-wing free-market fundamentalists, this despite the fact that the laissez-faire ideology of the latter (whatever sells, sells, naked girls and other blasphemies included) threatens the rigid social mores of the former. And despite the fact that an increasingly wealthy, increasingly powerful elite would seem at odds with the democratic ideal of equality for all, not to mention fair competition in business. This last dilemma did at least cause concern in the late-nineteenth century, precisely because of men like J. P. Morgan with his expensive, custom-rolled cigars.

Concern was widespread enough by 1890 for Congress to pass the Sherman Antitrust Act. Two years later, the state supreme court of Ohio used the act to break up John D. Rockefeller's megamonopoly, Standard Oil. Rockefeller, however, as if to prove fears of the pernicious influence of wealth entirely warranted, evaded judgment by moving his head offices from Ohio to New Jersey and reorganizing his business as a holding company. Standard Oil would be broken up finally but not until 1911. President Theodore Roosevelt made trust-busting a priority, notably, in 1902, breaking up a railroad conglomerate—the National Securities Company, one of several born of a consolidation effort directed by J. P. Morgan and others. Trust-busting was a priority as well for President Woodrow Wilson, whose vice president, Thomas R. Marshall, fed up with a Republican senator's long list of this country's needs, uttered the only words he is remembered for: "What this country needs is a really good five cent cigar!" Which was not only a wonderfully populist sentiment (whether he meant it that way or not), but sound business sense (whether he knew that or not), as cigarettes were going for about fifteen cents a pack, and taking market share away from cigars.

The response was to make cigars by machine, like cigarettes, and transform them from a luxury item into a product that the masses could afford, just as Henry Ford's assembly line had transformed the automobile into a product that the masses could afford. The response was also to get the message out to those masses through advertising, by then the method without which no business would flourish no matter how good and cheap the product. The upshot was that while machine-rolled cigars failed to cut into cigarette sales, they did cut heavily into the sales of hand-rolled cigars, taking over some 80 percent of the total cigar market by the late 1930s. Phillies, for one, became a brand name immediately recognized across the nation, if not for its flavor. It was just a cheap cigar, after all—as was Dutch Masters, despite the whiff of well-heeled old European sophistication (the masters were masters of art, shown on the box). Such brands were not for the wealthy, but were appropriate, as the American master Hopper might recognize, to a scene like the scene in *Nighthawks*.

The diner there is the type of place for people who would smoke a cheap rather than an expensive cigar. They are the cheap people, those who are not destined for wealth or to be members of the elect. They are the losers, for whom puffing on a cheap cigar may be the closest they will ever come to a semblance of success. Which means, ironically, that *Nighthawks* itself, with a few changes—brighten up the colors just a bit, the facial expressions, stick a cigar in the mouth of the man facing us—could be an advertisement for Phillies, cleverly giving the brand and the price through an advertisement within the advertisement. Or, with fewer changes—give him the cigar but keep the desolate mood, the dour facial expressions—a satire on such an advertisement.

Hopper knew perhaps more than he wanted to know about advertising, and about the strict requirements of commercial illustration. But a case might even be made that his popular, accessible, pictorial style owes something to his parents' and to some degree his own belief from early on that his talent should first and foremost be a means to provide for himself. The New York School of Illustrating on Thirty-fourth Street in Manhattan, which boasted "practical teaching" in "all the modern methods," may have left him dissatisfied, for he did soon switch to the more respectable New York School of Art. But upon graduating, he took a job as a commercial illustrator.

His work at C. C. Phillips and Company and as a freelancer (which together lasted the next twenty-odd years) included illustrations for movie posters and for advertisements, articles, and short stories in a host of magazines: *Sunday Morning, Edison Monthly, Bulletin, Everybody's, Tavern Topics, Profitable Advertising, Metropolitan Magazine, Hotel Management,* and *Scribner's.* He depicted movie theaters for *The Methodist* and illustrated advice on office life for *System, the Magazine of Business.* The indecorously erotic scene he later portrayed in *Office at Night* would be precisely the type of thing he would not be allowed to do for *System.* The painting might be a kind of impish rejoinder to the strictures under which he had to work before making it as an artist in the grander sense.

Like many a child of the middle class, Hopper was acutely aware that he must pay his dues. But also, like many a child of the American middle class, he resented this situation, wanted to follow none but his own rules, and refused more than three days a week of employment, using the rest of the time for his own painting.

Rebellion against commerce and his middle-class origins may have been more necessary for Hopper than for most. His father's business failures could have made commerce seem not like a way to get rich but a way to benefit the likes of J.P. Morgan, who held all the strings, and Hopper would have seen the damage that a depression could do to local industry in Nyack in the 1890s. Being an artist would be Hopper's way out, not of working but of the whole economic system. More: By including advertisements in paintings like *Nighthawks,* he would directly confront the bland vulgarity of commerce. His drive to do so is made overbearingly clear in *Drug Store* (1927), which, like *Nighthawks,* is an entirely urban scene, with no nature, and in this case no people, just a corner store, one Silber's Pharmacy, at night. Everything around the store is shadowed, murky. Buildings in the background might be empty or might not; they might hide some secret and profane activities or perhaps just people asleep, like the background buildings in *Nighthawks*. And as the diner in *Nighthawks* is lit up against the surrounding darkness, so Silber's large front window is brightly lit with a blue lettering across the front, two lines, both capitalized, the smaller top line reading PRESCRIPTION DRUGS, and the larger bottom line reading, EX-LAX. This is suggestive enough on its own, without Hopper having added beneath the blue letters a display of red and blue ribbons and blue boxes with red marks shown against bigger white boxes—a broken-up version of an American flag.

The Phillies sign does not overwhelm *Nighthawks* the way that "Ex-Lax" overwhelms *Drug Store*. But it does top the otherwise signless diner, like a false heaven that keeps the starlight out and the artificial light in. It might be saying that the pleasures of the afterlife can be achieved here on earth by spending a mere nickel for a machine-made cigar, just as in beer commercials paradise comes in a bottle, and a Model T Ford offers "hours of pleasure in God's open country." Yet the painting itself is not an advertisement, or even a satire on an advertisement, since the people in the diner can't see the sign, have no reaction and no particular relation to it. We may easily suppose the Phillies sign to be just another detail in a desolation they are used to. They have seen plenty of such advertisements before, are well aware that the sign is only a sign, the promise of a cheap cigar only a means of getting them to spend their money at a cash register, like the cash register in the empty storefront across the street. They might be the artist himself, who shows us the Phillies cigar sign but knows it for the vulgar appeal it is, a trick as cheap as the cigar it promotes.

The people in the diner can't see the sign, and would not, we might suppose, react much if they did. But they have no choice as to whether it is there or not, just as Hopper had no choice but to live in an aggressively commercial society. Even an artist has to sell to make money.

Much is made these days—and has been really ever since that rather messy writers collective known as the Beats made rebellion a crucial issue back in the materialist 1950s—of the disparity between our individual dreams and a culture that allows us only commercial possibilities. The artist has been defined as the one sort of person for whom capitalism is not only insufficient but antithetical, who must therefore refuse to "sell out." Art must demonstrate some higher consciousness and some deeper meaning than a song, say, written solely with sales numbers in mind or a movie designed solely to attract paying customers.

"I have seen the greatest minds of my generation," reads the first line of Allen Ginsberg's poem/manifesto *Howl* (1955–56), "destroyed by madness, starving hysterical naked," a sentiment he elaborates for some seventy lines in an incantatory Whitmanesque fashion. Then he asks the big question: "What sphinx of cement and aluminum bashed open their skulls and ate up their brains and imagination?" It was, says Ginsberg, "Moloch!," by which he means the entire twentieth-century, techno-industrial-commercial bludgeon.

The idea, or the imperative, becomes to avoid commerce and the demands of the "bean counters," the "suits." The songwriting pros of Tin Pan Alley, for example, however good their work, were finally no better off than factory workers. They were to be replaced by the singer-songwriter: individual, pure, like Bob Dylan or Jimi Hendrix, for whom making music they loved and believed in was more important than selling records. And then there was the do-it-yourself credo of 1980s punk rockers, who not only wrote their own songs but drew up their own catalogs and set up their own ragtag distribution networks. For them, making significant profit, being too successful, was proof of a kind of failure, as it was for Kurt Cobain of Nirvana, who denounced his own very profitable popularity with the song "Radio Friendly Unit Shifter" (1993) and committed suicide at the height of his fame.

Peter Biskind's recent bestseller—itself a suspicious phenomenon as we all know: Can it be any good and be a bestseller?—*Down and Dirty Pictures* (2004), chronicles the rise of the "independents," movies made without the backing of Hollywood studios by young "idealistic" directors. They did not like what Hollywood was putting out and, with some heroism and often at great financial risk to themselves, chose to make less commercial, more personal movies, without knowing how they would get the movies out before the public. The book contains a moment both revealing and immediately recognizable, which occurs after one of the directors, Quentin Tarantino, has won the Palm d'Or at the Cannes Film Festival for *Pulp Fiction. Pulp Fiction,* which was independently produced and independently distributed (by Miramax), was also a surprise hit, grossing more than $100 million at the box office. What happens is that another, less lauded independent film director, Alexandre Rockwell, warns Tarantino not to let success lead him off track: "You're a great filmmaker, don't compromise your vision. It doesn't matter how many people see the films."

Tarantino himself seems to have had no problem with success, with making tons of money, and doesn't seem to have a problem using his personal vision to make openly commercial, heavily advertised and marketed movies, either. He sells himself directly to the public, grants lengthy interviews with reviewers, and toots his own horn at awards ceremonies. He is arguably that rare talent who is both personal and commercial, and his work suggests just the opposite of what Ginsberg and many others would like us to think is the American paradigm for the artist: that personal and commercial are not opposed but can and even should function together. The personal and commercial did function together, for that matter, with the likes of Kurt Cobain and Bob Dylan and Jimi Hendrix, and with Ginsberg himself, who became a popular and financially successful writer because of *Howl. Howl,* too, was an act of selling, of advertising the anticommercial integrity and passion of the poet named Allen Ginsberg, just as being a portrayer of the American scene was a way of selling the very American painter Edward Hopper, as Hopper realized.

Ultimately Hopper did have the pleasure of turning down commercial offers, including one to sell cheap reproductions of his paintings and another to illustrate advertisements for Lucky Strike cigarettes. But that his art inspired such offers could have suggested to Hopper that he did the American scene all too well, all too commercially, even in paintings that made a nasty joke of commerce and the American scene, like *Drug Store.* He had, in fact, to emphasize the joke, he originally wanted to call that painting *Ex-Lax,* but was dissuaded by his agent for the very reason that it might not sell. But even such compromises aside, his very success may have troubled Hopper. In the late 1930s, when he was one of the most successful artists in the country, Hopper hit a long fallow period, during which he took time out to read the collected works of Herman Melville. Melville was likely a serendipitous choice—for the object lesson in what can happen to an ambitious artist who indulges a penchant for social critique, provided by Melville's career.

Melville, like Hopper, was the son of a failed businessman, but he found success relatively early with a pair of popular travel narratives, *Typee* (1846) and *Omoo* (1847), based on his experiences aboard whaling ships. He knew these were mainly entertainments, and while he wanted to earn a living as a writer, he saw no contradiction between that and his grander literary ambitions. These ambitions were given full scope in his third novel, the complex, trenchantly philosophical allegory, *Mardi* (1849). But *Mardi* turned off both the public and the reviewers, who might be expected to know better but could not understand why Melville had veered away from his earlier, more accessible style. Like the public, they wanted to be entertained, not disturbed. Melville's next book, however, *Moby-Dick* (1851), was also a complex, trenchantly philosophical allegory. The central figure, Captain Ahab, a whale hunter named after the most evil of Old Testament kings (husband to the notorious Jezebel and worshipper of false idols), might easily be read as America itself, in fevered pursuit of some impossible yet fixed ideal that would ultimately destroy it. *Moby-Dick,* although a masterpiece, hardly helped Melville's damaged reputation. He continued to write and publish after it had failed to sell, but he became increasingly unstable, and he was forced to work as a customs inspector at the Port of New York to support himself. This is precisely the type of fate Hopper had dealt with for two decades, and that he needed at this stage (respected, but in his fifties) to avoid. Hopper had no choice but to paint or to say, along with the inscrutable hero of Melville's short story "Bartleby the Scrivener" (1856), who chooses not to do his job, or any job, and refuses to say anything except "I would prefer not to." Hopper may have been tempted to imitate Bartleby, who represents a kind of reductio ad absurdum of his own lifelong tendency to silence and reserve. Of course Bartleby ends up in abject destitution, Hopper chose not to.

This is not to suggest that Hopper formed his style with sales uppermost in his mind. He did not "sell out" any more than

Quentin Tarantino did. Tarantino hit it big in independent films by breaking with the domestic, humbly emotional realism that pretty much defined indies in the 1980s, and going with his own honest love of pop spectacle and violent gunplay. He made the movies he wanted to see. Hopper, in rejecting modernist experimentation for his own peculiar style of realism, found a niche for himself that also paid well. This may have left him feeling profoundly misunderstood. But if Tarantino, say, decided to write and direct a melodramatic movie about a dysfunctional family, though authentically felt, it would only mark a betrayal of his true talent. Similarly, no one wanted Hopper to be America's French-influenced impressionist, and no one ever cared for his Paris paintings enough to buy them, partly because they were not very good. And no one wanted Hopper to be a sophisticated, cosmopolitan artist oriented toward world culture.

They wanted homegrown, homespun, and this is what he gave them despite his misgivings, allowing himself, for example, to be photographed by his woodstove with rolled-up shirtsleeves for the *Time* magazine profile of December 24, 1956. The profile begins with Hopper and Jo pulling into "a roadside diner" in a "white 1954 three-hole Buick sedan" to meet the interviewer, who slides quickly into Hopper's American-ness, which he approves, if tacitly, and concludes with Hopper offering such cornily gnomic nuggets as, "American women are pretty flat-chested on the whole" (not in his paintings, they're not) and "I like Emerson to read, I guess" (as opposed to Emerson to eat, I'm certain?). But Hopper never went so far as to flatter his audience in his paintings. The overt nastiness of *Drug Store,* with its equation of America with constipation, disappeared, but the will to present what William S. Burroughs once called "the worst features of America" remained in force at the time he painted *Nighthawks.*

Burroughs used that phrase in describing the Rio Grande Valley in his first novel, *Junky* (1953). The valley is where his heroin addict antihero Bill Lee briefly takes up farming, investing with a partner in a cotton field, from which he expects "to gross about $22,000" while hiring others to do the actual work. But the valley is a trap for small-time investors who think they'll make easy money. Crop yields are too uncertain, and only "the Big Holders" can survive from year to year. Small investors are, in fact, their easy prey: "You have to get up with the Big Holders or drop out and take any job they hand you." Yet many people come from all over the country to the valley, retirees and younger hopefuls wanting to escape the drudgery of the cities. They are lured there by the promise of riches and ease and by the connivings of Realtors, but they end up losing everything, sitting around, waiting to die. The valley, Burroughs says, is a like a "carnival. Soon the suckers will all be dead and the pitchmen will go someplace else." As does Bill Lee, wanderer, perpetual outsider, heading down to Mexico.

He is fleeing criminal prosecution, as did Burroughs himself, Lee being a romantic version of the author, who was the granddaddy of the Beats (and their one real genius, in this author's opinion). But it is easy to imagine him heading back up to New York City (where he scrambles for drugs near the beginning of the book) and finding himself in a diner like the diner in *Nighthawks.* This is especially the case for Burroughs, who always wore a fedora and suit jacket, had the high cheekbones of the man facing us and, like him, a thin downturned mouth. He would be at home there, in that diner, meaning he would be at home in his disgust, recognizing what he might call the "spiritually underprivileged" quality of the scene, the "basic American rottenness" there in the Phillies cigar ad and the cash register.

Even though Hopper put the sign and the register in the background, they still dominate the diner and the people in the diner. The cash register, for example, may be a ghostly silhouette, but it is in the center of the left-hand side of the painting, the only detail there to be picked out, to focus on. But by putting them in the background, Hopper is able to give their influence on daily life in America a more nuanced and yet more powerful presence in the painting, as if everything else we see is that way because of these greater economic imperatives. We are a nation defined by advertising and the need to sell. Even in the most local circumstances, our values, our customs, the very atmosphere in which we move, think, feel, eat, and lust, all reflect our commitment to commerce, as does our art.

Pop

Hopper might have foregrounded the Phillies cigar sign, for example, by showing the scene from a much higher angle so that the diner receded beneath the sign. If he had done so, or if he had (as he had wanted to) named his 1927 painting *Ex-Lax* instead of *Drug Store,* he would have more clearly anticipated the 1960s-era pop art ironies of artists such as Andy Warhol, whose reaction to commercialism in American culture was more accepting, if a bit on the nihilistic side.

Hopper and Warhol have a surprising amount in common. They were both New York City–based, Warhol arriving from Pittsburgh in the summer of 1949 and making a living for the next decade through commercial illustration. Like Hopper, he illustrated advertisements and magazine articles with titles that could easily have been used in *System, the Magazine of Business,* along with Hopper's drawings: "Success is a Flying Start," etc. They had oddly similar reactions to abstract expressionism. Hopper flirted with the painterly, emotional flourishes of French impressionism in his youth, before abandoning it for his more austere pictorial style, thus going in the opposite direction from the increasingly subjective modern trend that gave rise to abstract expressionism. Warhol, dealing with the fallout from abstract expressionism, rejected it and the painterly drips favored by the likes of Jackson Pollock (which had become almost a requirement in the 1950s for artists who expected to show at galleries) in favor of an entirely accessible, emotionless pictorial style. In Warhol's case, however, commerce and advertising did not provide small yet significant details in otherwise mundane settings. They were the primary, exclusive subject matter in many of his paintings, as if taking *Nighthawks* one step further meant simply reproducing the Phillies cigar sign on canvas. Warhol gained notice in the early 1960s for sculptures of boxes of Brillo pads that precisely reproduced boxes of Brillo pads found in supermarkets (1964) and for paintings such as *Campbell Soup Cans (Chicken with Rice, Bean with Bacon)* (1962) and *200 One Dollar Bills* (1962), which look exactly as their titles suggest.

Also like Hopper, Warhol developed a public persona that complemented his art and was, in Warhol's case, perhaps even more famous and more effective than his art. He fully embraced and sought to equate himself entirely with what he saw as commercial American culture—with spiritual emptiness, banality, and repetition, all of which he claimed to "like." For example, he claimed that he liked to eat alone at Automats, and that he wanted to found a chain of Automats called Andymats, where patrons would eat alone in television-equipped cubicles. He claimed that he had no identity besides that provided by commerce, by commercial technology, and money. "I am nobody," he said. "I have no memory." His stated ambition was "to be a machine" and he dubbed his Manhattan studio "The Factory," turning out a wildly prolific number of works, often difficult to distinguish from one another, with the aid of an assembly line's worth of assistants and hangers-on. He was openly after wealth and fame. More: He had no problem doing work for advertisements or in being a spokesman for a given product, or doing, say, a cameo on the television show *Love Boat.* He actively sought out such roles, as if determined to erase any line that might still exist between art and commerce. "Business," he insisted, was "the best art."

But unlike Hopper, who could trace his lineage back to seventeenth-century America, Warhol was the youngest child of Catholic immigrants from a farming community in Czechoslovakia. He grew up during the Depression and World War II, and his father died in 1942 from poisoned water he drank while working in a coal mine. His embrace of commercial America was both earnest and a grotesque parody of assimilation that belied origins he tried his best to obscure, though in fact he continued attending church throughout his life. It was the pose of someone who denied there could be anything behind a pose.

Yet Warhol was not only religious but moral, if slyly so, concerned with the commercialization and mechanization of life in the twentieth century. He did silk screens of fatal car accidents, suicide, electric chairs, and, in *Atomic Bomb* (c. 1963–64), a mushroom cloud like the one that rose up over Hiroshima, which was destroyed on the artist's seventeenth birthday. These were done in the same clean, often brightly colored style, with several copies of an image repeated on a large canvas that Warhol used to portray common products and movie stars, as if there was no appreciable difference between them. One of his electric chair silk screens bears the title *Lavender Disaster* (1963); another, composed of a news photo reproduced seven times, he called *Red Race Riot* (1963).

Yet the razor-sharp irony that makes this strategy significant is also razor thin; it is the irony of someone who absolutely refuses to concern himself with the very issues he raises, perhaps because he saw any moral stance as futile. Warhol became a leading figure of the 1960s, participating in and helping create the excesses of the era with his "happenings," his penchant for parties, nightclubbing, and his sponsorship of the rock band the Velvet Underground, with their melancholy anthems to perversion and drug addiction. But he shared none of that era's optimism, as the name of his art and music revue, "The Plastic Exploding Inevitable" suggests. When he took this show to Los Angeles in 1968, mass-media hippie chick Cher compared it to suicide. In San Francisco, according to a report in *The Village Voice,* the Haight-Ashbury crowd was "bewildered by the absolute malevolence of the Warhol entourage."

Rebellion was in, but in the main toward peace, toward some more authentic relation between people than business provided, toward improvement. But Warhol expressed no political interests, attended no antiwar rallies or civil rights marches. If he was moral, he saw no chance for improvement, just more of the same. He could simply reproduce the culture around him and mirror it in statements that, while showing up the contradiction, for example, of celebrating both individuality and machinelike efficiency, were utterly affectless. He could do this as if it did not matter.

But the culture Hopper reproduced in *Nighthawks* was his culture and did matter. He could not quite afford, personally or financially, to parody it. If cheap cigars were what that culture managed to come up with, what it promoted, then an ad for cheap cigars was what he would paint. But he could not simply accept the culture either, however ironically. Warhol embraced the garish surfaces of American commerce, while Hopper saw the shadows they cast.

Hip Creds

Everything, as they say, comes full circle. In 2004, a large detail showing the *Nighthawks* diner was reproduced on free start-up discs for Internet connections with no noticeable changes except for an open laptop on the counter as part of a marketing campaign for America Online. Full circle, yes, though we might wonder whether the painting had anything like a positive effect on AOL's not-so-wonderful reputation with the public or flailing stock price. Wouldn't a Rockwell have made more sense? Or even, given his hip creds, a Warhol? But perhaps they were not hoping for any such effect but were merely expressing, via Hopper, the state of their employees' morale.

Chapter Eight

How to Expect Failure and Avoid Disappointment

It was remarked early on in Hopper's career, in a 1930 monograph by his friend and fellow artist Guy Pène du Bois, that Hopper's religious background, the "Puritan" in him, became "the purist" he was as an artist. He was a purist in this sense: He believed that all art, not only his own, must be grounded in experience (du Bois wrote that Hopper would "not belie existing fact"). The Phillies cigar sign that tops the diner in *Nighthawks,* along with other telling details—the conventional suits and hats of the male customers, the sexy stylishness of the woman customer, the plate-glass windows, the server's uniform, and the silver coffee urns—tether the image to reality. This is what Hopper saw, and what we would see, in 1942, if we looked at America and wandered the streets of Manhattan. But the painting is purist in another sense as well, as a distillation of what we would see: So the cigar sign, for example, is also a symbol of the often harshly practical sensibility that defines the country.

We do not trust what cannot be experienced or precisely measured according to experience. Our use of statistics, in baseball and politics, is one example. Money is another: so much time and effort for so much pay, so many dollars for a car or a house, so many cents for a cup of coffee, a cigar. Seems like a good deal, doesn't it, a five-cent cigar, the only question being, will it make any difference in how it tastes if the cigar was rolled by hand or, more cheaply, by machine? If not, why spend ten cents when you can get the same experience for half?

Someone might object that there is an ineffable yet superior quality to a cigar that has been rolled by hand, a subtlety in the aroma, the way the smoke seeps into the brain. To which we may well accede, especially if the someone in question is wealthy, say, or important, and therefore has measurable standing in the world of experience. But we might also respond: This person is a pretentious ass, like an artist who won't do commercial illustration on the side and is supported by his parents, an intellectual who reads books on a subject but only understands, say, a car engine in the abstract, having never bothered to lift up the hood of his own car and look inside.

They "refuse to face reality," we say of such people and do not trust this refusal. We do not trust academics or "professional politicians." We may romanticize them, but we do not respect actual in-person starving artists and writers, though we do when their novels become bestsellers or we find their art adorning the cover of a magazine—when, that is, their creativity makes money and allows them to live well. Or if their art, novels, or poetry is made in direct response, not to a given theory or tradition, but to experience. The paragon of this would be Walt Whitman, whose poetry is of the highest order in sound, rhythm, formal experimentation, and ideas, but whose great subject is experience, all experience, ordinary and spectacular, monumental and humble, the mundane experience of labor, the epic experience of the Civil War.

With their long lines and encyclopedic catalogs of behaviors and occupations, Whitman's poems seem built to take in every conceivable encounter with external reality available in nineteenth-century America. From intimacy to chopping down trees to friendship to religious awe to loitering to fighting to sewing to death to a thousand or so others, all such encounters, even with despair, even with suicide, augment an ever-expanding vision of humanity and his country's destiny. "No dainty dulce affettuoso I," Whitman wrote in "Starting from Paumanok"—not your typical, sensitive, "poetic" poet, interested in lyricism and emotion for their own sakes—but a man among men, upon this solid earth: "Bearded, sun-burnt, gray-neck'd."

His near contemporary, the scholarly Emerson, graduated from Harvard College in 1821 and from Harvard Divinity School in 1826 but did not hold up intellectual facility as an end in itself. In his essay "Self-Reliance," he maintains rather that the "sturdy lad" who "teems it, farms it, keeps a school, edits a newspaper, goes to congress," etc., whose thinking, that is, is an adjunct to experience and activity, is far better than the "city doll" who holds a degree from a top university but cannot overcome even minor obstacles to his preset plans. Arguably the greatest American philosopher of the late-nineteenth and early-twentieth century, William James, unlike Emerson, did not forsake the institutional backing of a university and make his living as an independent essayist and lecturer; he did his most important work while safely ensconced at Harvard. And he was decidedly less colloquial and more abstruse than Emerson, more interested in describing a formal metaphysics. But he did so by deferring to experience as the final arbiter of all truth.

Truth might be defined as being independent of experience, as, that is, what is true on every occasion or, scientifically, for every repetition of a given experiment. But for James, there is no such truth, scientific or otherwise, only provisional beliefs that are true as long as they remain effective and should be discarded when found ineffective. Actions that result from these beliefs are more important than the beliefs themselves, and beliefs are valuable only if they inspire action. "He who refuses to embrace a unique opportunity loses the prize surely as if he had tried and failed," he wrote in *The Will to Believe* (1897). "Belief is measured by action," James also wrote—as succinct a summary of his ideas, alternately dubbed "pragmatism" and "radical empiricism," as there is. The term "radical" was well earned by his including in his purview what many of his countrymen would regard as the most significant belief of all, in God, consideration of which produced his treatise, *The Varieties of Religious Experience* (1902).

The emphasis is on an almost sensual awareness of the presence of the divine, and on the way such awareness stirs belief in a given individual, causing what might be called the "born again moment," and what James calls "sudden conversion." This occurs when we know as a fact, no less than we know we have hands, that "the spirit of God" is "with us" and we have been singled out for "election and grace" and "become partakers in the very substance of the Deity." But even this belief, however derived, must promote the believer's "adaptation" to the "fruits of this world's order." If, for example, the believer is inspired to help others, then that is the operative meaning of his or her belief in God: helping others. In more general terms, conversion produces a more intense, more effective relationship to experience, "new energies and endurances," and a heightened awareness of external reality which James describes as a "sense of newness."

Nighthawks might produce something akin to religious awe in the viewer. Note the gorgeous use of color, like stained glass: how the brightly lit yellow walls inside the diner glow against the shadows behind the diner; how the woman takes up the light with her orange hair and red lipstick; and how the jade green windowsill plays off both the light inside the diner and the murky green and blue tints of the sidewalk. Note the almost preternaturally coherent composition, with everything convincingly weighted and sturdy yet geometric, precise. But even all this would not produce awe at the presence of God so much as awe at an aspect of the world we recognize as real, or, more precisely, realistic, heightened by the talents and vision of a great artist. Say, then, super-real—the important thing being not fantastic, not abstract.

We can believe with *Nighthawks* that we might ourselves have looked at the diner on Greenwich Avenue that Hopper said he used as basis for the painting. And if we did look and did not see exactly the same scene, we would at least see a diner, and likely be able to trace the ways in which Hopper translated the diner into something worth putting on canvas. Still, Hopper must have felt this painting represented the real world as he experienced it.

Nighthawks, that is, makes an assertion regarding itself and reality. And we likely accept this assertion in the same way we accept the fact of a photographer being at an event represented by a picture in a newspaper, whether or not we regard the picture as a fair representation of the event itself.

———

Hopper had an intense and, due to nonrepresentational modern art movements, intensely self-conscious interest in the relationship between art and reality. Throughout his career, he insisted that for art to be "great" it must pay heed to reality. If, as Hopper said, Thomas Eakins, his favorite among nineteenth-century American painters, "used the facts of nature to express the 'cosmic,'" he accomplished this not through overt manipulation of facts he found but through an "almost photographic verisimilitude." As Hopper would later write in a statement for the magazine *Reality,* founded in 1953 by himself and a like-minded group concerned about the pernicious effect they feared abstract expressionism would have on younger artists, "life . . . implies all of existence and the province of art is to react to it and not to shun it." Shunning life, experience, the world-at-large was the irredeemable flaw with modern art movements, which must be corrected by coming generations of artists, although Hopper's own reaction to reality was hardly simple or direct.

Hopper was not after "verisimilitude," not in the sense of precisely reproducing a given piece of reality. His paintings might be based on what he actually saw, but they were altered, sometimes quite dramatically, sometimes less so. As he said of *Nighthawks,* "I simplified the scene a great deal and made the restaurant larger." Other paintings might distinctly resemble a given scene at a given location but actually be a "synthesis" that he "pieced together from sketches and mental impressions of things in the vicinity." In painting a house, for example, he might use a door from another house that was twenty miles away, which he liked better (or that better served his purpose). The roadside station depicted in *Gas* is actually a patchwork creation using bits and pieces that he sketched from several filling stations. Still other paintings might be wholly or nearly wholly invented. Hopper said *Office at Night* was inspired by a mere "glimpse" through a window from an El train, and he based another highly detailed scene (*Room in New York* [1932]) of a dreary couple in a dreary apartment on "glimpses of lighted interiors seen as I walked along the city streets at night."

None of this is especially surprising, considering Hopper did not have an especially exciting or eventful life, marrying late, having no children, and basically painting or worrying about what he would paint next: "I look all the time," as he put it, "for something that suggests something to me." He lived not directly, actively, in the muck of things but through his art. And he spent his leisure with other arts: going to the theater and movies, and reading, which he took for a deeply serious activity from his youth until he died (a lot of people are shown reading in Hopper paintings). Hopper was very much the sophisticated intellectual, as is evident in the way he described his paintings. If he attributed their origins to "experience and sensation," he defined the results not as situation or anecdote but conceptually, as "thoughts." In *Nighthawks,* he said, "I was painting the loneliness of a large city."* The furniture in *Office at Night,* he said, "has a very definite meaning for me," is not just furniture but a symbol, a metaphor.

Because of this, if Hopper was intensely self-conscious about the need for art to heed reality, he was also intensely self-conscious about what he as an artist brought to reality, of the "inner life. . . . a vast and varied realm." As he put it in his statement for *Reality,* the "element of imagination" is "essential" to

---

*That I have chosen to consider this statement nonexclusionary for the purpose of writing this book should be obvious. In any case, Hopper also said, "There are many thoughts, many impulses, that go into a picture—not just one."

art. The point was not that reality trumped subjectivity, but that for the very reason that a human being, and perhaps especially an artist, had such a vast inner life, abstraction and other nonrepresentational styles of painting failed to do it justice. Only the richness of reality, and the obstacles provided by reality, could be "stimulating" enough to force the inner life into some kind of recognizable shape.

Even when a given painting was wholly invented, he still enforced the rules of reality on the presentation of his subject to make the painting seem as if it could be real. He might, for example, bring "the main horizontal lines of the painting with little interruption to the edges of the picture" to keep the viewer "conscious of the spaces and the elements beyond the limits of the scene itself." He used this method to great effect in *Nighthawks*. The diner enters the scene from the right, rather than the scene being centered on the diner, and while the buildings across the street and the street itself are perfectly fitted into a self-contained composition, they can easily be thought of as continuing off the frame. Concentrating on this one particular corner, the painting makes the surrounding city real to the viewer.

Hopper also always tried to tie the images he used to real objects, even if that meant searching through Manhattan to find just the right-looking doorway or front stoop for a given painting, like a scholar seeking just the right bit of information to buttress an argument. The diner in *Nighthawks* being a case in point: Based on a real restaurant that seems to have evoked a certain set of ideas or a certain mood, Hopper then altered it to enhance that mood. In a preparatory sketch, the restaurant has its name stenciled on the plate-glass window, as actual restaurants generally did. Taking off the name brought the scene closer to what it evoked in Hopper's mind. The final result may not record reality exactly, but records a negotiation or a confronta-tion between reality and the artist: an attempt to discover art, not in a breathtaking mountaintop or cathedral but in what is es-sentially, as Hopper knew, only a diner, and imbue it with its own kind of beauty and awe.

This the painting does: In translating reality, Hopper succeeds in making us acutely aware of time and place. Very ordinary circumstances—New York City, pavement, plate-glass windows, fluorescent lighting—combine into a revelation: Oh! This is where we are now; this is how we live. Indeed. So much are we reawakened to the world of experience that the scene's mundan-ity and ugliness—the harsher, less palatable side of Hopper's realism—may not be immediately apparent.

To regard Hopper's realism as a confrontation between the artist's "inner life" and the life of the external world does not re-move him from the traditional American emphasis on the truth of experience over the truth of thought. Emerson argued for the superiority of the jack-of-all-trades who learns as he goes. But he did so in the context of his notion of "self-reliance": It is be-cause the superior man draws from internal resources, rather than outside authority, that he can deal effectively with what he experiences directly. Whitman attempted an ambitiously inclu-sive description of the America of his day, its people, its activi-ties, its natural phenomena. But there is a balance between that and the other great subject of his poetry, Whitman himself, a balance that sometimes gets lost, letting Whitman take over completely, as if America was invented solely to serve his partic-ular genius. In William James, our beliefs must be based in expe-rience and prove effective in the world of experience or be false. But the will to believe originates within us, and often our beliefs determine the experiences that in turn support those same beliefs: Someone, for example, faced with a jump over a crevice, will be more likely to make it across if he or she believes they can. James himself, after a sickly youth, suffered debilitating depression as a young man and spent much of his thirties in voluntary confinement at his father's house. Eventually he cured himself, he said, by deciding that "my first act of free will shall be to believe in free will."

There is a deep optimism in the notion that experience can be a better teacher than schools, books, ancient and recent authorities, and that the person who deals with experience directly may better triumph over it. This optimism trumpets our inner resources, the power of the individual self, and of will over fate and circumstance. It is given popular treatment in many places, in New Age self-empowerment seminars, and in the confidence-is-everything rhetoric of business leaders. Perhaps most notably, we have such inspirational guides as Norman Vincent Peale's classic bestseller, *The Power of Positive Thinking* (1952), which comes off as an unwitting (and redundantly verbose) parody of James's *The Will to Believe*.

His "simple philosophy," Peale tells us, resulted not from airy speculation but from "trial and error in my personal search for a way of life." Experience it is that has allowed him to glean not abstract truths or even beliefs but "techniques" the reader may employ to effectively counter "the problems, cares, and difficulties of human existence." These techniques, however, are what contemporary pop psychologists (who, as a group, are indebted to Peale) might call "coping mechanisms." They are not about how we live or what we do but about forming a mind-set that lets us deal with pretty much any obstacle. "You need be defeated only if you are willing to be," he writes. "This book teaches you how to 'will' not to be." This book, that is, advocates a form of denial. It is about experience and promises real world results, and toward that end Peale insists that the reader should be concerned with facts, and with changing facts to better achieve "happiness and joy." But this is accomplished by taking the correct "attitude" toward any given fact, which, however bleak it may appear, is susceptible to the perspective taken upon it: "a confident and optimistic thought pattern can modify or overcome the fact altogether."

Peale's "philosophy" might seem evidence of just how bleak and awful the twentieth century must have actually been for many Americans to make persuasive the idea that the best way to deal with it was to repeatedly insist (first thing each and every morning, Peale recommends) that we are happy. But Peale was the inevitable offspring of the marriage between optimism and experience found in Emerson and James. And he precisely fingered the pulse of mainstream America: our belief that thoughts are not only tools but are themselves part and parcel of experience, and our eminently practical reasoning that there is therefore no essential difference between a person thinking he or she is happy and actually being happy. This last is further evinced by our enthusiasm for antidepressants and sitcoms, our preference for celebratory songs and the inevitable happy ending. For us, a movie without a happy ending better be amazingly good so as not to threaten our own real happiness.

We cultivate instead a childlike innocence of sad endings, tragic endings, reminders of mortality, decline, the inevitability of failure, that our faculties will one day no longer be up to the task. And we cleave to this innocence. Like some magical virgin repeatedly raped but always made whole again, despite those many critical moments in which we are forced to doubt individually, through personal loss, or as a nation following such crises as the assassination of JFK, Watergate, 9/11, we do not find ourselves either literally or figuratively in some lonesome urban miasma drinking coffee late at night, wondering how it all could go so wrong. Rather, we return once again to that idyllic small town we may never have known, never have experienced, but that was helpfully portrayed for us piecemeal in the paintings of Hopper's near contemporary, Norman Rockwell (b. 1894, d. 1978).

Rockwell could be admired for his technical skill, his worldly success, his money, his fame (decades of covers for the *Saturday Evening Post*), and for the realistic verisimilitude of his portrayals of boys playing baseball, of barbershops, ironworkers, ice-skaters, worshippers, Thanksgiving dinners, etc. But realistic in Rockwell's work means thoroughly saturated with an amiable glow. He included few shadows in uniformly lit scenes relentlessly innocent of anything but good feelings, and was the perfect choice for the War Department to commission a poster in 1943. Only Norman Rockwell could portray with any conviction a soldier behind a large-caliber machine gun, "in a tough spot on the firing line," as he had said, and "about down to his last shot," with what looks like blood dripping from an eye—an eye hidden, here, by a rare shadow—yet give no sense that there is any chance of this soldier's returning home maimed or in a coffin.

This is more than rose-tinted glasses, it's rose-tinted neurons. He is the opposite of Hopper thematically. But Hopper is more than Rockwell turned on his head. He, too, might be in line with the power of positive thinking, by the very virtue of his turning to a diner at night and making great art out of such an unpromising subject. But whereas Rockwell was an indefatigable workhorse, Hopper was slow, methodical, given to self-doubt, and long periods of reluctance to try a new canvas. He might have been afraid of losing the confrontation with a reality that

Rockwell blithely transforms into what is as much pain-free fantasy as any suggested by the cinematic confections of a Steven Spielberg, a Frank Capra, or by Walt Disney theme parks. *Nighthawks,* however, is not just the result of a confrontation with reality; it is about such a confrontation and—contra Emerson, contra Whitman and James—about the blunting of the will, of the self, by a reality that provides the viewer little besides the beauty and awe with which Hopper has been able to imbue the scene.

A sense of this is present in the grimly downturned mouth of the man facing us; in the woman looking downward at her bit of sandwich; in the hunched shoulders of the man at the corner of the counter; and in the grimace of the server stuck behind the counter in his white uniform and white cap. There is nothing innocent about them: They are people who may not know much, but they do know that there is little they can do about their surroundings. The woman seems to have retreated inside of herself. The man facing us is as intense as the server is in their interaction, but in a remarkably understated way—we have to look closely to see it. They may be trying to get something, influence their place in the world, but such subdued anguish implies a fear that things may not get better, may just as well get worse, that facts are not amenable to their will.

This is where *Nighthawks* makes a deep and effective break from the foundation of American attitudes. When we lose our innocence, we also lose our ability to deny the unfavorable and "accentuate the positive"; we see not the grandeur but the loneliness of a modern city, for example, and so it is with more personal concerns. Obstacles seem larger, our goals further away. God's special dispensation comes under question: We sense not His presence but His absence. This is where *Nighthawks* (along with other Hopper paintings) becomes the cultural flash point behind so much art that came after, and so many movies, the dark stories of film noir leading to more recent classics such as *Blade Runner* and *Pulp Fiction* and *Taxi Driver*. *Nighthawks* is a door to an alternate way of viewing what's around us, our country, and of explaining our own lives to ourselves.

Nighthawks, a unique painting, multiplies, ramifies, becomes part of how we see ourselves in diners, corner cafés, coffee-houses, at lunch counters, becomes a thousand diners in a thousand movies. To make hay of one notable instance, it became the bleak background to the movie *Fat City* (1972).

Fat City

The absolute innocence of children is dogma with us. We harp on the need to shield them from the sexuality and violence that we think permeate our entertainment to an excessive degree. And we deem whoever carries such innocence beyond childhood morally spotless rather than immature—think of the über-naive idiot-as-hero Forrest Gump. Yet for adults, America is decidedly unforgiving.

Our economy is a free-for-all. We are aware of the unsavory underside of our own dreams in the streets where those who have failed for one reason or another end up: the cockroach-infested flophouses, the seedy bars where alcoholics gather, the gutters and doorways where dirty men lie, and crackheads and junkies and women lost to prostitution. We romanticize the ragged melodrama of petty crime we imagine takes place there, tell stories of the fallen. We speak of "street smarts" and "street cred" as a way of redeeming the people who overcome such deprivation and depravity and lift themselves into safety, affluence. We may even regard them as more "authentic" and envy them the length of their scars, evidence of a kind of experience we must deny ourselves. For we also say, "There but for the grace of God go I," or even more defensively, "There go the losers, whereas I am all about hard work, belief, determination." But has there ever been a more cynical group of human beings than American teenagers raised on soft fantasy, who come to realize how little help and encouragement society plans to offer them, that their survival is entirely their own concern? And worse: that in surviving, they will be forced to wear a smiling mask, and to pretend that they have not considered the possibility that the people who fail are no different from those who succeed?

Which is why it's not really sexuality and violence we reject in entertainment. We know the makers of such fare are in business, making gobs of money appealing to the masses, an innocent enough activity—we all want to be rich, relocate to "fat city." The more serious transgression is pathos: the story of failure told not romantically but straight, as in the movie *Fat City*. The title is doubly ironic, since its cast of characters are as far from anything resembling success as the movie itself was at the box office. Despite inspired acting from Stacy Keach and a young Jeff Bridges, and Hollywood veteran John Huston's considerable directing talents, *Fat City* was doomed by its own sense of doom, its utter lack of uplift.

Fat City, as it happens, is directly indebted to *Nighthawks,* rather than, as with many of the examples used in this book, through some more subterranean form of cultural exchange. The production designer, Richard Sylbert, used *Nighthawks,* along with another Hopper painting, *New York Movie* (1940), for the movie's color scheme. The yellow within the diner in *Nighthawks,* for example, becomes in *Fat City* the yellow of the buses that take the protagonist, Billy Tully—already a washed-out professional boxer at the age of twenty-nine—to his day-laboring jobs in the country, picking onions, say, at twenty cents per sack. The same yellow adorns a dress worn by a terminally alcoholic woman whom he picks up in a bar, which has the same rich mahogany counter as the diner in *Nighthawks,* and the walls of the small apartment where they play out a hopeless relationship. She waits for her usual man to get back out of prison; he waits until he can find the will within himself to get back into shape, return to the ring.

Tully once had a string of victories—he remembers this, we guess, as more impressive than it was—disrupted by a boxer who made cuts above Tully's eyes with a razor blade hidden inside a glove. Tully's wife left him soon after and he took to drinking and flophouses. The city in which he lives, Stockton, California, appears—from the opening shots of bums gathered on stoops and on corners with pale skin and defeated eyes—to have plenty of flophouses. But as if committed to regain his questionable former glory, he does, finally, sober up, train, and in the movie's climax fight again, coming back after a near knockout to slug his way to a sloppy victory over a Mexican opponent who we know is weak because we have seen him pissing blood before he enters the ring. Tully doesn't know this, but he seems to grasp that a single, improbable victory is essentially meaningless. He has been taught that he is a loser through hard experience. What he learns now is that he is a loser whether he wins or not. His expression after the fight might be that of someone beaten in the first round. All he wants is for his manager to pay him, and when the manager does, he returns to his drinking, his flophouses, his familiar downward spiral.

We might be tempted to regard the problem as Tully's own and the movie as a study of someone who can't overcome failure—a warning about the self-destructive effects of what we might term a negative outlook. We might be tempted to do so except for the movie's subplot, involving a young man named Ernie Munger whom Tully encourages to believe that boxing may be a way up from the streets of Stockton, and who joins with a group of neophytes on their first matches.

"If you don't have confidence in yourself," their manager, also Tully's manager, tells them, "you're never gonna get anywhere." In a key scene they are in the dressing room, getting themselves psyched up for the challenge ahead. One boxer mimics the bravado of Muhammad Ali: "Ain't nobody gonna get past me because I'm gonna be the world champ by the time I'm eighteen." He tells Ernie, "You wanna know what makes a good fighter? Believing in yourself." Confidence is all, a positive attitude, as Ali's own stupendously successful boxing career would seem to attest. But Ali had talent to spare, while the young boxers in *Fat City* go down in defeat one by one. They discover and will likely have to discover several more times before they accept what Tully already understands: They are simply not good enough at the sport to make it even close enough to the top to get away from Stockton and the crappy jobs at the canneries and the factories and out breaking their backs in the fields under the relentless sun.

It is Tully's understanding of this—despite being a failure, despite having no other talents, and not much in the way of brains—that makes him a character worthy of a movie. He also gets the strongest lines, in the movie's final scene, after having run into Ernie while drunk and disheveled and looked him in the face and insulted him. He calls Ernie "soft at the center," and when he does so, we are aware that he is looking at and talking not to Ernie but to his own younger self. Ernie may be aware of this too because he agrees to let Tully buy him a cup of coffee.

They end up at an all-night counter inside a bowling alley, their order taken by a server who must have been modeled on the server in *Nighthawks*—same all-white uniform, sans cap—except he's decades older now, wizened and horribly thin with age. He is the very embodiment of failure, still pouring coffee, having done, we guess, absolutely nothing but that his entire life. He becomes the focus of what Tully and Ernie manage by way of conversation. "How would you like to wake up in the morning and be him?" Tully asks, aware that for both Ernie and himself this is all too possible. "God," Ernie says softly, as if half in execration, half in prayer. "Jesus." "Waste," says Tully summing up: "Before you can get it rolling, your life makes a beeline for the drain."

And that's it: experience reduced to the hard, unavoidable fact of failure, a fact that does not care how you choose to look at it, how positive your attitude, already there in *Nighthawks* in the server. His job is the equivalent of taking orders at McDonald's, not for cash during summers off from college before the real career gets started. This is the career. This is what you have become, what you are, what you will remain, as the years pass, and life fades into death.

Ernie, at the very end of *Fat City*—figuring, correctly, that there is no more to say, Tully has said it all, gone to the very bottom—says he has to go, he's got a wife and a young child to return to. "Don't," says Tully. "Stay awhile. Talk." Ernie agrees. And they sit there at the counter with their coffee, not talking. Silent, in a despairing sort of way, but oddly comfortable for the first time in the movie. They have let go and, no longer believing themselves able to alter their station in the world, have found a semblance of peace—their own lives, however unpleasant, are only facts, unavoidable, immutable. And perhaps this is what makes *Nighthawks* less difficult to look at than might be supposed, what lies behind its odd beauty. Hopper has shown where experience does not enable us but overwhelms us—this diner, for no special reason, these people, this empty street, this Phillies cigar sign, which might have been a Camel sign or a Coke sign but is what it is—then lets us rest there.

Or maybe not. For if in *Fat City* Tully and Ernie have found some peace, we in the audience may still feel terribly disheartened, or perhaps we feel a tinge of fear that we don't quite want to admit to: What if they were us? Could we handle that? Wouldn't we be swallowing a scream? And don't we look at *Nighthawks* as if looking at exactly what we do not want but can enjoy only because it is after all only a painting, an experience that is not really an experience? We partake of it as we might a quick vacation in nowheresville before returning to our active pursuit of a better life for ourselves—a pursuit that does require belief, self-confidence. Could we confront the possibility that the painting really is us, after all, and surrender our claim to the American dream without screaming?

For *Nighthawks* is where the dream—or what it often enough boils down to; the practical, the material—is lost. Instead, we get facts, whether reflecting our own folly or not, that do not care about us, if we might prefer, say, to see some other sign than Phillies or no sign at all but a clear view of a star-studded sky. Such facts are what brought us out at night in the first place, to some nameless diner, to worry over the fact of our failure to improve our lot, sell more products, get promoted, move to a penthouse, smoke the best cigars, start a great business, or to get the job we always wanted, the one we believed we'd do better than anyone.

Now we doubt that any of this is up to us. The best we can do is to order ourselves a cup of coffee and sit awhile. But we can't quite let go, not yet; we still feel we should at least consider a plan B, some holding action; otherwise even this diner may soon be too good for us, the street become our final destination.

Chapter Nine

Desperate Schemes

> Your future is all used up.
> — *Touch of Evil*

If experience is how we learn about the world and our own place in the world, we do, on occasion, whether we admit to it or not, to anyone else or even to ourselves, experience despair. Perhaps we see a sudden, spreading hopelessness in, say, the breaking of the yolk of an egg we are frying ("Not again!"); in how the pale morning sunshine seems to glance without warmth off the front of the house we call home but owe too much on; in a pile of cardboard boxes we've been intending to take to the dump for too long now. It is the opposite of what we expect, the big-future-come-soon outlook that gilds the present and gets us out of bed in the morning to pop vitamin pills, take a jog, not smoke cigarettes, and grind away another day at the office, though we feel a raise is long overdue. And it is what critics address when they remark on Hopper's "silence" and "depression," as if in his confrontations with twentieth-century America he was rendered mute, paralyzed by despair, and expressed precisely this mute paralysis through his paintings.

We may very well see silence and depression in *Nighthawks,* especially if we feel ourselves not among the people in the diner but outside on the street looking in. We mutely contemplate a scene that has nothing to do with us yet may be a harbinger of our own fate, saying to us, "Here's the world you live in, get used to it." So that pile of cardboard boxes might say, "Here's your life, in essence: collecting cardboard boxes and taking them to the dump."

But if silence is in Hopper, he was not silenced as an artist, not so as to keep him from returning to the struggle between himself and modern society that took place on each new canvas. The longer we look at *Nighthawks,* the more we may notice if not hope in the people in the diner, then that they are vital and alive, despite the desolate feel of their surroundings, despite the way their environment seems to overwhelm them, and despite Hopper's own claim that he only "include(s) figures sometimes because I feel it's a duty to 'do' humanity." Even the woman's willful self-enclosure, her inordinate attention to a bit of sandwich she doesn't appear to want to eat, is vital in its way, just as in considering that pile of cardboard, we might overcome our sense of impotence by telling ourselves, "Let it sit there. Let it rot." Or, more extravagantly, in the surly manner of the man facing us in *Nighthawks,* we might think, "I know what to do, I'll pour gasoline on 'em and light 'em on fire and never go back to that dump"—though we'd probably only piss off the neighbors and get a summons for this minor rebellion.

Precisely this combination of silent despair overcrowding the atmosphere of a Hopper painting, and the perhaps futile vitality we find there also, in the cool, pale sunlight or in the people, must have been what struck a chord in those paragons of modern technology and money-driven art—moviemakers. Alfred Hitchcock used the mansion in *House by the Railroad* as a model for the mansion where the murderous roadside-motel owner Norman Bates lives with his mother's corpse in *Psycho* (1960). But Hopper's most notable influence was on moviemakers involved in a genre of B movie that has since become known by the French phrase, film noir.

Postwar, Eisenhower America was often portrayed at the time as a gleaming paradise of affluence, efficiency, and mechanized convenience, of TV and toasters and a car in every garage. The future of the nation looked bright following our having lifted ourselves out of the Great Depression, helped save Europe from the Nazis and Asia from imperialist Japan, and spent money to rebuild the countries that the war destroyed, benefiting our own economy and proving the virtues of American-style democracy. But film noir, which was having its heyday from the late 1940s to the mid-1950s, told a different story. Not one about the anxiety produced by the existence of the bomb—a weapon of unprecedented convenience and efficiency that twice wiped out entire cities full of vital human beings in a single blast—or by the cold war and the communist threat, though these do lurk behind film noir's severity and angst.

Many of those involved in the genre were directly or indirectly affected by the anticommunist hysteria that resulted in the House Committee on Un-American Activities (HUAC), which investigated Hollywood in the late 1940s and made a blacklist of suspected communists whose careers were often ruined. John Garfield, star of several films noir, refused to testify before the committee or to "name names," the concession commonly demanded in exchange for being left alone. He was hounded out of Hollywood by J. Edgar Hoover's FBI and died of a heart attack in 1952 at the age of thirty-nine. In the film noir *Kiss Me Deadly* (1955), the brutal private detective protagonist Mike Hammer greedily tracks down a suitcase full of what he'd been told is immensely valuable, but which turns out to be fissionable material. In a niftily absurd finale, he barely gets out of a beach house where he's been held hostage before it's engulfed by a mushroom cloud.

But the story that film noir told was not un-American by being sympathetic to our great enemy the USSR, but in a way which might also connect, for example, with the feelings of veterans of one of history's cruelest wars, who often returned stateside not covered in glory but weary and disillusioned. In dramatizing failure rather than success, hopelessness rather than redemption, film noir pointed toward America's own home-grown capacity for destruction, for producing despair. It told the story of people too desperate to worry about who was president, much less left wing versus right wing, people who were scrabbling along as best they could in the inferno of the big cities, haunting the slums and seedy bars and blind alleys. They were near enough to the hustle and bustle, the glitz and the glam, to get a taste of the grand opportunities to make something of themselves—but only a taste, for they had none of the power, none of the good fortune, and received none of the rewards on display in midcentury America. They were like members of the blacklist in finding themselves deemed—by fate, by society—undeserving, marginal. And like the blacklisted screenwriter played by Zero Mostel in the movie *The Front* (1976), who continued to work but had another writer (played by Woody Allen) submit his material, they resorted to subterfuge—to lies, to fraud, to con games—and also to robbery, and, quite often, to murder.

But they did so because they bought into the American dream, because they wanted to get their share of the goods, to make it from the bottom all the way to the top—or at least close enough to the top to keep them safe from ever hitting bottom again. Or they wanted to escape the urban miasma altogether and get back to the real, the true, the pastoral, the innocent, breathe clean air for the first or perhaps the second time in their lives, tend horses, milk cows. Dix Handley in John Huston's *Asphalt Jungle* agrees to take part in a jewelry heist only to pay off his gambling debts (he's a big, brutal stickup man, but he's got his honor) and buy back the Kentucky farm where he grew up. He does not make it, of course; he ends up betrayed and broke and lives only long enough to die of a gunshot wound upon arriving at the farm. The heroes of film noir have a marked tendency to die before or shortly after they get what they want, or thought they wanted, only to discover their dreams were as false and poisonous as the atmosphere of the streets they tried to rise above. Atmosphere is the real story of film noir, an overarching atmosphere no one ever manages to rise above because it goes all the way from the gutter to the penthouse, from the slum to city hall, and no one manages to escape because once there it filters into their very souls. They take it with them wherever they go, a mortal dose of corruption and vice, failure, and loss.

This atmosphere is concisely summed up by many a film noir title: *The Dark Corner* (1946), *The Street with No Name* (1948), *Night and the City* (1950), *While the City Sleeps* (1956), *Underworld U.S.A.* (1961). The last one suggests why atmosphere is key. Film noir not only tells hopeless stories about America but leads us down into a nightmarish realm where such stories have a certain inevitability. This realm is evoked by ominous shots of skyline silhouettes against slate gray dusks, by high-contrast black-and-white exposures that darken shadows and bleach out light. Action is set on subway platforms and in train stations, in shabby apartments and hotel rooms and dingy offices, on empty streets, or on crowded streets that might as well be empty for all the concern anyone has for the hero's increasingly tight predicament—even out in daytime among busy stores and rumbling traffic he might as well be chained down in a dank dungeon, awaiting his executioner. We might also see the impersonal hallways of government and the humbling vestibules of the rich, but the relative safety they provide is, we understand, bought through lies, bribery, the destruction of rivals, and the blood of the less fortunate.

The resulting aesthetic remains unique enough in the annals of American pop culture to have spawned something of an academic subdiscipline and a substantial body of literature. There it is rare for an author not to note the remarkable similarity between the feel of film noir and that of two nonfilm artists who excelled at atmosphere, one being the 1940s crime scene photographer, Arthur "Weegee" Fellig, the other being Hopper. Not coincidentally; Abraham Polonsky, for example, who directed the well-regarded *Force of Evil* (1948) before being blacklisted (he wouldn't direct again for twenty years), later said he got the look he wanted for the movie by showing his cameraman "a book of Hopper reproductions—Third Avenue, cafeterias, all that back lighting and those empty streets. Even when people are there, you don't see them; somehow the environments dominate the people." Yet the subject remains the people—in film noir as well as in Hopper, even when they are not included—in the process of being dominated.

The cheap pickpocket Skip McCoy from Samuel Fuller's

Pickup on South Street (1953) finds himself taking part in a bit of international espionage when he unwittingly lifts a microfilm of a chemical formula from the purse of a woman who is delivering said microfilm to a Russian spy. He is interested neither in helping the communist plotters nor in helping the FBI foil them. "Who cares?" he scoffs when a frustrated G-man asks him, "You know what 'treason' means?" He is solely and openly out for himself, to make as much money as he can from selling the item to whoever will pay, to buy his way out of the low and into the high life. He is a creature of the city for whom the city itself is the great and only adversary. The point is made clearly by an otherwise inconsequential shot, which if not based on a Hopper painting suggests that something more than coincidence is going on—rather a demonstration that cultural archetypes sprung from whatever confluence of historical trends draw strikingly alike imagery in each of us.

Skip, played by noir staple Richard Widmark, sits gaunt-faced and surly, in a fedora with a dark band and jacket and tie, smoking and sipping coffee from a large white mug at a counter where food is served but not visible—salt-and-pepper shakers are nearby. Behind him there's a large window, and beyond that a darkened street and beyond that the indescribable vastness of the city at night. The resemblance is striking: The shot must have been intended to reproduce the image of the man facing us from behind the counter of the diner in *Nighthawks.*

Although born before the advent of movies, Hopper got an early and intimate acquaintance with movies in 1914, when he designed posters for silent-era releases with wonderfully trashy titles like *The Dance of Mammon* and *Chasing a Million* and *She of the Wolf's Brood.* Part of this work entailed watching the movies themselves.

Hopper apparently enjoyed them, perhaps in spite of himself, and became a dedicated moviegoer. He would be a casual witness to the history of cinema: the relocation of the industry from New York to southern California in the 1910s, when slapstick was king and Charlie Chaplin the country's best-known actor; the rise of Hollywood, the studio system, and the star system; the regular production of predictable genre flicks in the 1920s; the gangster movies (he saw Howard Hawks's brilliant *Scarface*) and screwball comedies of the 1930s; and the introduction of sound (notably with *The Jazz Singer* in 1929) and color (notably with *Gone With the Wind* and *The Wizard of Oz,* both in 1939). Hopper saw John Huston's hard-boiled masterpiece, *The Maltese Falcon* (1941), considered by many to be the first full-fledged noir. And he remained interested in movies through the late 1950s and early 1960s, as he neared and then passed his eightieth birthday, seeing (among many others) *Rebel Without a Cause* (1955), *12 Angry Men* (1957), and Hitchcock's *The Birds* (1963).

Hopper may have felt an odd kinship with moviemakers, who, unlike many of his fellow painters, kept one foot squarely in a recognizable world, if for the sake of highly profitable mass entertainment. He did a number of paintings that might be considered homages to the movies, though like his depictions of the modern American scene in general, they are bleak, alien, lonely. In *The Circle Theatre* (1936), the front of the eponymous movie house is blocked from view by a large dull green subway entrance. In *Sheridan Theatre* (1937), we see a rather blowsy female figure from behind, small and accidental in the large open space of the movie house. Hopper's best-known and arguably most effective movie painting, *New York Movie* (1939), shows, off to the left, part of a movie screen with a movie playing and a section of the seating with the back of the head of a man watching the movie alone and the large hat in silhouette of a woman watching a row up from him, also alone. Off to the right, out of view of the screen, a young blond woman in a blue usher's uniform and heels leans against a wall. Her hand is raised to her chin, her head slightly bowed, and her eyes closed, not peacefully or as if sleeping on the job but as if intently focused on her own thoughts.

These thoughts seem to trouble her and make her, although still and silent, of dramatic interest. What is she thinking about? What is her life like outside of this movie theater? The painting seems to be not only about movie theaters but about movies themselves. The painting could be a very effective frame of a movie, even a crucial moment, one which will reflect in some sense the garishness of the colors surrounding this usher. The deep red of the curtain just beyond her, which is slightly parted (vaginalike) to reveal stairs leading up to the balcony, matches the red of the seats and the tiny lamp shades to the right of her head. The red is set off rather overbearingly by the greens in the carpet, as well as the paler green of the lower part of the wall and the ocher upper part of the wall. This is not a setting that promotes reasonable behavior but, rather, makes us wonder what dark deeds have occurred or may be occurring right now, up on that balcony while a few lone audience members sit absorbed in the day's feature. Is this what troubles our usherette? Or is it something she is trying to decide to do or not to do?

All of this suggests that Hopper did not enjoy movies without some internal conflict concerning the propriety of doing so. When he wrote home to his father from Paris in 1909, he mentioned that he went "to see the pictures (the cinematograph) of the Burns-Johnson fight," the parenthesis following the colloquialism is perhaps somewhat defensive. He was not in Europe, after all, for vulgar entertainment but to round off his education in fine art. And the staid denizens of Nyack would be suspicious of the movies as much as seventeenth-century Puritans were suspicious of the theater, because it was false, lurid, sensational, not conducive to reasonable behavior, to restraint, much less to contemplation of God. Antimovie (i.e., nickelodeon) regulations were passed even in New York City in the first decade of the century, to protect the morals of the mostly lower-class audience. Indeed, movies were considered lurid and sensational from the very beginning, a technology cum art form that might be confused with sorcery: "See the train go backward!" "See the men rob the bank!" Today Hollywood remains the locus of our most lurid fantasies, if not on screen then off, in the gigantic mansions built and rebuilt with decades of movie money, where stars and hot directors and big-time producers engage in dangerous and forbidden pleasures (at least in our supermarket tabloid-fed imaginings they do)—snorting mountains of cocaine, using starlet wannabes to sate their depraved lusts, etc.

Hollywood is our Sodom, tolerated as such because, well, this is a country that needs a Sodom if only to prove the rest of us relatively sinless. But also because the Hollywood establishment has made a deal: They will couch the sensationalism they purvey in stories that reflect our sense of right and wrong. Good people get happiness, and bad people are at least left without any substantial influence over events or are outright killed because they hurt good people. The inevitability of this is ingrained in our understanding of how narrative functions in movies. Even when a thoroughly nasty character like, say, Dirty Harry, is the hero, we assume he is basically good, and cheer him on as he commits acts that outside of a movie would be undeniably vicious. But the woman in *New York Movie* is an ambiguous figure, as if Hopper was portraying his own doubts about movies through her. She is just a woman working as an usher, yet a woman with something to think about that troubles her, a woman who is outside the movie being shown yet is herself in a lurid, cinematic setting.

Moral judgment is not absent. If we knew what she is considering, we may very well want her to come down on one side or the other of the question. What is absent is any way to pin her down, as we see her, as definitely good or definitely bad, deserving of reward or punishment. Perhaps she is guiltily considering some shameful action already accomplished. Perhaps she is but the innocent victim of an action committed against her. Perhaps neither or both. The luridness of the setting and her downcast appearance do suggest that she is morally compromised, which is part of what gives her a certain vitality and the painting its tension. If this were a frame in a movie like the movie being shown on the screen on the left side of the painting, this tension is what we would expect to see resolved. If she has acted shamefully and persists in her mistake, she will be brought to a bad end, while another character, the hero, is extricated from the results of her action; alternately, she may learn the error of her ways, right her wrongs, and be rewarded. But all we have is this one moment: We are left with the tension.

The situation is similar in *Nighthawks,* which Hopper gave movie screen–type proportions (152.4 cm. long by 84.1 cm. high; roughly a 2:1 ratio) and a perspective that would fit well in a movie. This is the middle distance shot, establishing the overall scene, just before we close in on the characters, witness the rise of conflict, the dramatic action. What conflict, what action? We don't know, precisely. But seeing the antagonism between the man facing us and the server and feeling dread in the very atmosphere of the painting, we can assume something dramatic and dramatically wrong is about to happen. These people, hanging out in this diner late at night at this otherwise empty street corner, are capable of behaving badly.

Again moral judgment is not absent. We may very well presume they will prove themselves damned. But we remain in a state of potential: of potential crime, potential punishment. We get none of the satisfaction of knowing how this will turn out, and whether the universe supports our moral values.

Film noir does provide resolution, generally of a violent and irrevocable sort, but only of the narrative, to confirm the hopelessness of the protagonist's plight, not whether the protagonist is sufficiently bad to deserve his fate. Dix Handley in *Asphalt Jungle* may simply want to pay off his gambling debts and get back to the honest life he left behind in Kentucky, and we sympathize with his sense of honor, skewed though it be, and with his desire for redemption. But he is also a thug who uses a gun to hold up passersby, coldcocks a patrolman, shoots a private investigator dead without hesitation, and is content to be hired muscle for a jewelry heist. We sympathize as well with the heist's elderly ringleader, Doc Riedenschneider, despite his seedy dream of dallying with young (too young) girls in South America. He bears himself with dignity and displays a neatly ironic turn of mind: "Experience has taught me never to trust a policeman. Just when you think one's alright, he turns legit." We may even sympathize with Alonzo Emmerich, the big-time but weak-willed lawyer with his fancy suits and big Victorian house. He bankrolls the heist while simultaneously planning on betraying and if necessary murdering the gang members when they bring him the jewels he's promised to pay them for. But we have seen him cowed before his doe-eyed mistress (yet who wouldn't be? She is played by Marilyn Monroe) and, poignantly, with his bedridden wife, both of them melancholy over what we come to understand was once a close, loving marriage. They all do and do not deserve their respective fates: Dix dying slowly, painfully, from a bullet in the stomach; Doc Reidenschneider arrested while tarrying in a bar to watch a girl dance to jukebox music; and Emmerich committing suicide after being caught and charged with murder.

Then again, did they deserve better? *Pickup on South Street* boasts one of film noir's rare happy endings. Skip, the unrepentant pickpocket, evades the police and a communist cabal, wins the love of a beautiful girl, and swears off his life of petty crime. But we have seen him stealing from strangers on the subway, slapping and punching the woman with whom he ends up, and generally being a cocky, callous, unsmiling, and self-serving human being—though he does finally beat up one of the communists, because the communist beat up the woman he has finally realized likes him. A happy ending for such a character is a provocation.* We don't dislike Skip necessarily. For an hour and a half, we have gotten to know him and to understand him. But we are unlikely to be convinced that he deserves the good life.

Who deserves what is an essential question in film noir. They are action-packed plot-driven movies, built for suspense, but with moral overtones. Could that nice girl actually be, as we are beginning to suspect, evil? Could that gruff, nasty, violent man be good? What makes these movies interesting, even alarming, is their refusal to answer the very question they pose. They muddy it instead. Everyone is morally compromised on some level, everyone sympathetic on another. The nice man, an accountant,

---

*Not just in theory: According to director Samuel Fuller's recent autobiography, *A Third Face* (2002), this movie provoked complaints from a no less dangerous defender of American values than J. Edgar Hoover. Fuller, for his part, in an interview included on Criterion's 2004 DVD version of the movie, insisted petty street criminals were among the most deserving people he knew.

has let himself be drawn along by a woman who could watch him die without any more emotion than she'd give a fly. Why? Because she's hardened, seen too much, breathed too much of the poison air of the city, spent too much of her life (although she's not old) in cheap nightclubs, cheap apartments, had too many men use and leave her: She's just another girl on the make. The struggle between the two of them could go either way. So could the romantic entanglement between an aging writer and a blond beauty in Nicholas Ray's *In a Lonely Place* (1950). He may not be guilty of murdering a hatcheck girl he had visit his apartment and read to him, but he is vicious and violent, and his newfound love-interest begins to wonder if he didn't, after all, in a fit of rage strangle the girl and dump her body on the side of the road. Suspicious, she refuses at the last minute to marry him, and when, only a day later, she finds out he is innocent, it is too late. He will not recover from her thinking him capable of murder.

Mere bad luck, perhaps, but there is something almost sacrilegious about film noir. It toys with a remarkably harsh (indeed a puritanical) form of judgment: One misstep and you're deservedly on the path to damnation, whatever virtues you might otherwise possess, however sad your childhood. If we are led to sympathize with the characters, so much the better: It is a lesson in learning not to sympathize with those who have made that misstep, who do not correct the error. Or would be except for the atmosphere of film noir, that shadowy loneliness that envelops its protagonists in dank alleys and in crowds, that miasma that reaches to the top, to those who have done well, but are often much worse—more confirmed in their crimes, because they brought them success—than those on the bottom. The characters in film noir do not receive any sign of God or evidence of anything like divine justice, though film noir generally makes no overt assertions or attacks regarding belief or disbelief. Neither did Hopper, who, despite his background, rarely played up religious symbols or themes in his work. One notable exception is a watercolor, *Methodist Church* (1929), in which a single gray, unmarked tombstone rises up before a plain white house of worship, as if to ask: Which is more true, the beliefs you purvey or the mortality I mark? The silence that critics have noted as seeming to suffuse Hopper's art may not indicate disbelief and despair but a suspension of belief, which is also well fitted to the dire drama of film noir. Indirectly, film noir does ask whether the universe upholds the type of moral order that would buttress faith by showing us humans who do not.

Similarly, the scene in *Nighthawks* is all too human. The desolation portrayed there is not that of nature or the universe, but of our own making; born of our own history, our own society, our own mores. The universe may or may not be so desolate, but it is silent as to the situation and potential activity of these few people in this diner on this dark night. This in America, where faith runs deep and strong, and where these days, even more than sixty-odd years ago, when secularism was less contended against than now, religion is hardly the opium, more the methamphetamine, of the people.

For us, religion is an especially ecstatic form of optimism. We do not look back to the Eden from which we've fallen in guilt, but look forward to the Eden to come with hope. The American God is a beacon for a future that in film noir is a will-o'-the-wisp leading us to destruction, and in *Nighthawks* it has been preempted by a prefab pseudoparadise with fluorescent lighting, machine-rolled nickel cigars, and cups of coffee anytime.

A film noir–influenced art movie of which Hopper "strongly approved" (according to his friend and interlocutor Brian O'Doherty), *The Savage Eye* (1959), unlike film noir and unlike *Nighthawks,* openly addresses the issue of religion.

While not a documentary, the movie incorporates documentary footage of an unglamorous Los Angeles: bars and salons, cafeterias, poker clubs and pool halls, burlesque shows, cafés, and clothing stores. At once gleaming and shoddy, this might have been "Hopper's L.A." had he lived there, except for the milling crowds of shoppers, drunks, and down-and-outs; later in the movie we get a series of bloody car crashes and crime scenes of a kind that attracted Weegee in New York in the 1940s. This is the milieu for film noir (car crashes are a noir staple) but is put at the service of a somewhat flimsy story, which might be termed psychological noir.

We follow around a recently divorced woman through a dull routine of wandering and trite amusements—yoga, poker, drinking, casual sex, etc. She is attractive enough, and empty enough, to be one of the corrupting vixens that parade through film noir. But she only waits for her monthly alimony checks; her schemes take place inside of her head, wishing vengeance on the husband who left her, wishing that he would stab the other woman. She is isolated, passive, like the woman in *New York Movie.* We are given her story and her thoughts in voice-over dialogue with an unseen presence. Called "The Poet" in the credits, this presence identifies himself as a fugitive aspect of her own psyche—"your angel" he explains, "your conscience"—with greater access to universal truth—"your God"—which is not the same as that purveyed by organized religion.

She visits a church, where healing and speaking in tongues is going on, only to flee the fraudulence of it; she gets into an accident and ends up swathed in bandages in an oxygen tank at a hospital where she dreams of her childhood, her lost innocence, her mother. Here the movie leaves noir behind for a left-wing epiphany. The blood she receives is from all sorts of people: poor, laborers, minorities, the homeless, etc. In receiving their blood, she rejoins in a deeper sense the human community that existed all around her but that she had been blind to before this near-death experience.

She is redeemed. The heroes and heroines of film noir are not. At most, they survive but remain lost and alone. If they have a conscience, if they have a God, it does not expand to any community but is locked away within them because they are desperate, scheming, taking whatever sliver of opportunity happens to come their way—"This diner must have some money in it somewhere, and be easy to rob, too!"—that they think will solve all their problems but will only get them in a far worse situation. Why? Because desperate schemes always require some interaction with other people, either as reliable partners or as unreliable partners whose moves must nonetheless be predicted. Because in film noir everyone has an agenda, a scheme of their own, hidden behind their noncommittal or smiling facial expressions, behind vows of loyalty, protestations of friendship, of love.

If God does exist in such a bleak and unfortunate universe, He exists only in ghostly form, within each of us, not among us, not binding us, and if God is present anywhere in *Nighthawks,* it must be in the only place left for Him. He must be locked away in the minds of the people in the painting, hidden, fugitive, His relationship to each of them unreadable to the others, to us, perhaps even to themselves.

God's Lonely Man

A cheap, vaguely disreputable form of entertainment in the 1950s, film noir receded during the 1960s, except in France, making Hopper at least a secondhand influence on New Wave directors such as Jean-Luc Godard and Jean-Pierre Melville, the latter so entranced by American culture that he adopted the writer's last name. They, in turn, brought film noir to the attention of American directors in the 1970s.

Brian De Palma combined Hitchcockian suspense with film noir's moral confusions and dread. His *Blow Out* (1981) ends with the unwitting witness to the assassination of a presidential candidate whom she was blackmailing being strangled to death in front of a giant American flag during a Liberty Day celebration in Philadelphia. Martin Scorsese's *Mean Streets* (1973) partakes of noir by portraying the criminal underworld of New York City to set off a drama about friendship and loyalty that is, however, specifically attuned to being Italian-American and Catholic. (The main character is a numbers runner for the mob who wants to be like St. Francis; Scorsese once considered joining the priesthood.) But Scorsese's *Taxi Driver* was scripted by Paul Schrader, who grew up in a rigid, Dutch Calvinist household and did not see a movie until he snuck off to one against his parents' wishes at the age of seventeen. Schrader considered *Taxi Driver* his spiritual autobiography. The movie makes the psychological isolation we find in the divorcée in *The Savage Eye* the cause of the moral confusions, lurid atmosphere, and explosive violence found in conventional film noir.

We are given a particular version of New York City: the bars, the liquor stores, the street people, the drug addicts and pimps and killers and crooks and prostitutes, the diners and 24/7 cafeterias, the neon lights reflected in rain-soaked pavement, the porn theaters and peep shows. This is all seen through the eyes of the taxi driver of the title, Travis Bickle, and filmed with dark shadows and blurred, overbright colors that might suit a carnival run by Satan and dedicated to pay-as-you-go mortal sin.

Travis is a marginal figure, a Vietnam-era former marine who takes on long, late-night shifts because he can't sleep. In the bleary dawns he is often left to wipe semen and blood off the backseat of his cab. But his lowliness is something of a canard. Whether we recognize him or not, he is us, a direct descendant, figuratively speaking, of the likes of Cotton Mather, repelled by what Travis sees as unmitigated degradation and believes will "one day" be "washed away" by a "real rain": a flood of biblical proportions. But Travis is utterly lost, alien, in a modern, mechanized, secular world and receives no sign of God's impending interference. God is only in his mind and he is, as he says, "God's lonely man," unable to connect, find a place for himself. His predicament is similar to Hopper's having to live in and paint a modern America he could not quite abide. Travis spends his off-hours in the very Times Square porn theaters that repel him, sometimes pointing a finger, like a gun barrel, at the people writhing on the screen and pulling an imaginary trigger.

What it comes down to, as it does in film noir, is one man versus the city itself. Travis buys a bunch of guns on the black market and tries to save a twelve-year-old prostitute named Iris whom he's befriended by going on a rampage, murdering her pimp and two other men. It's a decisive climax or should be. He saves Iris and is treated as a hero by the papers. But if this may be a godly act on some level, it is also an act of despair. Wounded and bleeding from the neck, on a couch in the tiny apartment where Iris turns tricks, Travis aims a pistol at his own head only to discover it is out of bullets. He has failed in any case, whatever the papers say. The city is too vast, too sinful, for one underage prostitute more or less to make any difference. Travis himself only returns, in the end, as the movie's title suggests he must, to driving a taxi.

We are left with a double perspective: Travis as prophet and Travis as psychopath, without any way, in the context provided by the movie, to decisively choose between them. We also have no way of knowing that the angst that drove Travis to his rampage won't build up again until he once again explodes, since his situation is much the same as it was before. We can, however, guess that if he does explode again, it will again be futile, and he will either die or once again be back driving his taxi—what else is there for him? We might similarly imagine that in the eternal present of *Nighthawks,* whatever these characters might be up to, they will affect no essential change in their surroundings or in their situation.

They will, whatever their desperation might lead them to do, only on some other night, end up back in this diner, or one more like it than not, drinking coffee. Hopper, meanwhile, having painted *Nighthawks* after having painted many other modern American scenes, will paint still another, and then yet another. He might be desperately attempting to evoke something more than silence out of his surroundings, some decisive meaning: Either the country has damned itself and we are defeated, truly and utterly, or we have retained some obscure access to God and He still exists, in however ghostly and fugitive a form, and still has something to say about redemption. But with each painting, Hopper is forced to content himself with a standoff.

This is the standoff we find ourselves in while viewing *Nighthawks,* looking over at the diner in the same way that Travis looks out at the city from within his taxicab. Part of what's keeping our attention is the possibility that we may enter that diner with our own desperate scheme: to stir up trouble, to make it reveal something of itself to us, to find out just where history has landed us, to salvage what we can. But we probably will not enter. We will stay out on the street, pass on by, knowing, perhaps, that any such scheme will be futile, at least for now.

America Noir

Such dreary streets! blocks of blackness, not houses, on either hand,
and here and there a candle, like a candle moving about in a tomb.

—HERMAN MELVILLE

When Travis Bickle in *Taxi Driver* shoots the pimp of the under-age prostitute whom he is going to save from the degradation of 1970s-era New York City, and enters the Third Avenue apartment building where she casually services her customers, he is channeling a Puritan-style rage at a country that should have been a shining city upon a hill but became a slough of venal sin. But he is also the archetypal American hero, the lone man of integrity with his come-what-may devotion to a self-imposed task. He is like Raymond Chandler's private detective, Philip Marlowe, who does his best to do right in a bleakly corrupt Los Angeles, where doing right brings no reward, no money, no beautiful women, only the satisfaction of having acted in accordance with values that he knows deep inside himself are good and solid. Travis knows beyond a doubt that no twelve-year-old should sell her body to whatever man happens along with a couple of twenties. And this gives him the right to kill, much as the right to kill is granted to countless heroes of westerns riding upright and armed against bad men who terrorize plain honest folks unable to muster the will to restore order to their small frontier town.

The makers of *Taxi Driver* understood this: They give us a scene in which Travis carefully polishes the cowboy boots he will wear during his rampage. But they did not give him a big white Stetson. Instead, he shaves his hair into a Mohawk, reminding us of a less savory version of American history, where we did not set up a fresh new civilization so much as force native populations off lands we coveted, wiping out entire tribes to establish a country devoted to tolerance and freedom.

This reminder calls into question the rightness of Travis's own behavior and also the good, solid values of the heroes of westerns. Perhaps those heroes were a bit too quick to resort to killing. Perhaps the bad guys were not so very bad as was presumed, the good not so very innocent, just as (we would now argue) the natives were not quite so savage as commonly and a bit too conveniently believed. Perhaps the very dream of setting up a civilization in which evil would always be correctly identified as such and go down in ignominious defeat to a better, purer, civilization than any that came before was too grand a dream, blindingly optimistic. It looks, from a slightly askew perspective—say, a reversed image—as pathological as Herman Melville's Captain Ahab in *Moby-Dick*. Ahab hunts the white whale to whom, in a prior struggle, he lost his leg. But the white whale does not hate Ahab and would likely leave Ahab alone, if only Ahab was not so obsessively determined to rid the ocean wide of an affront to what he has falsely presumed is his properly elite station in the universe.

Steeped in the Calvinist theology of the Puritans and rich in biblical and historical allusion, *Moby-Dick* is Melville's great American novel, itself an attempt to lasso a white whale, to define what it is about America that so signally distinguishes it from the rest of the world. The answer Melville provides is (roughly speaking) the scorning of limits, of mystery, in favor of belief in our ability to solve the human condition as if it were some mystical Rubik's Cube, through sheer, unadulterated willpower. It is not hard to read Melville's vision of America into the war in Iraq—justified, ultimately, as the first step in a wholesale transformation of Middle Eastern monarchies into terrorist-free, American-friendly democracies—or the hippie dream of peace spreading like ripples across the globe from the feelings of universal goodwill at Woodstock, or the attempt to determine the course of foreign governments and contain godless communism that brought us Vietnam. They are all various ways of taking over the destiny of humanity, of ridding the oceans wide of a notorious white whale.

The Vietnam parallel would have been uppermost in the mind of Hunter S. Thompson when he adopted "the White Whale" as the nickname for the Cadillac Coupe de Ville convertible he drove through the streets of Las Vegas in *Fear and Loathing in Las Vegas* (1971). He and his attorney are on the side of the hippies: They take lots of illegal drugs and bemoan the brutality of what they see as a thoroughly unnecessary and murderous military expedition. They are in Vegas, as the book's subtitle has it, on *A Savage Journey to the Heart of the American Dream,* which has been betrayed into a capitalist greedfest suitably represented by the overdone neon glitz and the con games practiced by casinos along the Strip. There the only value that matters is luck: A few are lucky and win, most are not, get taken, and retreat back to wherever they came from, beaten and humiliated.

The strict enforcement of draconian laws and informal codes—a bit of marijuana will put you in prison in Vegas, Thompson reports, and longish hair will get you in jail on a vagrancy charge or an involuntary escort out of town—undermine the wide-open individualism enshrined in the U.S. Constitution. Freedom of worship, of speech, freedom to believe what you want to believe, to refuse to conform, celebrated by Emerson, Thoreau, Whitman, and, in their way, by the hippies, is rooted out in favor of an overriding need to be on the side that's right because it is the side that's winning, i.e., to get lots of money. Vegas invites us to transcend common humanity, not morally, but in the sense that money means safety from being a loser and the ability to indulge a short list of accepted pleasures and luxuries. So in *Moby-Dick*, the otherwise skeptical members of the motley crew of the *Pequod* get caught up in Ahab's fervor and subordinate their better selves to help hunt down the white whale.

Wrongly they do so. Hunted down, Moby Dick turns attacker, rams the *Pequod,* and drowns the sailors. The sole survivor, Ishmael, grabs onto a wooden coffin: "for one whole day and night, I floated on a soft and dirge-like main." Thompson and his attorney flee the sleepless venality of the Strip in their giant brand-new white Cadillac, go looking for "coffee" and "to rest and regroup," and end up in the "shoddy limbo of North Vegas." This, according to Thompson, is "where you go when you've fucked up once too often on the Strip, and when you're not even welcome in the cut-rate downtown places around Casino Center." There in a neighborhood as desolate as the empty, shadowed street in *Nighthawks,* they enter the North Star Coffee Lounge, where they are served by a used-up former beauty with a "face slashed with lipstick and a 48 double-E chest." This "all-night diner," like the diner in *Nighthawks,* is a relatively uncomfortable excuse for a refuge. Thompson's waitress, like Hopper's grimacing server, is "passively hostile." Thompson's attorney quickly insults her by calling her a "Backdoor Beauty," and then, when she orders them to leave, he draws a large knife and demands a slice of pie.

The scene here and the scene in *Nighthawks* are defined by their distance from the optimism that makes America what it is. They imply a peculiarly American, peculiarly driven form of pessimism. We might imagine that if we found ourselves at the diner in *Nighthawks* on some lonely night when fear and doubt took over from our customary confidence, we would have brought that fear and doubt with us and we would find it in the other patrons as well. But we might also go further, and when we left the diner, instead of returning home to our comfortable beds and passing off the excursion as a mere anomaly, prick ourselves onward to discover if what we fear could possibly be true. Thompson and his attorney continue their search, not for the American dream, but for evidence that it is truly and finally kaput.

Asking around, they are directed to an establishment "on Paradise" that may once have been called the American dream: "a big black building" also known as "the old Psychiatrist's Club," which they discover "burned down three years ago."

Because our dreams are so grand and our optimism soars so high, our pessimism, when it comes, flows deep indeed. We leave ourselves no room for compromise, for simply being successful at getting through life without undue suffering. If we cannot build a city upon a hill, transform the world for the better, we will build nothing, besides perhaps a string of glitzy casinos. If we cannot catch our dreams on the fly, we will be nothing, accomplish nothing, only dry-hump lady fortune until she finally tires of our exertions and tosses us into the gutter. If we can't do anything to stop the brutality of the Vietnam War, Thompson implicitly argues in *Fear and Loathing,* the American dream is easily confused with a place called the Psychiatrist's Club, our optimism never anything more than a mass hallucination. We might be a band of sixteenth-century Spanish explorers who see the fabled land of infinite riches, El Dorado, glowing off on the horizon and elatedly rush forward, but when we get there discover only parched scrub and the scattered bones of those who arrived before us.

Of course, we are devastated. It does not occur to us that we should never have expected to find El Dorado, and that not finding El Dorado is the usual way of things on this earth and has been throughout history. Or that all we have to do is turn around, and we will soon find a nice enough place to set up camp and be no worse off than we should be. It does not occur to us, in short, that our sense of devastation is as much a delusion as our elation had been, that, for example, every country gets involved in useless foreign wars, loses on occasion. Instead, we blame ourselves, our lack of focus, belief, and commitment, when, after all, El Dorado may very well be close at hand, closer than we think, just a matter of regaining the optimism that brought us this far and going on a little further, or if a lot further then so be it. The bones we see around are but the remains of losers, true losers, the kind that give up when the going gets tough. If we lost in Vietnam, it was the fault of politicians who did not "stay the course." We shall not make that mistake again, we will win, and win the world over, with war in Iraq. If Hunter S. Thompson took a jaded view of the American dream in the Vietnam era, this did not stop him from continuing to search for his own version of the city upon a hill and to write nasty critiques meant to awaken us to our failures, to correct them and get us back on the better path. If there are those who think the ideal is not to win all wars but to eradicate war forever, then the various wars fought after Vietnam did not sufficiently deter them from waving signs with peace slogans once again against the war in Iraq.

There is a cycle at work. Melville ends *Moby-Dick* with his protagonist Ishmael floating on the ocean in a coffin, having no doubt seen enough of whaling voyages for the time being. But how far is his mood at this point from his mood at the beginning of the novel? There he tells us it is a "damp, drizzly November in his soul," and that he has taken to "involuntary pausing before coffin warehouses." He would surely consider suicide if it was not for the chance he has to do what he says he always does when he finds himself in such distress: Go whaling. For what choice does he have, really? He is a sailor. And what choice do we have as Americans? When depression takes over, when we see ourselves as powerless to determine our own fates or the fate of our nation, when everything seems lost, useless, we are advised from a hundred sources that everything is possible and all we need do is keep that in mind, decide to make our dreams come true, and proceed accordingly.

We are advised, that is, to get back on board, take the ride, forget that deeply pessimistic strain in the culture that runs from Melville through Hunter S. Thompson and informs not only film noir but the stripped-down, nearly nihilistic prose of Ernest Hemingway. A product, in part, of his traumatic experiences as an ambulance driver during World War I, Hemingway's style became central to what might be termed the American idiom. His writing prefigured the hard-boiled detective fiction of Dashiell Hammett and Raymond Chandler, where catching a killer hardly signifies anything in a society where mortal violence is a common method of getting ahead. Hemingway influenced such high literary standard bearers of disaffection as Joan Didion, Bret Easton Ellis, and, in her novel *Sleepless Nights* (1979), Elizabeth Hardwick. "Smoke and perfume," she writes at one point, "and somewhere a heart pounding." She is tersely yet pungently describing Billie Holiday, the jazz chanteuse whose singing rose above the sorrow it expressed until later in her life. Then her voice faltered and in faltering took on even greater power precisely because it could no longer rise above but only embody, sorrow. Holiday became an icon of despair itself.

This pessimistic strain also informs the pulp novels that have since become known as roman noir, practiced by James M. Cain—who might have a protagonist conclude his story of committing a cold-blooded murder just before being led off to the electric chair—and cult fave Jim Thompson. Thompson's titles alone recommend a seedy, desperate view of American life in the 1950s and 1960s: *A Hell of a Woman, The Killer Inside Me, The Golden Gizmo, The Grifters, The Alcoholics, Savage Town.* They became known as roman noir, just as certain movies became known as film noir, and for the same reason: a French phrase for a genre that the French saw the value of but we, in our dogmatic belief in the happy ending, decided was not much more than rank sensationalism.

A deep pessimism also informs well-celebrated, classically ambitious novels like Richard Wright's *Native Son* (1940). Wright's hero, Bigger Thomas, child of Chicago's segregated slums, listens to his well-intentioned lawyer give a long-winded dissertation on why he did what he did and how he might re-deem himself. But Bigger decides that for him, a pair of murders not only is justified but is precisely what has already redeemed him. Murder is his upside-down version of the American dream. The hero of Thomas Pynchon's *Gravity's Rainbow,* U.S. Army Lieutenant Tyrone Slothrop, is, like the author, a descendant of New England Puritans. But as he discovers the tragic dimensions of a century given over to rampant capitalism and technology, which has brought humanity not to a new crest of greatness but to the brink of annihilation, he also discovers that he himself is "preterit," i.e., not graced but damned. He loses his very identity in the chaos of postwar Berlin, from which he will never return. Jay Gatsby, meanwhile, of F. Scott Fitzgerald's *The Great Gatsby* (1925), has, in Horatio Alger fashion, through hard work and great optimism in his own abilities, gone from poverty to fabulous wealth, lives in a mansion, throws enormous parties. He is a member of the elect, has realized the American dream. But he misses a love from his youth who has since married, and commits suicide, causing the novel's narrator to ponder the fail-ure of "the fresh green breast of a new land" met by "Dutch sailors' eyes" centuries before to fulfill the sense of promise it in-spired, "the last and greatest of all human dreams."

Nighthawks certainly finds a place among such works, their pessimism there for us when the latest adventure in confident ac-tion toward a grand goal comes a cropper. They help us keep our sanity when we are left for a period without our usual sense of self on a mission to improve our lives and our society, when the whole project seems hopeless. They define the bottom from which we will inevitably once again begin to scale the heights.

Most of us will. But for some of us such works might even provide a second home, as a nearby diner gives regular relief from a stuffy apartment. We have gotten off the good ship America and will hunt for whales no more. Perhaps we have failed to regain our confidence, our will to succeed, in this our nation. We accept, albeit mournfully, that we will never be in the party, meet the honorable undersecretary of state for lunch, invent some hot new cutting-edge technology, or see our names spelled out in red plastic letters across a movie marquee. We will not receive due mention in the sober black on white of *The New York Times,* discover our picture in *Rolling Stone* magazine, or *Forbes,* or *People*—not even in the background, at, say, a celebrity-studded charity event. We will never, in short, amount to much of anything. And more: Perhaps we have, through successive failures of our own or through witnessing those of others, become honest skeptics, not merely of our own potential for success but of our culture's values in general. We do not believe that anything is possible, that good fortune is just around the corner for anyone but the few and very lucky, that anyone perpetually reawakens to a perpetually new dawn.

Well and fine: Such pessimistic works allow us to be failures (relatively speaking), to be skeptics. They tell us what we need to keep in mind if we are to live with ourselves, that it is okay to drive a beat-up old Chevy rather than a luxury SUV, to smoke cigarettes, to drink to excess for no reason on a Tuesday, for our abs to not be as hard as a washboard, for our erections to wane prematurely, for our marriages to not be faithful, for our children to not attend the most prestigious of kindergartens. They shield us from being especially surprised when we get laid off, from berating ourselves for not looking forward to trying to get another job, or to getting another job and staying late at the office, being excessively productive, etc.

But can we really remain pessimistic? William S. Burroughs once remarked that "the U.S. drag" is "unlike any other drag in the world." He identified it with an overwhelming despondency that might ambush us upon entering a typical American cocktail lounge, or when strolling through a recently constructed subdivision only to hit a dead end. It is unlike any other drag because it's validity is so stridently denied. How can we even comprehend a dead end when signs all around us insist that we should be cruising at top speed down a six-lane highway? How can we live in an America that betrays the ideal, sells out the dream? How can we abide even mild failure when success is all we talk about, sustain a pessimistic outlook when optimism defines us? We would almost have to pursue the drag, in the same rigidly willful way as we are meant to pursue the dream, which cannot be easy, as if we were desperately striving to fail. And what of writers and artists who insistently evoke a deeply pessimistic vision of America? What of Hopper, wondering if he still has something new to say about alienation, about loneliness in the big city, about the strangely devastating effect of shadows on an empty street, yet going forward, meticulous and disciplined, to take up the brush and complete the self-imposed task once again?

We might think of him as pursuing the American dream in reverse, and might also note that desire is not absent from a painting like *Nighthawks*. This diner, despite the surrounding darkness, the empty street, despite being a small, limited place, despite the discernible lack of enthusiasm among the people we see there, despite its strangeness, its anonymity, has a lush, alluring quality, a kind of siren call: "Let's get lost!" It is as if someone were offering a potent narcotic that we know we will regret for the time and energy it will steal from our more serious goals, or as if we found ourselves entering the adults-only section at the local video store, knowing the false excitements provided by the DVDs displayed therein will leave us only more frustrated.

Will we take the drug anyway, rent the porn? Will we enter

that diner and sit down to listen in on whatever the man facing us and the server are angrily discussing and drink hot coffee? Will we ignore the danger that we will find, the anonymity and desolation outweighed by temporary relief from all those big hopes and dreams, stay longer than we feel we should, return again, make a habit of it . . .

Norman Mailer's true-crime masterpiece, *The Executioner's Song* (1979), begins with the release of Gary Gilmore from prison, where he has already spent a good portion of his life. Now in his thirties, remanded to the care of near relations, he tries to integrate himself into a clean-living community of Utah Mormons. He gets a job, a girlfriend, but abuses painkillers for what he claims are severe headaches, spends his spare money on large quantities of beer, starts stealing, misses days of work and does little work when he's there, gets into fights. He himself is a Mormon, a believer, who wants to be good and knows he's behaving badly, heading into trouble, and will likely find himself back in prison. He remains a believer even after he goes all the way into crime, murdering, in cold blood, for no particular reason, the cashier at a gas station and the owner of a small hotel, and does find himself back in prison, on death row.

There he demands, in the face of numerous challenges from outside groups and protests against the death penalty (Gilmore's case received national attention), that his sentence be carried out. This is partly because he is sick of being behind bars. But he is also continuing an Ahab-like quest for "Truth" from his youth, which he describes as "very rigid, unbending, a single straight line that excluded everything but itself," a quest in which he was "never quite satisfied" and that now takes death as its object. He wants to be free of the confines of the flesh and make, so to speak, an American-style fresh start in the afterlife, where, he is convinced, he will be reunited with his loyal girlfriend and be redeemed by love. But he also, in a letter to her, at one point gives way to a revealing despair. "What will I meet when I die? The Oldness? Vengeful ghosts?" he writes. "Will I be called to and clutched at by lost spirits? Will there be nothing?"

Critic Louis Menand comments that the most compelling character in *The Executioner's Song,* and one of Mailer's greatest achievements, is not Gilmore himself but his girlfriend, Nicole. She, too, has a Mormon background but has drifted off into a life of petty crime, drugs, and promiscuity long before she met Gilmore. An obviously confused person, she allows herself to be drawn into Gilmore's mystical death quest in the way that Melville's Ishmael allows himself to be drawn into Ahab's quest to defeat the white whale. But after Gilmore's execution, perhaps significantly stronger for having gone as far as she did with Gilmore, she does not commit suicide as she promised him she would. Instead, argues Menand, she is "for life." Accurate enough, and a positive development, but just as the gloomy, shambling Ishmael has none of Ahab's tragic grandeur, so Nicole has none of Gilmore's dark glamour: Getting off at the last moment before crossing the border into hell is not quite the stuff of a hero.

Gilmore's dark glamour is that of the thoroughgoing rebel. Not the rebel who refuses to conform because he knows a better way, a surer path, but the rebel who heads heedlessly into a nightmare. We get a suggestion of the power of such a figure while watching James Dean in *Rebel Without a Cause* (1955) or Marlon Brando as Johnny, the leader of a motorcycle gang in *The Wild One* (1953). When asked what he is rebelling against,

Johnny responds, "What have you got?" We find it in many of our fast living and on the edge movie stars and rock and rollers, and in such legendary bank robbers as Jesse James, Ma Barker, John Dillinger, and Bonnie and Clyde. It is behind the continuous appeal of William S. Burroughs, who made a literary career out of drug abuse, and Charles Bukowski, the hard-drinking poet of skid row, and a legion of chart-topping gangsta rappers who brag of their thuggishness, their crimes, their depravity. They go all the way the wrong way and we want to know whether, with personal perfection and the city upon a hill still out of reach, could taking such a perverse path somehow prove the real way to finally satisfy our quest for ultimate truth?

This is the question that gives *Nighthawks* its alluring quality: What would happen if we entered this scene where everything we believe in—capitalism, democracy, progress, productivity, the bounty of nature—is either absent or turned into a negative? What if we let that diner draw us in, away from the confidence, the optimism, the perpetual dawn of the dream, and instead sought out the shadows, the emptiness, the loneliness, the desolation? What would become of us then? Would we, as Gilmore said, be "clutched at by lost spirits?" Would we find only "nothingness," a sort of living death? Or would we find, as Gilmore also suggests, an "energy" of some kind on the other side, a side we cannot see correctly from this side of life or from this side of the plate-glass window in *Nighthawks,* not until we enter that diner, sit down, order a cup of coffee.

There is a wonderful scene toward the end of *The Executioner's Song,* which takes place on the night before Gilmore's execution. He is visited by a host of people: journalists, his lawyers, relatives—good, law-abiding, and mainly God-fearing people. They keep company with a vicious murderer as he drinks and pops pills that have been snuck into Utah State prison for him. Judgment of his crimes is suspended for now. They know this man, have learned to like him, to care about him, and do not want him to die. It's as if Gilmore has, after all, found some kind of redemption, belatedly been invited to join the human community. Or as if we are getting an idea of what the afterlife might be like—that Gilmore will be reunited soul to soul with Nicole, because love does win out over all other considerations—and we are not, as Gilmore himself puts it, "judged and sentenced, as so many churches will have us believe."

The scene, like the diner in *Nighthawks,* holds intimations, if only intimations, of a kind of sinner's heaven, or of a fantastic netherworld hereby christened America Noir. It is a shadow America, full of ghosts, those who have died to the normal way of things, to the cycle of optimism and pessimism, to the driven pursuit of perfection and the jarring realization that we have missed the mark, but that only means we must try again and try harder—the cup is half full, lets get it up to the brim this time, shall we, boys? Instead, we have the likes of Tyrone Slothrop, Jay Gatsby, Bigger Thomas, Gary Gilmore, and John Dillinger. We have long-faded B movie stars and street punks and serial killers and penny-ante pickpockets and cancer-ridden chain-smokers and venereal salesmen and terminal drunks. We have a vast crowd of people who have not entered into the common culture, the wayward, the lost, the damned, all bums of one kind or another, and all given sanctuary, not in spite of their being failures but for that very reason. And just as America Noir is a dark version of America, so perhaps these ghosts, these people dead to the normal way of things, are a part of ourselves, our own suppressed Gary Gilmores, shadowy doppelgängers who, when they intrude on the normal realm, appear only evil.

Modern America is haunted by just this possibility, the intrusion into daylight of the darker nighttime America. A seemingly normal in every way and very friendly guy we meet in a lobby kidnaps and tortures innocent children and buries them in his well-manicured backyard. A usually placid, if a bit quiet, home-owner one day wanders into his office with an automatic rifle and begins shooting his coworkers before putting the barrel into his mouth and pulling the trigger. A husband and father of three takes on a hundred-dollar-a-day cocaine habit and beats his wife. A kindly schoolteacher has a series of kinky affairs with twelve-year-olds. A newspaper reporter tricks his editors and reports sensational fiction as fact. A politician, whose every word is a complete lie, manages to fool enough of the voters with his caring tone of voice to get elected. A high-flying businessman with a calfskin attaché case and Armani suit has none of the contacts he says he has, no job at all in fact, no MBA. A total imposter, he takes investors for their money and moves on.

They are citizens of America Noir. We may not be citizens, quite, but we do make excursions there. We might let ourselves be tempted into the adults-only section of the video store and pick out a DVD and with some inevitable shame carry it up to the cash register. Or we might purchase drugs we should not take. Or we might while away an evening drinking cheap gin and tonics at a garish little cocktail lounge, leering at the waitress between sips, although we are supposed to be preparing for an important meeting scheduled for the next morning, bright and early. An excursion, that's all, we tell ourselves; we will be back to normal soon enough because we don't want to go all the way, like Gary Gilmore. We do not even want to run across anyone resembling Gary Gilmore. We do not accept the possibility of dying here. We would—we must—die in sunshine so bright as to obliterate all evidence that we ever set foot in that other, darker country, gave in to our other, darker selves. We expect meaning and achievement to survive us, not hopelessness and emptiness— as if our entire existence added up to no more than time wasted in some nowhere diner.

We are split, however, because of our excursions, into pure day and pure night. We are like Robert Mitchum in the movie *Night of the Hunter* (1955; the first-time director, actor Charles Laughton, would not helm another) as the suave, good-looking, hymn-singing pseudopreacher Harry Powell. He talks to God as he drives his jalopy through Norman Rockwell–esque small towns in Depression-era America, marrying widows with whom he refuses to have sex—sex would compromise his absolute devotion to God—and then murdering them. He has the word *hate* tattooed across the knuckles of his left hand and *love* across the knuckles of his right. We are split, like Travis Bickle is split. We know that we are not what we should be, that America has fallen way beneath its ideal, that our history, like the history of all nations, is bloodied with injustice, against Indians, against slaves, against the North Vietnamese. Still we think there is something to be done, to revive the purity and innocence of the ideal.

And we are split like Hopper. We are alienated from the very country we have built. We have lost our innocence, our individualism, and our strict small-town morals to mechanization and industry, to the harsh demands of capital, to overcrowded yet lonely cities, to unrestrained lust, to a mobility that makes us strangers and transients. Yet we are entranced by the modern world, and struck by the chance that there may be great beauty in this ugliness after all, there may be desire in this desolation, and that in our very failure we have founded a sort of paradise, if nothing like the one we thought we would found.

Nighthawks, desolate, alien, denatured, perverse, desperate, is nonetheless undeniably alluring, as if offering a decidedly oblique glimpse of what is just beyond there, just on the other side of that canvas, of where we wanted to get to all along.

Notes on Sources

Introduction

An analysis of the Declaration of Independence and prerevolutionary American religious life can be found in Jayne Allen's *Jefferson's Declaration of Independence: Origins, Philosophy, and Theology* (Lexington: University Press of Kentucky, 1998). Information on Hopper's ancestry is from Levin (see notes to chapter 1), p. 5. Information on Joseph Smith and the Mormons and the Finney quote are from Robert Vincent Remini's *Joseph Smith* (New York: Viking Press, 2002). The influence of *Nighthawks* on *Fat City* is mentioned in John Gregory Dunne, "Guys Who Worked on the Movie," *Harper's*, February 2003.

For the "Me, Hopper's *Nighthawks*, This Book," section, I consulted *Edward Hopper and the American Imagination*, edited by Deborah Lyons and Adam D. Weinberg (New York: W.W. Norton and Company, 1995); Robert Hughes's *American Visions* (New York: Alfred A. Knopf, 1997); and *Edward Hopper*, edited by Sheena Wagstaff (London: Tate Publishing, 2004).

Chapter 1. The Making of the Painting, or How to Be a Stranger in Your Own Land

For information on and an understanding of Hopper's life and career, I used *Edward Hopper* by Lloyd Goodrich (New York: Harry N. Abrams, 1971); *Edward Hopper* by Robert Carleton Hobbs (New York: Harry N. Abrams,

1987); and *Edward Hopper: An Intimate Biography* by Gail Levin (New York: Alfred A.Knopf, 1995).

In "The Artist" section, the concurrence of Pearl Harbor with the start of Hopper's work on *Nighthawks*, and Jo Hopper's reaction in her journal is in Levin, p. 348; the concurrence of these two events, explored further in chapter 3, is also remarked on in Hobbs. The buxom woman in *Soir Bleu* is identified as a prostitute by Levin, pp. 98–99; the "Exhibition of Paintings and Drawings by Contemporary American Artists" is discussed on pp. 74–75, and Hopper's difficulty in producing new work in the late 1930s, pp. 283–319. The importance of nativist attitudes among art critics for recognition of Hopper's work in the 1920s, and his slow, meticulous way of coming up with and executing a new painting are both discussed in Goodrich. The "changes and corrections" quote, and the quotes used toward the end of "The Artist" section, including remarks on the American scene, his ancestry, "The man is the work," and "I am trying to paint myself," are from an interview in Katharine Kuh's *The Artist's Voice: Talks with Seventeen Artists* (New York: Harper and Row, 1962). The quote about Eakins is in Levin, p. 377; and the original title of *Skyline Near Washington Square* on p. 193. Hopper used the phrase "personal vision" in a statement written in 1953 for *Reality* magazine, reproduced in Goodrich, p. 164. The lighting in *Nighthawks* is identified as fluorescent by Hobbs, p. 125.

In "The Man" section, Hopper's ancestry, his religious background, and his childhood are detailed in Levin, pp. 3–26; I also used Goodrich and the village of Nyack's home page, www.nyack.org. Hopper is perhaps most famously discussed as a "Puritan" by Guy Pène du Bois in *Edward Hopper* (New York: Whitney Museum of American Art, 1931). The significance of the shift from Victorian America to the twentieth century for an understanding of Hopper and his art is a central theme of both Hobbs and Levin. Hopper's decision to take up commercial illustration is discussed in Goodrich, and more thoroughly in Levin, p. 26. Hopper described Nyack as "intolerably stupid" in a letter to his mother quoted and discussed in Levin. The "for the money" quote is from the profile in *Time* magazine, December 24, 1956. Josephine Nivison Hopper's background, Hopper's marriage and its significance to his art, and Jo's sexual dissatisfaction are detailed and discussed in Levin. Hopper's marriage is also discussed and analyzed in Vivien Green Fryd's *Art and the Crisis of Marriage: Edward Hopper and Georgia O'Keeffe* (University of Chicago Press, 2003). Levin blames the sexual troubles on Hopper's possible premarital use of prostitutes (p. 181) and his "old, selfish vision of male sexual dominance" (p. 182); Fryd notes that he "harbored rather Victorian notions about woman's roles [*sic*] at home and in the bedroom" (p. 49). The Brian O'Doherty quotes on Jo Hopper and Edward Hopper are from "Hopper's Look" in *Edward Hopper,* edited by Sheena Wagstaff (London: Tate Publishing, 2004), p. 96 n. 6 and p. 85, respectively. Jo Hopper's "lifetime stretching canvases for me" quote is from Goodrich, p. 83. Hopper's move from impressionism to the tradition of American realism is argued by Goodrich.

In the "Both Old and New" section, the discrepancy between nineteenth-century individualism and twentieth-century American culture is discussed in Hobbs. Hopper's opinion of Picasso is in Levin, p. 467.

In "The American Scene" section, Hopper's dislike of the *Time* magazine profile is in Levin, p. 507; his refusal of invitations to attend the inaugurations of Kennedy and Johnson, on p. 541 and p. 569 respectively. The Raphael Soyer quote is from Hobbs, p. 123. Hopper's return to his Washington Square apartment to die is in Goodrich, p. 169, and his burial in Nyack is noted at www.nyack.org.

Chapter 2. One Man, One Big Damned City

The Lewis Mumford quote comes from "The Metropolitan Milieu," included in *America and Alfred Stieglitz* (New York: Aperture, 1979). The Thomas Bender quote is from his *The Unfinished City* (New York: The New Press, 2002). Information on, insight into, and quotes by Robert Henri are from *Robert Henri: His Life and Art* by Bernard B. Perlman (New York: Dover Publications, 1991). The relationship between Henri and George Bellows is discussed in *The Paintings of George Bellows* by Michael Quick, Jane Myers, Marianne Doezema, and Franklin Kelly (New York: Harry N. Abrams, 1992). Robert Hughes's *American Visions* (New York: Alfred A. Knopf, 1977) helped on information about Bellows, Georgia O'Keeffe, Jacob Riis, and Joseph Stella. The Stella quote can be found on p. 377. Brief quotes on the Empire State Building are from *Manhattan '45* by Jan Morris (New York: Oxford University Press, 1987). For information on and insight into Weegee, I consulted *Weegee's World* by Miles Barth (New York: Bulfinch Press, 1997); *Weegee's New York* (Munich: Shirmer/Mosel, 1982); and Weegee's own *Naked City* (New York: Essential Books, 1943). Hughes describes Hopper as "a conservative Wendell Willkie Republican, who loathed the New Deal," on p. 423. Hopper denied any sociological significance to his paintings in Kuh (see notes to chapter 1). That Hopper's Washington Square apartment served as a retreat, or "refuge," is remarked by Hobbs (see notes to chapter 1) on p. 127. His reluctance to move is discussed several times by Levin (see notes to chapter 1). Jo Hopper's complaint regarding Hopper's conversational skills is from the December 24, 1956 *Time* magazine cover story.

In the "Jazz" section, information on and insight into Pollock is from *Jackson Pollock: An American Saga* by Steven Naifeh and Gregory White Smith (New York: C. N. Potter, 1989). The words attributed to Clement Greenberg were found on the flyleaf of *Hopper* by Rolf G. Renner (Cologne: Taschen, 2002). Hopper's claim to the term "improvise" occurs in his interview with Kuh. The metronome–Charlie Parker fact comes from *The Oxford Companion to Jazz*, edited by Bill Keihner (New York: Oxford University Press, 2000), p. 324. I also consulted *Visions of Jazz* by Gary Giddins (New York: Oxford University Press, 1998); the line about Miles Davis occurs on p. 349. Hopper called his color schemes "simple" in Kuh. Hopper's unwillingness to flaunt, to court admiration through emotionalism or technique, is noted and discussed by Peter Schjedahl in "Hopperesque," in *Light Years* (New York: Hirshl and Adler Galleries Inc., 1988).

Chapter 3. The End of the World Came Sometime Yesterday

Some of the information used to describe New York City as a giant machine comes from *Imperial City: New York* by Geoffrey Moorhouse (New York: Henry Holt, 1988), p. 261. Information about the introduction of time zones is from *Victorian America* by Thomas J. Shleveth (New York: Harper Collins, 1991), pp. 30–31; the statistics on movie houses and attendance is on p. 200. The "recent American history" referred to is in *The Story of orling America* by Allen Weinstein and David Rubel (New York: Dorling Kindersley, 2002), and the quote is from p. 516. I consulted *The History of Invention, Revised Edition* by Trevor I. Williams (New York: Checkmark Books, 2000). Goodrich (see notes to chapter 1) discusses Hopper not painting skyscrapers, the New York skyline, or "rushing traffic" on p. 98. Levin (see notes to chapter 1) discusses Hopper not painting skyscrapers or airplanes on p. 229. Information and insights on Cotton Mather (including quotes), and the quote from James Wilson come from *New World, New Earth* by Cecelia Tichi (New Haven: Yale University Press, 1979). The Thomas Jefferson quote is from *Writings* (New York: Viking/Library of America, 1984), p. 818. The Meriwether Lewis quotes are from *The Journals of Lewis and Clark* (New York: Mariner Books, 1997), pp. 92 and 99. Quotes by Washington Irving, Rockwell Kent, and Edward Abbey are from *The Norton Book of Nature,* edited by Robert Finch and John Elder (New York: W. W. Norton and Company, 1990). Hopper's admiration for Henry Beston is suggested in passing in Levin, p. 436. The Hopper quote on nature is from his "Notes on Painting," published in 1933 in the catalog for his retrospective at the Museum of Modern Art and reproduced in Goodrich, p. 161. The quote regarding his interest in sunlight is in Goodrich. The division between technology and nature, the significance of the automobile for Hopper's portrayal of nature, and the way that farms in his paintings seem to have fallen into disuse are discussed in Hobbs (see notes to chapter 1). The "I don't work from nature anymore" quote is from Kuh (see notes to chapter 1). The Lewis Mumford quote is from "The American Milieu" (see notes to chapter 2). The Bruce Sterling quote is from "Why Europe Has No Taste for the Future: Unfounded Fear Is Choking Off the Next Green Revolution," in *Wired* (February 2004), p. 82. The object that the woman in *Nighthawks* holds in her hand, often unrecognized as such, is identified as a "sandwich" by Jo Hopper in her notes on the painting, reproduced in *Edward Hopper: A Journal of his Work, Volume 2* (New York: W. W. Norton, 1997), p. 63.

For the "That Cigarette" section, I consulted *Ashes to Ashes* by Richard Kluger (New York: Alfred A. Knopf, 1996) and *Smoking Not Allowed* by Gilda Berger (New York: Franklin Watts, 1987); quotes are from the latter. The photo of Hopper smoking can be found in Levin, p. 346, discussion of same on p. 345.

Chapter 4. When Freedom Means You Don't Know Who You Are

Information on Thoreau is from *The Days of Henry Thoreau* by Walter Harding (New York: Dover Publications, Incorporated, 1982). Hopper's tendency to overindulge in coffee outside the apartment when unable to paint is noted in Levin, p. 292. The quote from the letter to *Scribner's,* applauding Hemingway's "The Killers," is in Levin (see notes to chapter 1), who relates the story to *Nighthawks* on p. 350. Information on diner history and the origins of the diner is from *American Diner: Then and Now* by Richard J. S. Gutman (Baltimore: Johns Hopkins University Press, 1993). Hopper's interest in hotels and the sense of transience one gets from many of his paintings are discussed in Hobbs (see notes to chapter 1). Hopper's habits while traveling, including his staying in cheap motels, is discussed in Alain de Botton's *The Art of Travel* (New York: Pantheon, 2002), and referred to by Peter Wollen in "Two or Three Things I Know About Edward Hopper" in *Edward Hopper,* edited by Sheena Wagstaff (London: Tate Publishing, 2004), p. 71.

For the "Those Cups of Coffee" section, I consulted Mark Pendergrast's *Coffee Grinds* (New York: Basic Books, 1999).

Chapter 5. Wayward Lust, Part 1: Hard-core *Nighthawks*

Newt Gingrich's terms are from *Global Sex* by Dennis Altman (University of Chicago Press, 2001), p. 149. Information on the Puritans is from *Sexual Revolution in Early America* by Richard Godbeer (Baltimore: Johns Hopkins University Press, 2002); *The Pelican History of the United States of America* by Hugh Brogan (New York: Viking Penguin, 1986); and *From Dawn to Decadence* by Jacques Barzun (New York: HarperCollins, 2000). Barzun contrasts the harshness of the Puritans and the overweening righteousness of the Victorians, as does Henry F. May, in "Changing Ideas" from *The American Sexual Dilemma,* edited by William L. O'Neill (New York: Holt, Rinehart, and Winston, Incorporated, 1972). Information on Alexander Comstock is also from May. Hopper's anxious interest in George Santayana's *The Last Puritan* and a discussion of that book, including Santayana's use of Emerson and Hopper's sense of himself as a Puritan, are in Levin (see notes to chapter 1), pp. 275–77. The Hopper quotes on Paris are in Levin, pp. 57–58; Levin argues the importance of Paris in the erotic sensibility of many of Hopper's paintings. Also relevant here is Hopper's praising of fellow artist Charles Burchfield as "one of those who, in each generation, naturally and honestly liberate their subjects from the taboos of their time," quoted in Goodrich (see notes to chapter 1), p. 124. The quote on *Office at Night* and the painting's original title are in Levin, p. 129. An understanding of Stieglitz's antagonistic relationship to American sexual mores comes from Lewis Mumford's "The American Milieu" (see notes to chapter 2). Information on Stieglitz and Georgia O'Keeffe is from *O'Keeffe and Stieglitz: An American Romance* by Benita Eisler (New York: Doubleday, 1991); the photos I describe by Stieglitz of O'Keeffe have been reproduced there. The Anaïs Nin quote is from *Incest* (New York: Harcourt Brace Jovanovich, 1992), p. 210. The Henry Miller quote is from "Obscenity and the Law of Reflection," in *Sexual Revolution,* edited by Jeffrey Escoffier (New York: Thunder's Mouth Press, 2003). *Grindhouse* by Eddie Muller (New York: St. Martin's Griffin, 1996) helped on sex in American movies. The sexuality of *Office at Night* is seen as repressed by Hobbs (see notes to chapter 1). The suggestion that Hopper's paintings represent sexual fantasies, with Jo Hopper as an active participant, is made by Wollen (see notes to chapter 4), p. 71, and by Rolf G. Renner (see notes to chapter 2), who argues that Hopper was "channeling [illicit sexual fantasies] into the licit confines of marriage" on p. 47. Levin discusses Hopper's difficult sex life using quotes from Jo Hopper's journals on pp. 178–83. The "affirmation" quote is from *America and Alfred Stieglitz* (New York: Aperture, 1979). Information on nineteenth-century sexuality and the Oneida Community (including the Noyes quote) is from *Religion, Society, and Utopia in Nineteenth-Century America* by Ira L. Mandelker (Amherst: University of Massachusetts Press, 1984). *The Marriage Revolt* and its implications are discussed in May. The statistic on divorce rates in the first decades of the twentieth century is taken from William J. Bennett's *The Broken Hearth: Reversing the Moral Collapse of the American Family* (New York: Waterbrook Press, 2001). Vivien Green Fryd (see notes to chapter 1) also discusses the difficulties of Hoppers' relationship with respect to changing sexual mores, and compares the Hoppers to O'Keeffe and Stieglitz.

Chapter 6. Wayward Lust, Part 2: Wicked Women and Weak-Willed Men

My understanding of the color scheme in *Nighthawks* throughout this book but especially in this chapter was aided by conversations with Kimowan McClain, professor of art at the University of North Carolina at Chapel Hill. Information used in the first and second paragraph of this chapter is from James R. McGovern's "Changing Behavior," in *The American Sexual*

Dilemma, edited by William L. O'Neill (New York: Holt, Rinehart, and Winston, Inc., 1972). Information on Mae West is from Kenneth Anger's *Hollywood Babylon* (New York: Dell, 1981). *Playboy* quotes from early issues of the magazine are reprinted in FAQ section of the official *Playboy* Web site, www.playboy.com. The argument that Hopper's first view of female anatomy occurred in art school is pursued by Levin (see notes to chapter 1), p. 39. Levin identifies the Republic Theater as the location for *Girlie Show* on p. 335. Information about the striptease and the Republic Theater can be found in *Stripping in Time* by Lucinda Jarret (San Francisco: Pandora, 1997). Muller's *Grindhouse* (see notes to chapter 5) contains useful information on Russ Meyer. Women as the moral center of the Victorian household and the upholders of sexual standards is from May (see notes to chapter 5), p. 10–11. The theory that Hopper's mother fulfilled this role and more, and the significance of this for Hopper's portrayals of women is argued by Levin, pp. 23–25; but whereas Levin considers this an atypical "inversion of psychological roles" in Hopper's parents (p. 25), I suggest that it was typical with a vengeance; it may even be typical of the American experience in general. (Note, for example, psychologist Erik Erikson's midcentury contention that a signal aspect of American identity resulted from a lack of paternal authority during the Great Depression. Note also the role played by the matriarchal Barbara Bush, who may never have held elective office but whose decisive influence over her husband and her powerful sons, particularly with respect to moral values, is commonly accepted. Hence the obsessive American fetish for oversize breasts?) The Camille Paglia quote is from *Vamps and Tramps* (New York: Vintage, 1994), p. 111. Information on Bettie Page is from *The Real Bettie Page* by Richard Foster (New York: Citadel Press, 1997).

For the "Crumb" section, Hughes (see notes to chapter 2) remarks on the similarity between Hopper's women and "Robert Crumb's dream girls," p. 427. Information on Crumb is from the documentary *Crumb* (1995, directed by Terry Zwigoff). Crumb's comics have been reproduced in a multivolume set published by Fantagraphics Books.

Chapter 7. Cheap Cigars and Ex-Lax

Information on Henry Ford and ad quote are from *The Wealth of the Nation* by Stuart Bruchey (New York: Harper and Row, 1988), p. 147, as is the quote from John Winthrop. Information on cigars comes from *Tobacco and Americans* by Robert K. Heimann (New York: McGraw-Hill, 1960). Social Darwinism and J. P. Morgan are discussed in Louis Menand's *The Metaphysical Club* (New York: Farrar, Straus, and Giroux, 2001), Morgan on p. 302. Levin (see notes to chapter 1) suggests that Hopper's father's business failures militated against him becoming an artist on p. 26; I am suggesting that they may have also been a motivation behind his becoming an artist. Levin discusses the New York School of Illustrating and quotes from their advertising on p. 28. Hobbs (see notes to chapter 1) treats *Drug Store* as a critique of American materialism, p. 61. Levin notes the symbolic importance of the red, white, and blue in the window display and discusses the change in the painting's name from *Ex-Lax* to *Drug Store,* pp. 210–11. The fact that Hopper read the collected works of Melville in the late 1930s is in Levin, p. 305. Hopper's turning down of commercial offers in the 1930s and thereafter is also in Levin.

For the "Pop" section, Hobbs notes Hopper's importance as an antecedent to pop art on p. 102. On Andy Warhol, I used *Warhol* by David Bourdon (New York: Harry Abrams, 1989), and culled quotes from there and from *The Philosophy of Andy Warhol (From A to B and Back Again)* by Andy Warhol (New York: Harcourt, Brace, Jovanovich, 1975).

Chapter 8. How to Expect Failure and Avoid Disappointment

The Guy Pène du Bois quotes are from his monograph *Edward Hopper* (New York: Whitney Museum of American Art, 1931). My understanding of the balance, unity, and geometry of *Nighthawks* is from a discussion in Goodrich (see notes on chapter 1), pp. 141–51; Goodrich also describes the painting's colors as "garish." The quote on Thomas Eakins is from Levin (see notes to chapter 1), p. 377. Hopper's statement for *Reality* magazine is reproduced in Goodrich, p. 164. The "simplified the scene" quote is from Kuh (see notes to chapter 1). The "synthesis" quote, information on the development of *Gas,* and "lighted interiors" quotes are from Goodrich, p. 129. The "I look all the time" quote and Hopper's calling his paintings "thoughts" are from *Time* magazine, December 24, 1956. Brian O'Doherty (see notes to chapter 1) remarks on the number of figures Hopper portrayed reading, on p. 88. The "experience and sensation" quote is in a letter from

Hopper to Charles H. Sawyer, dated October 29, 1939, and is reproduced in Goodrich, pp. 163–64. *Nighthawks* as an image of "loneliness" and the footnoted Hopper quote are both from Kuh. The remark on the furniture in *Office at Night* can be found in Hobbs (see notes to chapter 1), p. 16. The "horizontal lines" quote is from the Sawyer letter cited above. The Rockwell quote is from *Norman Rockwell: Illustrator* by Arthur L. Guptill (New York: Watson-Guptill Publications, 1946), p. 133.

Chapter 9. Desperate Schemes

A critic who makes a strong case for Hopper's "silence" is J. A. Ward in his *American Silences: The Realism of James Agee, Walker Evans, and Edward Hopper* (Baton Rouge: Louisiana State University Press, 1985). Hitchcock's use of Hopper's *House by the Railroad* is noted in *Alfred Hitchcock: A Life in Darkness and Light* by Patrick McGillan (New York: HarperCollins, 2003), p. 589. The relationship between film noir and HUAC and the fate of actor John Garfield are discussed in *Dark City: The Lost World of Film Noir* by Eddie Muller (New York: St. Martin's Griffin, 1998). The Abraham Polonsky quote is from *Street with No Name: A History of the Classic American Film Noir* by Andrew Dickos (Lexington: University Press of Kentucky, 2002), p. 193. Hopper's movie habit is discussed by O'Doherty (see notes to chapter 1), who mentions his seeing *Scarface* (1932); by Wollen (see notes to chapter 4), who mentions Hopper seeing *The Maltese Falcon* (1941); and is returned to throughout Levin (see notes to chapter 1). Hopper's work designing movie posters is described and discussed in Levin, pp. 95–96; what was revealed in his letter to his father is discussed on p. 78. Hopper's admiration for *The Savage Eye* (1959) is noted by O'Doherty on p. 85.

For "God's Lonely Man" section, information on Paul Schrader is from Peter Biskind's *Easy Riders, Raging Bulls* (New York: Touchstone, 1998), pp. 288–89.

Chapter 10. America Noir

Louis Menand's essay on Norman Mailer can be found in *American Studies* (New York: Farrar, Straus, and Giroux, 2002), see especially pp. 160–61.

Acknowledgments

Special thanks to my editor, Sean Desmond, and my agent, Joe Spieler.

Copyright permissions continue from page iv.

Edward Hopper (1882–1967). *Gas,* 1940, oil on canvas, 26¼ × 40¼". Mrs. Simon Guggenheim Fund (577.1943). The Museum of Modern Art, New York, N.Y., U.S.A. Digital Image © The Museum of Modern Art/Licensed by SCALA/Art Resource, N.Y.

Alice Doesn't Live Here Anymore. Courtesy Warner Bros, Inc./Photofest.

The Asphalt Jungle. Courtesy Metro-Goldwyn-Mayer/Photofest.

Taxi Driver. Courtesy of Columbia Pictures/Photofest.

Pulp Fiction. Courtesy of Miramax Films/Photofest.

Edward Hopper. *Office at Night,* 1940. Oil on canvas. 56.2 × 63.5 cm. Collection Walker Art Center, Minneapolis, Minn. Gift of T. B. Walker Foundation, Gilbert M. Walker Fund, 1948.

Edward Hopper (1882–1967). *Night Windows,* 1928. Oil on canvas. 29 × 34". Gift of John Hay Whitney. (248.1940). The Museum of Modern Art, New York, N.Y., U.S.A. Digital Image © The Museum of Modern Art/Licensed by SCALA/Art Resource, N.Y.

Edward Hopper. *Summertime,* 1943. Oil on canvas, 74 × 111.8 cm. Delaware Art Museum, Gift of Dora Sexton Brown, 1962. DAM#1962-28

Faster, Pussycat! Kill! Kill! Courtesy Eve Productions, Inc./Photofest.

Edward Hopper. *Drug Store,* 1927. Oil on canvas, 73.66 × 101.92 cm. Museum of Fine Arts, Boston, Bequest of John T. Spaulding, 48.564. Photograph © 2004 Museum of Fine Arts, Boston, Mass.

AOL 8.0 Plus CD-ROM mass mailer. The AOL.com triangle logo and AOL are registered trademarks of America Online, Inc. The America Online content, name, icons, and trademarks are used with permission.

Fat City. Courtesy Columbia Pictures Industries, Inc./Photofest.

Force of Evil. Courtesy Enterprise Productions Inc./Photofest.

Edward Hopper (1882–1967). *New York Movie,* 1939. Oil on canvas, 32¼ × 40⅛". Given anonymously. (396.1941). The Museum of Modern Art, New York, N.Y., U.S.A. Digital Image © The Museum of Modern Art/Licensed by SCALA/Art Resource, N.Y.

Pickup on South Street. Courtesy Twentieth Century–Fox/Photofest.

Index